A Democracy of Despots

In *A Democracy of Despots* well-known Canadian Broadcasting Corporation correspondent Donald Murray provides an eye-witness account of the struggle for power in Russia under Mikhail Gorbachev and Boris Yeltsin and shows how both men used and abused the democratic institutions they helped make possible.

A history of Soviet and Russian experiences in developing democratic institutions during the period from 1988 to 1995, *A Democracy of Despots* tells the story of the men and women who began the experiment in democracy, only to find themselves at war with one another five years later.

Arguing that Gorbachev and Yeltsin used the democratic institutions they created to crush political opponents and increase their own personal power, Murray concludes that the rise of Vladimir Zhirinovsky and the war in Chechnya are not aberrations on Russia's road to democracy but the logical extension and consequence of Gorbachev's and Yeltsin's despotism.

DONALD MURRAY was the Moscow correspondent for the Canadian Broadcasting Corporation and Radio Canada from 1988 to 1994.

A Democracy of Despots

DONALD MURRAY

McGill-Queen's University Press
Montreal & Kingston • London • Buffalo

© Donald Murray 1995
ISBN 0-7735-1353-1 (cloth)
ISBN 0-7735-1360-4 (paper)

Legal deposit third quarter 1995
Bibliothèque nationale du Québec
Printed in Canada on acid-free paper

McGill-Queen's University Press is grateful to the Canada
Council for support of its publishing program.

Canadian Cataloguing in Publication Data

Murray, Don, 1947–
A democracy of despots
Includes bibliographical references and index.
ISBN 0-7735-1353-1 (bound) –
ISBN 0-7735-1360-4 (pbk.)
1. Gorbachev, Mikhail Sergeevich, 1931–   2. Yeltsin,
Boris Nikolayevich, 1931–   3. Soviet Union – Politics
and government – 1985–1991. 4. Russia (Federation) –
Politics and government – 1991–   1. Title.
DK510.763.M87 1995   947.085'4'0922   C95-900582-X

Typeset in Sabon 10.5/12.5
by Caractéra inc., Quebec City

Contents

Acknowledgments

As the correspondent in Moscow for the Canadian Broadcasting Corporation from 1988 to 1994, I was a witness to most of the events described in this book. As well, I conducted seventy-five interviews with political leaders, their advisers, and deputies of the three legislatures in this period. Almost all offered their comments and analysis freely, at great length and on the record. I would like to thank the staff of the CBC Moscow bureau, and in particular Corinne Seminoff, for their help in this work.

Above all, I would like to thank my wife Věra whose research, interviewing, editing, and knowledge of Russia contributed enormously to the final shape of this book.

Chronology

11 March 1985 – Mikhail Gorbachev becomes the general secretary of the Communist Party of the Soviet Union.

January 1987 – Gorbachev presents proposals to the Central Committee of the Communist Party for competitive elections to party posts.

October 1987 – Boris Yeltsin attacks Mikhail Gorbachev's leadership style at a Central Committee meeting. He is later stripped of his Politburo position and his post as Moscow party leader.

February 1988 – Gorbachev and his advisers begin drawing up plans for competitive elections to a Soviet Congress of People's Deputies.

May 1988 – The Central Committee publishes Ten Theses calling for greater democracy and competitive parliamentary elections.

July 1988 – The Nineteenth Conference of the Communist Party adopts a plan to create a Soviet Congress of People's Deputies and to hold elections in the spring of 1989.

March 1989 – Competitive elections take place to elect members of the Soviet Congress of People's Deputies. Only individuals, not parties, may compete. The Communist Party remains the only legal political party in the Soviet Union. Boris Yeltsin, Andrei Sakharov, and approximately four hundred so-called radical democrats win seats in the 2,250 seat Congress.

May 1989 – The first Soviet Congress of People's Deputies meets. Mikhail Gorbachev is elected chairman of the Congress and effective head of state. The Congress elects from its ranks 542 deputies to become members of the Supreme Soviet, the permanent parliament which will sit eight to ten months a year.

June 1989 – The Supreme Soviet holds its first session.

July 1989 – The Interregional Group, bringing together radical democrat deputies in the Congress, holds its founding convention. It elects five co-chairmen, including Boris Yeltsin and Andrei Sakharov.

December 1989 – The Second Soviet Congress of People's Deputies narrowly rejects a proposal by Andrei Sakharov to debate Article 6 of the Soviet Constitution which guarantees the leading role of the Communist Party. Mikhail Gorbachev opposes any constitutional change. Andrei Sakharov dies on 14 December.

February 1990 – The Central Committee of the Communist Party endorses a plan put forward by Mikhail Gorbachev to create an executive presidency for the Soviet Union and to amend the constitution to drop Article 6.

March 1990 – Competitive elections are held to elect deputies to legislatures in the fifteen republics of the Soviet Union. In elections in the Russian Federation Boris Yeltsin is elected a deputy of the Russian Congress of People's Deputies.

The Third Soviet Congress of People's Deputies amends the Soviet constitution to eliminate Article 6, which guarantees the leading role of the Communist Party, and to create the post of executive president. The Congress then elects Mikhail Gorbachev to the post.

May 1990 – Boris Yeltsin is elected chairman of the Russian Congress of People's Deputies, thus becoming the leader of the Soviet Union's largest republic. The Congress chooses from its ranks deputies to sit in the Russian Supreme Soviet, the republic's working parliament.

June 1990 – The Russian Congress of People's Deputies adopts a resolution on Russian sovereignty.

July 1990 – Mikhail Gorbachev and Boris Yeltsin agree to draw up a joint 500-day plan to lead the Soviet Union to a market economy.

October 1990 – In the face of strong opposition from his prime minister and the Communist Party leadership, Gorbachev abandons the 500-day plan.

December 1990 – Soviet Foreign Minister Edouard Shevardnadze resigns, warning of an approaching right-wing coup. The Soviet Congress of People's Deputies elects Gennadi Yanayev, a Communist Party Politburo member, to the newly-created post of Soviet vice-president.

January 1991 – Soviet troops attack and seize key buildings in the capitals of Lithuania and Latvia, killing more than twenty people. Mikhail Gorbachev disclaims all responsibility for the attacks.

March 1991 – In a referendum organized by Mikhail Gorbachev, voters in nine republics, including Russia and Ukraine, vote to remain part of the Soviet Union. On the same ballot, voters in Russia endorse the idea of an executive president of Russia elected directly by the people.

April 1991 – Boris Yeltsin defeats an attempt by Communist deputies in the Russian Congress of People's Deputies to strip him of his post of chairman.

May 1991 – Mikhail Gorbachev launches negotiations with leaders of nine Soviet republics on a new Union treaty to create a far more decentralized Soviet Union.

June 1991 – Boris Yeltsin is elected as the first president of the Russian Federation.

August 1991 – A putsch organized by his vice-president and other Soviet leaders to topple Mikhail Gorbachev fails. Boris Yeltsin and the Russian parliament lead the successful opposition to the putsch. In its wake the parliaments of Ukraine and other Soviet republics vote declarations of independence.

September 1991 – The Soviet Congress of People's Deputies agrees to disband itself in favour of a new confederal parliament whose deputies would be named by parliaments in each Soviet republic.

November 1991 – The Russian Congress of People's Deputies votes to allow Boris Yeltsin to rule by decree for a year.

December 1991 – The leaders of Russia, Ukraine, and Belarus sign a document creating a Commonwealth of Independent States to replace the Soviet Union. On 25 December Mikhail Gorbachev resigns as Soviet president. The Soviet Union ceases to exist.

January 1992 – The Big Bang of price liberalization ends the system of Soviet centralized planning and price controls. Inflation rages but goods are once again seen in stores.

December 1992 – The Russian Congress of People's Deputies renews Yeltsin's power to rule by decree only until the spring of 1993. Yeltsin demands a referendum to ask voters who should rule Russia, the president or the Congress.

March 1993 – Boris Yeltsin announces he is imposing special rule, bypassing the Russian Congress until a referendum can be held.

April 1993 – In a referendum Russian voters endorse Yeltsin's presidency and his economic reform program and vote in favour of early legislative elections. The leadership of the Russian Congress says the result is not binding.

June 1993 – Yeltsin organizes a constitutional conference to draw up a new constitution instituting a presidential republic. The Congress leadership boycotts the conference.

September 1993 – Yeltsin announces he is dissolving the Russian Congress. The Congress leadership barricades itself inside the parliament building, the Russian White House.

October 1993 – After riots and an attack by parliamentary supporters on the Russian television centre, Yeltsin orders the army to attack the White House. After an all-day battle on 4 October, the Congress leaders surrender and are taken to prison.

December 1993 – In a referendum Russians vote by a small majority in favour of the new constitution proposed by Boris Yeltsin. In simultaneous elections for the new Federal Assembly, the party led by ultra-nationalist Vladimir Zhirinovsky wins 23 per cent of the vote for the lower house, the Duma.

January 1994 – The new Federal Assembly meets for the first time. The Duma elects Ivan Rybkin, a Communist leader of the Russian Congress, as speaker.

February 1994 – The Duma votes to grant amnesty to the leaders of the Russian Congress still in prison.

April 1994 – Boris Yeltsin and the leaders of two hundred political parties and social organizations sign a Pact on Civil Accord in the Kremlin. The Communists and their allies in the Duma refuse to sign.

June 1994 – Yeltsin signs an anti-crime decree which abrogates several clauses protecting civil rights in the constitution.

December 1994 – Yeltsin orders the army to enter the breakaway republic of Chechnya to keep it from leaving the Russian Federation. A bitter war begins. Radical democrats in the Duma denounce the offensive and Yeltsin but the majority of deputies refuse to consider measures to end the fighting or to limit the president's power.

A Democracy of Despots

Introduction

Soon after reaching the pinnacle of the Soviet political system, Mikhail Gorbachev made a discovery: absolute power applied over decades breeds a state approaching absolute inertia.

On 11 March 1985 Gorbachev had become the general secretary of the Communist Party of the Soviet Union and chairman of its Politburo. This was a small committee of aging men (at fifty-four Gorbachev was by several years the youngest among them) with vast power – ten full members with the right to vote and four alternate, non-voting members who participated in the committee's discussions. The Politburo had the authority to do everything from declaring war to raising the price of milk, or vodka, for 285 million people.

Its members were not elected. They were selected by the general secretary from the ranks of the Communist Party Central Committee, three hundred men (and a handful of women) who met twice a year to debate and approve major policy decisions proposed by the Politburo. Central Committee members were, in practice, Communist Party leaders of Soviet republics and Communist Party bosses of major provinces and regions in Russia. Their careers and advancement depended on the favour of the Politburo and, above all, on the general secretary, who proposed their membership to the Central Committee himself. If the Politburo was composed of the aging princes of the regime, Central Committee members were its barons. This mechanism of power had been conceived by Lenin. It had been the centrepiece of seven decades of one-party rule. In theory the Politburo stood behind the prime minister, his cabinet, and his government and advised them. In practice it was the highest echelon of government, dictating all key policy and personnel decisions. In 1985 this committee included the prime minister, the defence minister, the head of the KGB, and the party leaders of key cities and regions such as Moscow, Leningrad, and Ukraine.

When Gorbachev took power the system was virtually unchallenged. Organized opposition was unthinkable; individual dissenters had been forced into prison, into exile, or into silence. Yet the system's very power to suppress debate and dissent had frozen it into immobility. The energetic new general secretary set himself a task: to modernize the political system which he had inherited and to restore its vigour. It was a brave quest but a doomed one. This was due, in large measure, to the senescent rigidity of the one-party system itself. It was also due, in part, to Gorbachev. He was a man of Soviet power who understand well its flaws but still believed in the virtues of socialism with a Soviet face. Ten years after becoming Soviet leader he said: "By 1988 I understand we would have to make changes outside the traditional confines of the system, but not outside the confines of socialism."[1]

So Gorbachev tried to change the political structure of his state without fundamentally altering its economic foundations. His reform involved the creation of a new legislature, the Soviet Congress of People's Deputies, which Gorbachev saw as a new locus of power and an arena for debate and decisions to stimulate the evolution of Soviet socialism. This book will describe the creation of that legislature and its role in the momentous upheaval which brought about the collapse of the Soviet Union. It will also examine the role of parliamentary institutions in the bitter struggles which have marked the first years of the independent Russian Federation, the largest state to emerge from the rubble of that collapse. The tragic paradox of Russia's uncertain march to democracy has been that the men who championed those institutions, first Mikhail Gorbachev and then Boris Yeltsin, did so for motives only distantly related to their belief in the need for a democratic parliament in their country. Rather, each saw the legislature he first dominated and then struggled against as a weapon to reinforce his power and to remould the country according to his vision.

The book makes no attempt to paint a broad picture of Soviet and Russian society in this eventful period. Rather, it concentrates on a group of men and women – they numbered no more than one thousand in all – whose ideas, arguments, and decisions drastically altered the face of their country. The Leninist political structure had succeeded, after seven decades, in severing the organic link between the political elite in Moscow and the people on behalf of whom the elite claimed to be working. The leadership of the country operated in a self-imposed political vacuum. The introduction of competitive elections under Gorbachev only partially modified that. Having elected their representatives, the voters then watched, largely unconsulted, as the political struggles unfolded around the Kremlin. And so, at this time of profound political transformation, individuals and personality played an outsize role.

The period was dominated by two men, Mikhail Gorbachev and Boris Yeltsin, whose backgrounds and careers were strikingly similar; their personalities were not. Gorbachev was thoroughly at ease in the established structures of power. He wanted change and talked of change, indeed of revolutionary change, but his instinct was always to compromise, to stop short of drastic innovation. He was, as one colleague put it, a parliamentary politician. This helps explain the enormous amount of time and energy he devoted to the parliamenatary institution he created, the Soviet Congress of People's Deputies. It also helps explain the extraordinarily positive response he evoked in the West. He was the first Soviet leader whose pyschology seemed understandable to westerners. They felt at ease with him. But in reality, his vision of parliamentary politics was rooted in Russian tradition, or more properly in Leninist tradition. Gorbachev believed in Lenin and sought, as the book will show, to imitate his creation and his achievement.

Boris Yeltsin was a personality of another order. He proclaimed himself a man set apart by fate, a rebel, but at the same time a man destined to rule. If compromise was at the heart of Gorbachev's approach to power, it was anathema to Yeltsin. Crisis and confrontation was the crucible which forged his talents and demonstrated his leadership. He would seek new conflicts even after he had bested his political enemies in Moscow and created a constitution and a structure of power to fit him personally. With the collapse of the Communist Party in 1991 it was this confrontational style which became the model for political leadership in the institutional vacuum of the Russian Federation.

In the past ten years the political road travelled by Russians has been long and often dangerous. The country has been freed from the stagnation imposed by one-party rule. But in the uncertainty and anarchy of post-Soviet Russia, inertia and one-party rule are now remembered nostalgically by many older people. Russians have created the forms of parliamentary democracy but few are yet persuaded their country has embraced its content.

CHAPTER ONE

An Oasis of Liberty

It was 25 December 1991. It was cold; a state had just died. At 7:32 p.m., almost surreptitiously, two men took down the Soviet flag, the flag of the October revolution which had flown over the Kremlin for seventy-four years. They hoisted in its place the flag of the February revolution, the tricolor which had once symbolized the overthrow of the czar and now proclaimed the new state of Russia.

On Red Square almost no one noticed. A few people trudged home through the wind and snow. A handful of communists waved red flags in front of Lenin's tomb. A couple, out for an evening stroll, tried to grasp the idea that they had been born in the Soviet Union but would die in another country. I'm sorry, a woman said, that a great country is falling apart before our eyes. I don't give a damn, said one man with protective Soviet cynicism, nothing will change anyway.

On the day after the death of the Soviet Union the lineup was long on Red Square to see the corpse of the founder. "We were taught he was a great leader," they said of Lenin. "He was a saint. Don't move him."

A kilometre away, the last perquisites of power granted to the last leader of the dead state were barely visible. Two enormous black Zil limousines crouched before the President Hotel, chauffeurs in place, motors perpetually running. Inside, a scene of consummate political surrealism. Mikhail Gorbachev was holding a cocktail party.

The night before, as he said farewell on national television to his country and his power, he had looked small and forlorn. In a twelve-minute speech he had warned of coming conflicts and said, in effect, it's not my fault. He had done everything in his power to prevent the end of the Soviet Union.

This evening, in the hotel built by the Communist Party for its leaders, he seemed another man. Trailed by his aides, he moved about the room, smiling, talking, and toasting his guests with lemon vodka. His guests, Soviet and foreign journalists, were puzzled. Gorbachev was behaving like a politician celebrating a triumph, not like a leader whose career had ended in the ashes of his own state.

"Mikhail Sergeyevich believes he's left office victorious." The explanation came from a small, wizened gnome of a man. This was Georgi Shaknazarov, Gorbachev's chief constitutional adviser. "Even if the structure of the state collapsed," Shaknazarov said, "Gorbachev has given liberty to his people."[1]

4 October 1993. Just before 9 a.m., seven T-80 tanks rumbled down Kutuzovsky Prospekt, briefly drowning out the crackle of rifle fire in central Moscow. They trained their gun barrels on the White House, the home of the Russian Supreme Soviet. At that moment Russian television announced that Boris Yeltsin was about to address the nation.

"A handful of men who call themselves politicians made an attempt to impose their will on the entire country," Yeltsin said. "Those who unleashed this bloody battle in the middle of a peaceful city are criminals. Everthing that we see happening in Moscow is a well-planned armed mutiny. It has been organized by communist revanchists, by fascist leaders, by some of the former deputies, representatives of the Soviets. Now the whole world can see the means with which they wanted to rule Russia: cynical lies, bribes, stones, sticks, rifles and machine guns.

"The armed mutiny is doomed."[2]

His tone was as savage as his words. Yet he was talking of Alexander Rutskoi, his elected vice-president in 1991, and Ruslan Khasbulatov, his choice to succeed him as Russian parliamentary chairman. These men had stood by him when he had climbed onto a tank just two years earlier in front of the same building to proclaim the legitimacy of the Russian parliament against the illegitimacy of the putsch which sought to oust Mikhail Gorbachev from power. Then he had said: "We are faced with a reactionary and unconstitutional right-wing putsch. The use of force is unacceptable. We are obliged to declare illegal the so-called Committee which has taken power. A Congress of People's Deputies must be convened immediately."

Yeltsin had added a premonitory rhetorical flourish: "You can build a throne with bayonets, but it's difficult to sit on it."[3]

Two years later, the Russian army, at Yeltsin's order, was pounding the White House into submission. Crack rifle regiments kept up a steady barrage of bullets into the offices of the building while crowds of Moscovites watched from the Novy Arbatsky bridge, almost in the line of fire, as if at a football game. Once an hour, a tank loosed off precisely two rounds into the White House tower, where the parliamentary leadership was thought to be holed up.

The leaders were, in fact, on the fifth floor. Khasbulatov, almost catatonic, sat numbly, dressed in a windbreaker, holding a pipe. "Yes, we will all die," he said. "But in some other city, our comrades will gather a Congress."

Alexander Rutskoi raged and pleaded. The man sworn in as president by the self-proclaimed 10th Congress of Russian People's Deputies on September 21, the man who had vowed to die defending the White House, was now on the phone to Valery Zorkin, the chief judge of the Constitutional Court.

"Valera, they will kill us all! Call the foreign embassies ... Do something! They are murderers; do you understand that or don't you?"[4]

The first clumps of parliamentary loyalists emerged from the White House, waving white flags above their heads, just before 2 p.m. Four hours later, Khasbulatov and Rutskoi were taken in a bus, through jeering crowds, to Lefortovo Prison. Officially, forty-six people had died in the assault on the White House, but almost no one believed the death toll was that low. Nevertheless, it seemed that Boris Yeltsin had won a complete victory.

But within days doubts were being voiced within the Kremlin itself. Echoing the warning about thrones built on bayonets, one of Yeltsin's own advisers, Sergei Stankevich, asked aloud if the bloody confrontation hadn't also fatally diminished the moral authority of Russia's president. "It's necessary to find the basis for civil compromise. Russia cannot be reformed by a man standing on top of a tank."[5]

11 January 1994. In the living room of his shabby apartment in Moscow's Sokolniki district, Vladimir Zhirinovsky looked at the unmade fold-out bed and barked at an aide to deal with it. He shouted at a bodyguard to bring his coat and hat.

He was living the role he had slowly perfected over the past three years, that of the decisive, authoritarian leader who would raise Russians from the trough of humiliation, cleanse them of impurity, and strike fear into the hearts of their enemies ("the world won't follow America's orders. If necessary, we'll fight a nuclear war!")

Now he was exultant. "This," he said, "is the day I've been waiting for all my life."

It was 9 a.m. on the morning of the opening of the Russian Duma, the newly elected lower house of the new parliament. One hour later the man whose party had taken 23 per cent of the vote, the largest share in Russia's first post-Soviet elections, entered the building temporarily housing the Duma. In the Duma his party had sixty-four of the 444 seats.[6]

The world media paid him chaotic homage. A crowd of two hundred reporters and cameramen surged around him, pushing and yelling, as he marched to his seat. The score of the ultra-nationalist leader of the Liberal Democratic Party had stunned the world. It had particularly stunned forces loyal to Boris Yeltsin. So would his opening speech in parliament.

"You are waging war on Russia," he shouted, pointing at the deputies of Russia's Choice, who had championed radical economic reform and the destruction of the Russian Supreme Soviet. "For you democracy is the annihilation of Russians. That's your democracy! Don't cut me off! SHUT UP! I'm the one talking now. Out of the hall! You're all candidates for the psychiatric asylum!"

And when Anatoli Chubais, a deputy from Russia's Choice and the minister of privatization, pointed at his watch to signify that Zhirinovsky had gone over time, Zhirinovsky shouted: "Mr. Chubais, you can show them your watch in Lefortovo [prison] when it's time for your lunch there!"[7]

Russia's experiment with representative institutions and parliamentary democracy began in the spring of 1989. By the spring of 1995 it had survived the collapse of an empire and two military confrontations in the heart of Moscow.

These snapshots of three critical moments in this six-year evolution would seem, at first glance, only to confirm the description of parliamentary government once offered by the nineteenth-century Russian thinker Alexander Herzen as "a trap called an oasis of liberty. It merely defends the right of property, exiles men in the name of public safety, and keeps men under arms who are ready, without asking why, to fire instantly as soon as ordered. Little do naïve democrats know what it is they believe in, and what the consequences will be."[8]

But the snapshots show more.

For Mikhail Gorbachev, searching already for his niche in history, liberty was a gift he had bestowed on his people, even at the price of the death of the Soviet Union. This was, in December 1991, an idea both revealing and false. Gorbachev, on leaving power, was casting himself in the historical mould of the good czar, in the tradition of Peter the Great and Alexander II, who, seeing the need, launched revolutions from above.

Yet the testimony of Gorbachev's own advisers indicates that his goal, in decreeing competitive elections and establishing a quasi-parliament, was not so much to give liberty to his people as to give himself more power in his battle with the recalcitrant establishment of the Soviet Communist Party. To that end he set out to create a separate power centre, one with the legitimacy conferred by electoral competition but one which he could still dominate. Both advisers and opponents agree that what he did not foresee was how quickly the new parliamentary body would assert its separate identity. In trying to tame one monster, as one of his advisers put it, he created another.[9]

And so Gorbachev resorted increasingly to the technique of parliamentary coups, bold manœuvres which ignored, short-circuited, or simply broke the existing rules and which depended on his ability to overpower political resistance by the force of his personality and position. It was a technique he used briefly with great success, until his opponents began to use the same methods against him. But unlike Gorbachev, his opponents and his successors were willing to move beyond the breaking of parliamentary rules to get their way. Tanks, troops, and blood would ultimately be the decisive factors as political battles were transformed into real battles in Russia's capital.

The struggle for power in the dying days of the Soviet Union was complicated by institutional confusion, created largely by Gorbachev himself. It was he, inspired by a mythical golden age of Leninist political participation embodied in the slogan "All Power to the Soviets," who chose to create the Soviet Congress of People's Deputies which placed supreme legislative power, including the power to rewrite the constitution, and executive authority in one body. Its chairman, chosen by a vote of the deputies, became both the speaker and the executive head of state. Thus the distinction between executive and legislative power became blurred at a crucial time of crisis.

His rival and successor, Boris Yeltsin, also looked backward into Russian history, searching for a mythical age of limited Russian democracy, and chose to resurrect the Duma, first created under the last czar.

Yet the representative forces thus unleashed helped topple the first leader and will, in all likelihood, outlast the second. That is the theme of this book.

The period from 1989 to 1995 dramatically illustrates another, more disturbing theme. It is the theme of political extremism that lurks just below the surface of Russian political life, ready to explode in armed confrontation as in October 1993, or in the presence of Vladimir Zhirinovsky in the new Duma, with his taunts and threats and his vision of a new Russian empire to which leaders of republics of the former Soviet Union would come crawling on their knees, tears in their eyes, to beg for admittance.[10] It is a theme which Russian leaders and thinkers have pondered for almost two hundred years, offering explanations reaching back across the centuries to find the roots in early communal society or alternatively in the Bolshevik tradition of political debate as war, to be won by any means.

Whatever the explanation, the following description of the Russian political class, written by Alexander Herzen in the middle of the nineteenth century, sounds eerily contemporary: "We are great doctrinaires and raisonneurs. To this German capacity we add our own national ... element, ruthless, fanatically dry: we are only too willing to cut off heads ... With fearless step we march to the very limit, and go beyond it; never out of step with the dialectic, only with the truth."[11]

CHAPTER TWO

Searching for the New World

Later, after the Communist system and the Soviet empire had collapsed, Alexander Yakovlev, one of Mikhail Gorbachev's closest lieutenants, would use a startling metaphor of faith and betrayal to describe what had happened: "We tried to destroy the Church in the name of religious truth and the truth of Jesus, only to discover that our religion was one of lies and our Jesus was counterfeit."[1]

But in December 1985, just eight months after Mikhail Gorbachev became the general secretary of the Communist Party of the Soviet Union, Yakovlev was still a believer in socialism. He was also a secretary of the Central Committee. That month he sat down and wrote Gorbachev a memo. In it he outlined a plan to begin what could only be termed a new political revolution in the country.

I tried to establish the imperative need to split the Communist Party of the Soviet Union into two parties and hold elections. This would create democratic competition and both parties would be rejuvenated. They would alternate in power. It was a necessary process of democracy; it was democracy itself. A monopoly of power denies democracy, a monopoly of property denies democracy, and a monopoly of ideology denies democracy. I believed in this because I thought it was the way to perfect socialism.[2]

Gorbachev showed the memorandum to no one. He was a successful politician, not a revolutionary. Wait, he told Yakovlev, it's too early.

But Yakovlev was not alone. Among Gorbachev's advisers, discussions about free elections and democratization had started almost from the moment he was chosen party leader in 1985. They took place at a string of government dachas, vast country houses just beyond Moscow's ring road. Here, behind high green fences which resembled nothing so much as prison walls, the counsellors of the new prince ate and drank, while they argued and strolled the vast, unkempt grounds, their wants catered to by a small army of KGB servants. This was the ultimate privilege of Soviet power. Even the vodka came from a special production line of the giant Kristall distillery in Moscow reserved for the Central Committee.

In the first spring of perestroika, these retreats bore no resemblance to the drunken banqueting favoured by Stalin and his successors. They were, instead, rambling seminars on politics stretching for hours into the night. In April 1985 the Gorbachev team gathered at the Volinskoye dacha to prepare his first report as general secretary to the Central Committee. Here Gorbachev's principal advisers, Yakovlev and Anatoli Lukyanov, then the head of the Central Committee Organization department, first argued over Yakovlev's idea to split the party in two. "It seemed to me," Lukyanov said later, "a little artificial to create two wings in one party which would be competing against each other."[3]

In that first report to the Central Committee there was, in fact, no mention of political reform. Instead Gorbachev talked of the need for perestroika and "acceleration." He still believed that, with more discipline and effort, the socialist system, under the guidance of the Communist Party, could be reformed.

But the discussions over political reform at the party dachas were important, and so were the men who participated in them. They would set in motion, through their ideas and initiatives, forces which would destroy a totalitarian state.

They were unlikely candidates to launch a political revolution: men in their fifties and early sixties, intellectuals who, like moles, had chosen to spend a lifetime tunnelling up the party hierarchy, carefully covering their doubts and dreams, while loyally serving the old regime. They were, with the exception of Lukyanov, political schizophrenics. What they dreamed of was democratization, not democracy. Almost all of them saw no contradiction in talking of competitive elections in a one-party state. Their allegiance was still to the Leninist ideal. And for the first among them, Leninism was more than an ideal; it was a passion. Mikhail Gorbachev was a true believer, an acolyte who loved the man as much as his system.

When Alexander Yakovlev reflected on those discussions in August 1993, he was still sitting in an office in the Staraya Ploschad complex next to the Kremlin. This had once been the nerve centre of the Central Committee. Now Yakovlev served another master, Boris Yeltsin, and the room was stripped of the traditional portrait of Lenin. In all other respects it remained the office of a high Soviet official. A long conference table dominated the monastic room. On a smaller table next to Yakovlev's desk stood ten white phones. One, in the middle, still bore the hammer-and-sickle crest: this was the direct line to the president's office.

Yakovlev was a Communist believer, and the son of a Communist believer. His father had fought for Lenin's side in the Civil War and he would fight again, along with his son, in the Great Patriotic War. But he had also carefully kept the Bible presented to him on his graduation from grade four. It was from this Bible that Alexander Yakovlev first learned the letters of the Cyrillic alphabet, with the help of his grandfather. "When I was in the second grade, women in the village asked me to read to them from the Bible. What did I understand in it? To be frank, nothing. But I still read it."[4]

Yakovlev had a heroic war. Grievously wounded at the front near Leningrad in 1942, he returned home to a village near Yaroslavl, an invalid on crutches. In 1944, at the age of twenty, he joined the Communist Party. Several years later he was sent to the Higher Party School in Moscow. In 1956, with other party workers from the Central Committee, he listened from the balcony as Nikita Khrushchev made his secret speech to the Twentieth Party Congress on Stalin's crimes.

It was the first profound shock to the foundation of his Communist faith. "I remember how we came down afterwards from the balcony and none of us could look each other in the face. We were all stunned, and ashamed."

A dozen years later, another shock. Yakovlev was sent to Prague in August 1968, the day after the Soviet invasion of Czechoslovakia. As the deputy head of the propaganda department of the Communist Party Central Committee, he was to oversee Soviet journalists and help direct the Czech media. Instead he found himself a virtual prisoner in the Soviet embassy.

"In the streets I saw gallows with effigies of Soviet soldiers hanging there. People were shouting 'fascists, fascists.' I wondered why we had come." He quickly applied, and was allowed, to go home.[5]

Five years later Yakovlev was sent into what he describes as political exile, as ambassador to Canada. The catalyst, ironically, was a paper he had written denouncing the glorification of Russian nationalism and the pre-revolutionary past among a new breed of conservative writers. It incurred the wrath of Politburo member and ideology chief, Mikhail Suslov.

Yakovlev spent ten years in Canada. In 1993 he still talked of farms in Saskatchewan where four people did the work that dozens would do in the Soviet Union. There were other memories that marked him, notably those of his many conversations with Prime Minister Pierre Elliott Trudeau. "We sometimes had long private sessions without ever talking politics," Yakovlev said. "We discussed philosophical issues, Dostoyevsky and Pushkin."[6]

And for ten years, from his vantage point in Ottawa, he watched the workings of competitive party politics, both in Canada and the United States. Then, in 1983, Mikhail Gorbachev came on an official visit, as a Politburo member. The two men had met before but now they spent hours in private conversation and realized they shared many views. Within a month Gorbachev had arranged for Yakovlev to return to Moscow.

"Yakovlev came back from Canada with the idea of a two-party system," Anatoli Lukyanov said. "It was all quite interesting, with its democratic side, and its difficulties. These 'Westerners,' as they're called here, who see the advertisements and intellectual window displays of the West and then come back and recommend that we adopt such a system, I call that their attempt to create a New World."[7]

Gorbachev chose other advisers from the party hierarchy, such as Georgi Shaknazarov, Anatoli Chernayev, and Ivan Frolov, men who saw themselves as intellectuals, as outsiders working inside the party, hiding their doubts. They had also spent time outside the Soviet Union, in this case Prague, working at the Communist periodical, *Problems of Peace and Socialism*.

Shaknazarov insisted his doubts had already crystallized by the end of the Second World War. Despite that, he joined the party. "My point of view was social-democratic even then. I would say that 10 to 15 per cent of the party shared my view. There was no freedom, personal freedom. I felt that the methods used, without democracy, were completely unacceptable. A dozen men decided everything for the country. Any intelligent person could see it didn't work."[8]

In fact, it took Gorbachev more than a year in office as general secretary to come to the same conclusion. It was forced on him when he realized that the party hierarchy was simply sabotaging his economic reforms contained in new laws on cooperative enterprise and factory self-financing. These laws were intended to free parts of the economy from the dead hand of central planning. Factories would be allowed to keep a much larger share of their profits and the new cooperatives would be small private enterprises in all but name. But in many parts of the country party bosses refused to implement these laws.

According to Chernayev, Gorbachev began to understand that his idea of turning the party into the leader of perestroika simply wasn't working.[9]

The first battle was joined in the fall of 1986. Gorbachev was now searching for a weapon to bring the party hierarchy to heel. Democratization, his advisers suggested, could be the sword. The party leadership was preparing a full meeting or plenum of the Central Committee to deal with the question of party officials or "cadres." "Every Soviet leader chose his own method to clean out the party," historian Roy Medvedev said. "Gorbachev wanted to use the election system to get rid of the dead wood."[10]

He proposed to the Politburo a modified system of workers' self-management, where party managers in industry and agriculture would be elected by their workforces. This, so the thinking among the general secretary's advisers went, would ensure that younger, more energetic managers would take over who would carry out economic reforms. The Politburo, made up largely of men appointed by Leonid Brezhnev, reluctantly agreed.

But Alexander Yakovlev urged Gorbachev to go further with reform, to push for political democratization with genuine competitive elections.

The final package accepted by the Politburo bore the scars of painful compromise. Rather than competitive elections, it sketched a plan to "perfect" the existing system of electing one carefully vetted candidate per riding to local soviets (councils). Instead, several candidates would be proposed at electors' meetings and pre-election conferences. Elections would be held in larger constituencies, with several deputies being elected from each. It also included a proposal to elect first secretaries of party committees, right up to republic level, by secret ballot from a choice of candidates. This was little more than reheated Leninism, according to Roy Medvedev. Gorbachev was merely proposing to restore the system in effect in the 1920s and abolished by Stalin.

But the barons of the Central Committee resisted even this. When a date to hold the plenum in January 1987 was finally agreed on, Gorbachev personally met with almost every one of the three hundred members of the committee, inviting them out to his dacha. He was a man supremely confident that his personal charm, his arguments, and his smile would persuade them, as it had so many others, to accept his view, and his reform.[11]

And then Gorbachev abruptly changed tactics.

His opening speech at the Central Committee meeting was a frontal attack against corruption by senior party officials "who abused their authority, suppressed criticism, sought [personal] gain, and some of whom became accomplices in, if not organizers of, criminal activities." Political reforms, he said, were needed to carry out perestroika. The introduction of democracy would make the party more efficient, allowing the better-educated men and women of talent and ambition to replace those officials "who view initiative and activism of people as something little short of a natural calamity."[12]

This was greeted with stony silence. No one spoke out directly against Gorbachev's proposals. There was reluctant agreement to extend the principle of competitive elections to the soviets and to enterprises. But as for competition within the ranks, the final resolution of the plenum merely "noted the fact that the Politburo raised the question of the need to widen democracy within the Party." As a consolation prize the Central Committee agreed to Gorbachev's proposal to hold a special party conference the following year.

By the end of the two-day plenum Gorbachev's irritation was evident. His closing speech was a warning and a call to arms; the war for control of the party had only begun. "We need democracy like air. If we fail to realize this, or if we realize this but take no really serious steps to broaden it, promote it, and draw the country's working people extensively into the perestroika process, our policy will get choked, and perestroika will fail."[13]

The frontal attack against the party barons had failed. So now Gorbachev chose the guerilla tactics of glasnost. He made speeches urging local organizations to implement his plans "experimentally." Newspapers began printing letters from readers openly questioning the existing one-candidate electoral system. On a tour in Latvia, he suggested the Baltics would be a good place to start with competitive elections. "What do you think?" he asked the audience. There was loud applause. "Hold on," Gorbachev laughed, "let's not rush into things!"[14]

Public criticism had turned the existing simulacrum of a parliament, the Supreme Soviet, into a public joke. All members were pre-selected by the Communist Party, all elections had only one candidate. When it met, once or twice a year for a few days, the Brezhnev Supreme Soviet was an astonishing sight: serried ranks of old men endlessly applauding themselves, after the most decrepit among them had ploughed through a speech he barely understood. And to complete the tableau, a forest of arms rising, as one, to approve the bill at hand. Under this system the Supreme Soviet passed an average of one to two laws a year. The real legislature was the presidium, or executive committee of the Supreme Soviet, which adopted five to six hundred decrees a year. And all of these had previously been approved by the Communist Party Politburo.[15]

Georgi Shaknazarov was one of the last to be elected to it in 1987:

I had just become the first deputy head of a department of the Central Committee, and the party considered that I should be a member of the Supreme Soviet. And right away a seat was opened in Turkmenia. I was invited to go, I went, the signal had been given by Moscow, everybody was ready in the local party organization. I had never had anything to do with Turkmenia but everybody at the election meeting voted yes, and the same same day I became a deputy.

It should be said that local officials in the republics were interested in getting someone from the Centre. Because the Centre could help them. It was the Soviet variation of lobbying. And since I was a member of the party hierarchy, I could phone a minister to ask him to give help to the Turkmen district where I was elected; trucks from the Afghan war, for example, or building materials to complete the local school building plan.[16]

By June 1987 the guerilla campaign was showing modest results. In elections on June 21 for local soviets, the recommendation to start "experimenting" with competition led to races with more than one candidate in ninety-three ridings. Still, this number has to be set beside the total number of local deputies elected that day: 2,321,766.[17]

Guerilla tactics would soften up the enemy; they would not win the war. What changed the balance of power was a battle for possession of the past.

Once again the initiative was Gorbachev's. He had decided to use the occasion of the seventieth anniversary of the Bolshevik revolution in November 1987 to deliver a landmark speech, nothing short of a fundamental official revision of Soviet history. Throughout the summer he worked on a draft of the speech. On 21 October he read it to the Central Committee. It was a powerful indictment, containing figures on the slaughter of the Communist Party and army leadership under Stalin. Even more heretical was Gorbachev's conclusion that all the "triumphs" of Stalinism – in the building of socialism, in the Second World War, and in the postwar reconstruction – were achieved *despite* Stalin, not because of him.

When he rose to speak in the ornate Kremlin hall on 2 November 1987, rumour, speculation and word-of-mouth had raised expectations to feverish heights. Many in the hall hoped, and many more feared, that this was to be a dramatic divorce with the past. But his public speech was but a pale shadow of his private indictment. He did condemn Stalin's crimes as "enormous and unforgivable," but then said that Stalin's terror had cost not millions but only "many thousands of lives." As for the "triumphs" of Stalinism, publicly Gorbachev now said there had been no alternative to crash industrialization and collectivization of agriculture. It was in almost complete contradiction to his conclusion behind closed doors two weeks previously.

His plan had been derailed by the man who was to be his nemesis and, ultimately, his political executioner. But in October 1987 Boris Yeltsin seemed bent on political suicide, not execution. He was a alternate (non-voting) member of the Politburo and the man in charge of the Moscow party organization. He had been picked by Gorbachev for the job and had made a reputation as a reformer attacking corruption and privileges in the capital. But at the Central Committee meeting, just minutes after Gorbachev had read the incendiary draft of his anniversary speech, Yeltsin went to the podium to submit his resignation from the Politburo. It was unprecedented. Equally unprecedented was his speech, a confused but devastating attack on the party leadership. It even included a direct attack on Gorbachev for encouraging a "cult of personality" around him.

Yeltsin's speech brought swift retribution. Twenty-five speakers took the floor in succession to denounce him in the bitterest terms for everything from excessive ambition to immaturity and vanity. Within weeks he was released from the Politburo and fired as

Moscow party chief. But the unexpected attack left Gorbachev exposed. Those committed to reform in the Politburo were in the minority and now this minority was further weakened by Yeltsin's suicidal initiative. Gorbachev's plan officially to rewrite Soviet history in one dramatic speech was abandoned.

The battle for possession of the past was now engaged. The counter-attack came in the form of a letter from a Leningrad chemistry teacher, Nina Andreyeva. It was called "I cannot betray my principles" and was published on 13 March 1988 in the newspaper *Sovietskaya Rossiya*. It was a ringing defence of Stalin's achievements and the leading role of the Communist Party, and a direct attack on perestroika, which was now in the hands of "left-wing liberal intellectuals."

The next day Mikhail Gorbachev left on an official trip to Yugoslavia. It was then that Yegor Ligachev, the number two man in the Politburo, made his move.

Like Gorbachev, Ligachev was a provincial party secretary, brought to Moscow from Tomsk by former Soviet leader Yuri Andropov. He was a pure product of the party, a simple man who believed in the virtues of hard work, a teetotaller who decreed that party meetings in Tomsk take place on Saturdays. Unlike Gorbachev, he saw no need to reform the existing system. Six years later, reflecting on these events, he still spoke in communist clichés, and believed them:

Under the direction of our Party, our country became a superpower. The Communists took a backward country and made it a great power; they triumphed over fascism and saved humanity, they went into space, and created a planned economy.

In the first three years of perestroika, we achieved many successes: the volume of production and construction went up. But when Gorbachev and Yakovlev started down another path, not of reform but of the transformation of society ... its destruction, then we're talking about revolution, or rather counter-revolution.[18]

Ligachev called in the editors of Communist party newspapers and news agencies, praised the article by Andreyeva, and recommended they use it as a guide in carrying out their work. The message was clear. The director of TASS, the Soviet news agency, at once issued a recommendation to provincial papers to reprint the Andreyeva article. Glasnost was abruptly frozen.

It took time for Gorbachev to organize his troops. Finally, at a two-day meeting of the Politburo which began 24 March 1988, he insisted that every member take a stand for or against the Andreyeva article. Ligachev defended it as a natural reaction against attempts to blacken Soviet history. The majority lined up behind Alexander Yakovlev, who described it as anti-perestroika from beginning to end. "It's filled with a desperate nostalgia for the strongman of the past, combined with an attempt to re-evaluate more recent developments. Perestroika doesn't yet have strong roots, either in people's thinking or in life. Such an attack can't go unanswered."[19]

Yakovlev was instructed to write an article to be published in *Pravda* repeating his criticisms of Ligachev and his denunciation of the Andreyeva article. Gorbachev was triumphant. Now, he told his colleagues, it was time to look to the future. And the future, for Gorbachev, was Leninist.

"We have to begin work on the Theses (proposals) for the party conference, comrades. On the strength of my position I've already devoted some thought to this. We must begin to clarify how to put forward once again the Leninist slogan about the Soviets in the context of perestroika. And what should the relationship be between the party and the Soviets?"[20]

In fact, he had already secretly started the work at the Novo Ogarevo dacha outside Moscow. Later this dacha would become synonymous with Gorbachev's doomed effort to draw up a new constitution, a Union Treaty, for the Soviet Union. But in March 1988 a half-dozen aging apparatchiks were engaged in nothing less than a quest to invent democracy. Alexander Yakovlev, Georgi Shaknazarov, Anatoli Lukyanov, Vadim Medvedev, Ivan Frolov, Anatoli Chernayev – each came armed with his own vision: presidential government along the American model, a parliamentary system, two socialist-communist parties competing for power, a return to true Leninist competitive democracy.

According to Vadim Medvedev, at that point a Central Committee secretary and later a non-voting member of the Politburo, Gorbachev and his inner circle argued for days on end about these ideas. "Many times," Medvedev said, "there were fierce disputes where the target was Gorbachev, despite his position."[21]

For these political schizophrenics, having long served a state whose sclerotic structures they secretly wanted to change, this was the chance, very likely the unique chance, to see their beliefs translated into reality. Some among them, notably Yakovlev and Lukyanov, were trying for the second time. Twenty years earlier they had attempted to persuade the Brezhnev party leadership, then engaged in drafting a new constitution, to open the door to limited democracy.

"In 1969, we were preparing a draft for the Politburo," Lukyanov said. Both he and Yakovlev worked in the Central Committee. "We attached a note, signed by Yakovlev, myself and three others, outlining various possibilities: alternative elections, the election of a Congress of People's Deputies, and the election of the Supreme Soviet ..."

Their suggestions were ignored. But now a new leader wanted their help to modernize the political structure.

"Medvedev and Shaknazarov wanted to create a presidency where the posts of general secretary (of the Communist Party) and president would be held by one man," Lukyanov said. "Yakovlev felt it would still concentrate too much power in the hands of one man. Who was against it? I was, and in the end, so was Gorbachev."

Medvedev remembered his position differently: "We should have opted for a classical system, either the English system, in which the leader of the party which wins the election forms the government and is responsible before parliament, or the American system or some mixture of presidential and parliamentary systems as in Europe. But there should have been a division between executive and legislative functions."

The system adopted contained at its heart the Soviet Congress of People's Deputies, a giant assembly of 2,250 members, which would meet once or twice a year. Its power would be based on two things: competitive elections conferring political legitimacy on the elected deputies, and a radical change of role for the Communist Party. Gorbachev and his advisers saw the party stepping back from its day-to-day control of all decisions and allowing the Congress a free hand to debate and pass laws and the government leeway to execute them. The party's role would be to draw up the general orientations of policy and to play a watchdog role. Its authority would flow from the fact that the majority of deputies in the new Congress would be party members. The chairman of the Congress would be both Speaker and effective head of state. This, everyone agreed, would be Gorbachev's job. There would be three groups of deputies: 750 would be elected in so-called national territorial districts,

750 in republican districts, and 750 from so-called social organizations. From the ranks of the Congress a full-time working parliament of 542 members, the Supreme Soviet, would be elected.

The creation of this monster was largely due to three men. Anatoli Lukyanov was the man who proposed the structure and defended it ardently. A stocky man, with the face and voice of a basset hound, he had toiled in the Kremlin for more than thirty years. He boasted of knowing Molotov. Anastas Mikoyan, who had survived revolution, civil war, and Stalin's purges to reach the summit of the Soviet state and die in bed, became his patron and delivered to him the secret of political longevity: "In politics you have no friends." One who thought he was Lukyanov's friend was Mikhail Gorbachev. They had known each other for almost forty years since meeting at Moscow State University where they had both studied law.[22]

Alone of the Gorbachev advisers, Lukyanov was not politically schizophrenic. He had never apparently questioned his Marxist beliefs. On the contrary, he had spent years writing a doctoral thesis on the history of Lenin's legislative organ, the Congress of Soviets.

Now he seized the opportunity to recreate the Congress. Tirelessly he preached the Leninist doctrine of the Congress as a true mirror of society.

That's why we opted for a system of three separate forms of representation at the Congress ... one third elected by ridings, one third through republican and autonomous republic elections, and one third through social organizations. For us it was a key question. Otherwise, there was a threat that women, the working classes, collective farm workers who had always represented the majority in the Supreme Soviet wouldn't be represented. This way the Congress achieved the goal of being a mirror, a collective portrait of society.

In those closed-door discussions, I put forward another reason for the Congress. I said to the comrades, with this major change to our political and social system, parties and blocs will develop. Struggles may start. Therefore a large, powerful organ will be needed to keep the country from confrontation and conflict.[23]

Other advisers were dubious. Far from seeing it as a mirror of society, they feared the Congress would be seen as yet another attempt by the party to manipulate society. They were particularly uneasy about the elections from "social organizations," in effect

Communist-front organizations. Such a concept had no parallel in the world. It was a flagrant violation of the concept of one citizen, one vote.[24]

Shaknazarov was both Lukyanov's principal collaborator in writing on the Theses on the new political structures, and his main opponent. Shaknazarov was in favour of a normal parliament with an upper and lower house. He argued that history had graphically demonstrated that the Congress could not fulfill the role Lukyanov claimed for it. "I said to him: Anatoli, what do you find so special in this institution? In fact, it failed, it collapsed. It was unable to act as a rampart against the dictatorship of Stalin or the resulting disorders. He destroyed it in a day, don't you see?"[25]

Despite their earlier arguments over the future of the Communist Party, Lukyanov received tactical support in this debate from the second key participant, Alexander Yakovlev. He had so far failed to convince Gorbachev to split the party. Now he saw, in the creation of the Congress, a roundabout way to pursue his goal. The key was the resurrection of the slogan "All power to the soviets." "I personally saw this proposal as a way of limiting the power of the Communist Party," he said later. It was exactly the same logic, he pointed out, which led Andrei Sakharov to brandish the slogan at the First Congress of People's Deputies.[26]

The third man, the man who was persuaded and the man who counted, was Mikhail Gorbachev. "Gorbachev liked it," Vadim Medvedev said. "He talked about the tradition of the soviets, all power to the soviets, the Leninist tradition. Through the soviets, the party, having won the elections, would organize executive power."

Gorbachev was a mysterious man, even to his colleagues. One said he carefully hid his true self behind layers of camouflage. A Communist Party member at twenty-one, he became, at thirty-five, the Communist Party first secretary of the Stavropol region, the youngest regional first secretary in the Soviet Union. In 1979, at the age of forty-eight, he became the youngest member of the Politburo. Six years later he was the leader of the country. There is no trace, at any stage of this remarkable ascent, of any public questioning of the basis of the system. Even his revelation in 1990 that both his grandfathers had been victims of the Stalinist repression of the 1930s was made to underline his faith, not to question it. "Should I turn my back on my grandfather, who was committed to the socialist idea?" he said in a Soviet television interview.

Some biographers suggest one clue to the mystery of Gorbachev was his choice of law as a student in 1950 at Moscow State University. At the time it was an unusual choice. The study of law, which meant western bourgeois law, had been all but eliminated at the end of the 1920s. Even in the late years of Stalin's rule only a small minority of university students were enrolled in law faculties where they had the opportunity to read authors such as Rousseau, Locke, and Montesquieu along with standard Communist works. The intellectual impact of those studies on Gorbachev seems clear. The theme of the "law-based state" was one he preached with growing insistence when he became Soviet leader. Yet the mystery remained. Reflecting on Gorbachev's personality and the changes he wrought, a close aide concluded that Gorbachev was perhaps simply a reformer by nature, a reformer who spent years hiding his true instincts. "The general secretary was something like a 'genetic error' in a system which reproduces itself by cloning."[27]

Another clue to Gorbachev's behaviour was his identification with Lenin. The general secretary was a rarity, even in his own party: for him, the corpse in the mausoleum on Red Square was a living presence. Lenin's revolution had been a great breakthrough. Its achievements may have been perverted by his successors but the answer was not to abandon the system but to return to Lenin.

Gorbachev quoted Lenin, not only in his public speeches, but also to bemused colleagues at meetings of the Politburo. He kept the collected writings of Lenin on his Kremlin desk and subjected his staff to readings. "He would often pick a volume up and read aloud," wrote Valeri Boldin, his one-time chief of staff. "He liked to compare Lenin's comments to the current situation and extoll the author's perspicacity."[28]

This consuming quest to identify with the father of the revolution led Gorbachev, ironically, to Alexander Solzhenitzyn. In public the Politburo would denounce Solzhenitzyn's historical novel, *Lenin in Zurich*, as a disreputable slander on the founder of the Soviet state. It would never be published in the Soviet Union. In private, Gorbachev devoured the book hungrily. Have you read it, he asked Chernayev at the end of a long evening of work. Chernayev hadn't and found himself listening to a two-hour monologue about the book ("a powerful piece of work, malicious but talented") and the man, frozen in exile on the eve of a revolution he didn't foresee:

He was 47 then. And he hadn't done anything! He was irritable and testy. He had fought and split with everyone. No one could get close to him. Look, here's Inessa Armand (a French radical feminist and Lenin's lover). She loved him passionately from 1908 to 1920. That's no joke! Do you remember, in "Onward, Onward, Onward," when Misha Ulyanov (an actor well-known for his portrayal of Lenin in a famous glasnost play by Mikhail Shatrov) throws himself on her breast. I thought it was blasphemy! But now I've read Solzhenityzn and I see it in human terms. Anybody can take a great hero and reduce him to an ordinary man-in-the-street. But this is no caricature. You'll recognize the real Lenin!

"Blasphemy," "a great hero" – Gorbachev's passion was almost religious. His fascination with and emulation of Lenin may appear somewhat strange. In fact, there are many psychological similarities between the two men, heightened perhaps by the attempt by Gorbachev to "absorb" his hero. Like Lenin, Gorbachev used the force of his personality and his intellect to overwhelm his audiences, his arm slashing and poking the air in unconscious imitation of the founder of the state, who was frozen in bronze in this pose in hundreds of squares in cities around the country. Like stern school masters they rained down facts and arguments on recalcitrant pupils until, finally, the pupils relented.

Despite the public-relations radiance of his smile, Gorbachev, like Lenin, was indifferent to colleagues and subordinates. His prime minister, Nikolai Ryzhkov, in a book tellingly entitled *Perestroika: a History of Betrayals*, begins by bitterly recounting how Gorbachev casually discarded him after he suffered a heart attack in 1990, adding to the wound by "consulting" with him about his successor after the choice had been made. Even a close adviser like Alexander Yakovlev complained in 1988 that Gorbachev, in the five years that they had known each other, had never once thanked him for his work.[29]

This indifference sprang from the same source. Gorbachev, like Lenin, was obsessed by power: how to achieve it and how to keep it. To this end, Lenin was ready to resort to any tactical manœuvre. It was precisely this quality which Gorbachev admired and underlined to colleagues. "Lenin never thought the road to socialism would be straight," he told them. "Whenever life demanded it, he was capable of changing slogans. And he never allowed himself to become the slave of decisions already taken."[30]

And so the man who loved Lenin seized the occasion to build a political monument to him. But the majority of his advisers at the Novo Ogarevo dacha remained unconvinced. They continued to point to the cracks in the structure. To end the debate, Gorbachev finally resorted to a technique made famous by Nikita Khrushchev – the appeal to a larger forum, packed with loyalists. In April 1988 he called in the chief of the Central Committee legal department and other legislative experts. The question of parliamentary structures was put to a vote. These loyal party men obediently voted for the leader's choice.[31]

It was not coincidental that Gorbachev would make use of a tactic of Khrushchev. He was the second Soviet leader who filled his thoughts at this time. Gorbachev was haunted by the fall of the only general secretary to try to reform the party. Years later he reflected, with irony, on his own efforts to avoid making the same mistakes. "Khrushchev destroyed the nomenklatura and I often said to my colleagues when we began perestroika: If we don't think up something new we will meet the same fate as Khrushchev. Then we started on the first free elections."[32]

First, however, he had to convince the Politburo. Here Gorbachev proceeded carefully. He had been seared by the Nina Andreyeva confrontation. "We mustn't frighten the geese," he kept repeating at the dacha, speaking of his Politburo colleagues. "This will stun them," he said, contemplating the new political structures. "For most of them, there'll be no place at the top."[33]

It would certainly surprise the world when he unveiled his ideas at the party conference on 28 June 1988. But the story that Gorbachev sprung these changes on unsuspecting members of the Politburo on the eve of the conference is a myth.[34]

Instead, Gorbachev slowly brought them along. In April he called 150 provincial party leaders to Moscow to talk of his ideas for resuscitating Lenin's concept of the soviets. The Politburo debated the new parliamentary institutions at least three times during the spring, according to Anatoli Lukyanov, during which he was called upon to explain and defend his concept of a Congress of People's Deputies.

On 23 May the Central Committee published "Ten Theses for the 19th Party Conference." The homage to Lenin was unmistakable. For it was in April 1917, immediately after his return from exile, that Lenin published his Ten Theses, a call to socialist revolution and a glimpse of the new utopia: a proletarian state which would be governed by soviets of workers' and peasants' deputies, where the police, the army, and the bourgeois bureaucracy would be abolished.

The Theses gave the Soviet public its first glimpse of the parliamentary future. The commitment to competitive elections was clearly spelled out. Gorbachev's idea that the party would step back from its day-to-day control of the state was also outlined. It would abandon its administrative functions and revert to the role Lenin had intended for it, that of "political avant-garde" debating and deciding broad policy goals. The prime minister and his government, who until now had merely been lieutenants carrying out the orders of the Politburo and the Central Committee, would assume greater executive responsibility. They would report to the Congress, where the Communist Party would exercise authority through its expected majority of deputies. No parliamentary model was specifically proposed but Soviet citizens were urged to study carefully Lenin's Congress of Soviets which helped launch the 1917 revolution, along with "different variations and proposals," including the idea of turning the Supreme Soviet into a virtual full-time parliament and of electing some members from "social organizations."[35]

It was vague but the effect was electric. Russians gathered in thick knots in front of newspaper billboards to read the leaden prose of Gorbachev's advisers. Foreign journalists, arriving by the thousands in Moscow for the Gorbachev-Reagan summit, watched in astonishment as Soviet citizens, for the first time in decades, argued openly in the streets about politics.

Curiously, despite Gorbachev's apprehensions, the arguments in the Politburo were far less heated. In retrospect, participants and advisers suggested different reasons for this: no one wanted to criticize openly "democracy," the Leninist model stifled many potential objections, the old men in the Kremlin were complacently convinced that all this was merely cosmetic, that the party would continue to pull all the key strings. Yegor Ligachev offered a simpler explanation: "Of course, there were arguments [about competitive elections and a new Congress] but they weren't nearly as violent as those about the interpretation of our history. Those were the really important discussions: sometimes, history is more important than current events."[36]

Indeed, the most telling objection came from a man who loyally supported Gorbachev in the Politburo, his prime minister, Nikolai

Ryzhkov. And he would object precisely to the Leninist model itself, saying it completely blurred the line between the executive and the legislative. It was a recipe for confusion and disaster, he warned, in the final discussion before the party conference. "Either we clearly separate the three branches of government and define their functions or, since you've chosen to transform the soviets into powerful bodies, we go all the way and give them all state power. I don't see any other way. Otherwise, the state may lose its ability to govern."[37]

Ryzhkov found himself in what he called "the sad minority," his arguments swept aside as special pleading on behalf of his own power base, the Council of Ministers, the Soviet cabinet.

On 28 June 1988, Gorbachev opened the 19th Party conference with a marathon four-hour speech. The five thousand delegates found the contents distinctly unsettling. They applauded infrequently and, when he had finished, denied Gorbachev the traditional standing ovation.

There was, in fact, something to displease everyone in the vast hall. Gorbachev developed the themes of "socialist pluralism" and a "law-based state." Against this background he unveiled the structure of his proposed new two-tier parliament, with its Congress of 2,250 members, from which deputies would be chosen to sit in the 542-member permanent Supreme Soviet. The structure was ungainly but the elections to select its members would be competitive for the first time in decades. At the same time the party would withdraw from day-to-day government administration. Party economic departments, which duplicated government ministries would be abolished. The party bureaucracy would be slashed. To provincial party leaders in the hall, all this sounded ominous.

Liberals were scarcely encouraged by the patently undemocratic features of this package. There was, naturally, the matter of the 750 seats reserved for "social organizations" controlled by the party. There was also the unexpected comment from Gorbachev that, as a rule, the first secretary of a regional party organization would be "recommended" for the post of chairman of the regional soviet.

There was, in fact, so much grumbling about this idea that Gorbachev was forced to return to the podium two days later to defend it. It was then that he suggested that party secretaries would first have to be elected, in competitive contests, to the soviets before they could be nominated as chairmen. Several of his advisers said the intent of this manœuvre was clear: Gorbachev was counting on voters to accomplish what he so far had not been able to – that is, eliminate the deadwood and reactionary forces from the provincial party structures.[38]

In retrospect, the conference can be seen as a trial run for the first Congress of People's Deputies the following year. In an astonishing break with Soviet tradition, large chunks of the proceedings were televised each evening. Viewers saw a delegate openly attack the party leadership and call for the resignation of its most decrepit members. There were calls from reformers for faster change and denounciations of the slow pace of reform. All the while Gorbachev presided, intervened, and ceaselessly improvised. It was a masterful performance, all the more so since the Soviet leader knew that the majority of delegates was opposed to his sweeping plans.

On the fourth and final day, Gorbachev's instinct for improvisation combined with luck to provide the excitement and distraction he needed to slip his plan through. Luck took the bulky form of Boris Yeltsin, striding down from the balcony to demand time at the podium. Yeltsin had been dropped from the Politburo and fired as Moscow party chief but Gorbachev had allowed him to stay in Moscow as vice-minister of construction. He was a delegate at the conference. Gorbachev overruled his colleagues and gave him the microphone. Yeltsin's speech was an attack on the sclerosis of the party which had so far paralysed perestroika. He attacked the hidden network of party privileges. And he called for his own political rehabilitation.

Immediately, a bitter counter-attack was launched by Yeltsin's principal enemy in the Politburo, Yegor Ligachev. It was nasty and personal. You Boris, Ligachev repeated like a mantra, are wrong. It was a naked confrontation of conflicting ambition, it was stunning political theatre, and it was broadcast to the nation that night.

In the end, like some Soviet Solomon, Gorbachev weighed the arguments before the delegates and the country. He deftly produced a transcript of the secret Central Committee meeting in October 1987. He read out a passage in which, under questioning from Gorbachev himself, Yeltsin admitted his error in criticizing the party's reform program. Yeltsin would not be rehabilitated. But Gorbachev also implicitly criticized Ligachev: the party had to democratize itself, and couldn't reform society by resorting to old command-style methods.

The conference was agog and hours behind schedule. It was the opening Gorbachev was waiting for. He had just finished warning the delegates that there must be no repeat of the January 1987 plenum, when the Central Committee had passed resolutions to make the party more democratic, and most of the provincial bosses had simply ignored them.

Ivan Laptev was the editor-in-chief of the government newspaper *Izvestiia*, and a delegate to the conference. He understood Gorbachev's dilemma. "We'd always adopted good resolutions at party congresses. But most of them had become dead letters, either because there were no mechanisms to apply them, or because there was no timetable. So there we were at this party conference. Everybody had spoken and expressed his point of view, we'd agreed that we had to organize competitive elections. But the party elite stayed completely calm. They said to themselves that they could put off the elections for as long as they wanted."

Laptev described what happened next as Gorbachev's "magic trick."

It was right before the end of the conference, I remember it well. Gorbachev was at the podium, he'd just finished his closing speech, and suddenly he pulled a piece of paper from his pocket. He hesitated, and shifted from one foot to the other. He was clearly very nervous. Then he read out what was written on the paper. It was a resolution setting the date for elections: the spring of 1989.

Then he quickly asked the delegates to support the resolution. We all raised our hands. That was it! As we were filing out, I remember several provincial secretaries asking: what have we just done, what have we done?[39]

What they had done was open the door to forces which would sweep them and their leader away.

It was, associates and observers say, the high point of Gorbachev's time in power. Politically and intellectually, he set the pace and forced the party elite to follow, while the country watched, rapt. Yet at the heart of this process is a question: not so much what had they done, but *why* had they done it?

Alexander Yakovlev and Georgi Shaknazarov both agree the answer, paradoxically, lies in decades of discipline instilled in Communist Party members.

"The paradox is that they were such believers that the system was eternal, that it couldn't be changed," Shaknazarov said. "But when the general secretary said this is the decision, the party and the Politburo have decided, that's the way it went. Nobody dared disagree with the general secretary."

"What the West never understood is that democracy was introduced because of the inertia of the party. This was the inertia of discipline," Yakovlev said. He compared membership in the Politburo to that in the Mechenoz, a German secret society of the sword in the Middle Ages. "It gave us the power to do anything we wanted. All we had to do was show our party card. We would have never been able to break the backbone of the totalitarian regime in Russia without this instrument – this totalitarian party."[40]

The inertia of discipline had begun as democratic centralism under Lenin. The theory was that there would be internal debate and discussion in the party until the decision was taken and then unquestioning obedience. In fact, Lenin's personality was such that discussion and contrary opinion became irrelevant when he made his views known. The tendency to bow before the leader's view became the rigid rule under the regime of fear of Stalin. No succeeding leader had the unchecked power of life and death which Stalin had possessed but the tradition of obedience had been learned. Gorbachev understood it and used it to achieve a goal he knew most delegates feared. But in this moment of triumph did Gorbachev himself truly understand what he had done? Did he realize that the mechanism he had created would lead to a multiparty system and the end of his regime?

In hindsight, his advisers were persuaded that the general secretary saw the future as they did. Alexander Yakovlev put it a touch poetically: "Gorbachev was a child of his times. He had one foot in the past and one in the future. And he did something of great importance for Russia when he decided to take that step into the future. It was clear that by doing so we were all going to lose power. For each it was different experience. For some it was painful."[41]

But almost every utterance of Gorbachev, then and later, suggests that this is a gentle delusion. At the party conference, he emotionally defended the idea of the Leninist one-party state. He compared suggestions to limit the party's role to a dangerous virus, a gift to the enemies of the perestroika. "Anyone who calls into question the role and meaning of the party will be decisively repulsed. Some are saying that to break with the past, we have to put limits on the party. No, this is not the way, comrades! This isn't the way."[42]

In the months before the conference all Gorbachev's thinking had been directed toward the goal of weakening the grip of party secretaries, not in order to create the foundation of a multi-party system, but to reinforce his own power. As early as January 1988 he had mused about creating an executive presidency to avoid the fate which befell Khrushchev. In June he returned to the idea with his advisers. "Maybe I should open the section of my report on political reforms by announcing that I shall leave the post of general secretary and then proposing that the job be combined with that of chairman of the new Supreme Soviet. Then the conference and later the Congress of People's Deputies could decide."

But he rejected that dramatic idea, saying he didn't need any new burdens. In fact, he clung to the job of general secretary for three more years, accumulating titles and powers until, on paper, he had more than any Soviet leader before him. Rather than initiate the process of multi-party democracy, he resisted until events gave him no choice.

And after it was all over, from the rubble of the Soviet state the voice of the last Leninist could still be heard, explaining again what he had really tried to do. "I wanted," Gorbachev said in 1993, "to develop democratization in a one-party system."[43]

CHAPTER THREE

The First Campaign

In January 1989 the Central Committee of the Communist Party published a directive, which it proudly described as its election platform. It urged Soviet citizens to choose "active supporters of change, and those who think and act for the good of the state with bravery, responsibility and boldness."

But fear, not bravery or boldness, was the dominant emotion among Communist Party leaders at the beginning of this campaign. "What the members of the Politburo, every one of us, feared was democracy itself," wrote Nikolai Ryzhkov.[1] They expected that, given a choice, the voters would reject them.

And so, in the first symbolic act of the campaign, they decided not to give the voters that choice. The senior leadership of the Communist Party, including Gorbachev, Yakovlev, and all the advisers who had so strenuously argued for undiluted democracy, would enter the new Congress as deputies elected by a social organization – the Communist Party itself. One hundred seats were reserved for the party; there would be precisely one hundred candidates. They would become known as the "Red Hundred."

"The idea for the Red Hundred came from Gorbachev himself," said Anatoli Chernayev. "For him, it was a question of loyalty, or solidarity. He knew that 90 per cent of the Politburo wouldn't get in otherwise."[2]

This was controlled democracy with a vengeance. Gorbachev himself approved all the names on the party list. To give it a faint whiff of choice, 641 "electors," composed of Central Committee members and specially invited guests, were eventually allowed to vote for or against each candidate. Twelve voted against Gorbachev.[3]

Reflecting on this election years later, several of Gorbachev's advisers insisted on the validity of this decision. The Politburo ruled the country; it had to be represented in the legislature. (Gorbachev had decided that Politburo members who were regional leaders, such as the party heads of Moscow, Leningrad, and Ukraine, would have to face the voters in constituency elections.) At the same time, the pruning of the list eliminated many of the most reactionary members of the Central Committee in favour of fifty-two workers and peasants and several liberal intellectuals. To have allowed the electors any choice at all would have meant the elimination not only of Alexander Yakovlev (he received the highest number of negative votes, seventy-eight) but also of Yegor Ligachev (he was the second most unpopular man on the list with fifty-nine negative votes).[4]

The advisers merely shrugged or chuckled at the title bestowed on the chosen few by Soviet journalists. Yet the name was devastating, conjuring up associations with the Black Hundred, the extreme right-wing nationalist movement of the early 1900s which had encouraged roving gangs of thugs to perpetrate anti-semitic pogroms around the Russian Empire.

The elections were a quest for legitimacy, a bid to renovate a tottering system and the party which was its main pillar, but the first one hundred deputies were tainted even before the Congress assembled. In their wake would come the deputies elected by such representative "social organizations" as the Association of Inventors (five nominees for five seats) and the All-Union Voluntary Temperance Society.

Yet in the cold, grey days of late January 1989 something momentous was also taking place. In certain cities in Russia and Ukraine, and in the Baltics, citizens were rising up. By force of number and determination, they overran the legal fortress erected by the Communist Party to protect its troops in the electoral struggle. Not a shot was fired, but the events of the next two months could be compared to the fall of the Bastille: they constituted a revolt which would lead to a revolution.

On Sunday, 22 January, in central Moscow, several thousand people crowded around the side entrance to Dom Kino, the cinematographer's union hall. Inside, eight hundred people already filled the hall. They represented many of the capital's cultural elite, mixed in with former political prisoners and young organizers of the so-called informal political clubs that had sprouted in recent months. They were, in the words of the man they had come to honour and nominate, "the impoverished proletariat of intellectual labour."[5] That man was Andrei Sakharov.

"People have waited decades for this," a young teacher said. He had managed to squeeze into the hall. "But it's difficult to be optimistic. There's a slight hope something will come of it, but I wouldn't be very sure."

Sakharov sat, still as a monk, as speaker after speaker praised him as "the conscience of the Soviet people." It was only two years since he had been freed from internal exile in Gorky. Then, in a reedy, nasal voice, he read out his election platform: freedom for political prisoners in Armenia, freedom of speech and travel, powerful legal controls on the KGB, and electoral reform.

It was this last point which provoked the greatest applause. Sahkarov was unanimously nominated to run in Moscow's national-territorial district, but no one in the hall knew whether his name would actually appear on the ballot.

The new electoral law, passed on 1 December 1988, contained several protective "filters," agreed to by Gorbachev to placate anxious members of the Politburo. For the voters gathered at Dom Kino, the most disturbing was article 38. It established district commissions which would intervene after nominations to weed out "unacceptable" candidates. The law offered no guidelines on the composition of such commissions or on what basis they would accept or reject candidates. It was, in fact, an invitation to district party officials to pack the ballots with loyal followers of the regime.

But the party hadn't reckoned with the people's revolt. In riding after riding in Moscow and other major cities, they literally stormed the district commission meetings. The meetings themselves often resembled sieges which dragged on for six, eight, sometimes twelve hours.

Unhappy party officials seeking office found themselves facing a barrage of written questions about their mismanagement of local affairs. Loud and prolonged confrontations over procedure between supporters of the establishment candidate and those of "dissidents" were interrupted for long stretches while the protagonists retreated to seek a negotiated solution. While they consulted, local poets offered readings of their latest works. And frequently, when the votes were counted, the party standard-bearer found himself rejected. Instead, the final ballot would feature a dissident historian such as Roy Medvedev, or a thirty-one-year-old scientist calling openly for multi-party democracy, such as Arkadi Murashev. Or Boris Yeltsin.

Yeltsin had been refused admittance to the Red Hundred by Gorbachev. Now he was besieged by more than two hundred requests to run in ridings around the country. He chose to run in Moscow. The setting chosen for the district commission meeting at which Yeltsin was one of ten hopeful candidates was thick with history. This was the Hall of Columns in central Moscow, once the Club of the Nobility. Here Lenin, Stalin, Andropov, and Chernenko had all lain in state. And here, in the notorious Stalin show trials of the 1930s, Mensheviks, Trotskyists, and finally old Bolshevik companions of Lenin had abjectly confessed to imaginary crimes and grotesque conspiracies before being taken away to be shot.

The meeting on 22 February was also planned as something of a show trial. Yeltsin's aides had quickly discovered that eight hundred of the one thousand people in the hall were loyal troops of the Moscow party hierarchy. They had come with orders to put the names of only two candidates on the final ballot: Yuri Brakov, the director of the Zil automobile factory, and the cosmonaut Georgi Grechko.

Each candidate was required to answer written questions, and then oral questions. Yeltsin received more than a hundred written queries, almost all hostile, and some openly abusive. He said later he knew the hall was filled with people primed with more provocative questions, only waiting for the signal from the organizers to stir up controversy. Yeltsin chose to answer the most hostile written questions first, thus puncturing the organizers' strategy of mounting confrontation and abuse.

The meeting had started at 2 p.m.; it was now past midnight. Just before voting began, there was a surprise announcement which left the party hierarchy's strategy in tatters. By prior arrangement with Yeltsin, the cosmonaut Grechko now stood up to say he was withdrawing his candidacy. With no contingency instructions, the Moscow party troops were thrown into confusion. When the results were announced shortly before 3 a.m. Yeltsin had obtained the votes of more than half the "electors," enough to assure him a place on the election ballot.[6]

Faced with nominated candidates such as Yeltsin, Medvedev, and Murashev, local party committees turned for guidance to the Kremlin. They were told not to interfere. Some senior party figures were baffled, and furious.

Yegor Ligachev read with incredulity directives from the Central Committee telling local party committees to stay above the fray, not to make recommendations or indicate who to vote for. It was, he concluded bitterly, a huge mistake, or worse. "They were turning democracy on its head," he said. "Every party fights for power. That's its reason for existence. And here we were, standing aside in elections for the new centre of power. I believe now it was all part of a carefully worked-out plan to push the party out of the political arena and then out of the economic sphere."[7]

In mid-February, Viktor Chebrikov, the former head of the KGB and the Politburo member in charge of legal affairs, broke silence. In a bitter speech, published in *Pravda*, he called on the party to ignore the directives and to wage war against "independent, so-called informal organizations which pose a great threat to our mighty, positive social movement."

In fact, in much of the Soviet hinterland, the party remained in control. The new electoral law provided for no legal regulation of apportionment and districting, so regional party secretaries had carte blanche to gerrymander the districts they chose to run in. According to Russian political scientist Vladimir Kolossov, in three-quarters of the ridings in the Russian Federation – the largest republic in the Soviet Union with a hundred and fifty million people – the number of eligible voters varied by more than 20 per cent. In a more than a dozen cases, the spread was 400 per cent between the largest and smallest ridings.[8] And, despite the official commitment to competitive elections, on election day there were still 384 ridings (of a total of 1,500) where only one candidate was running.[9]

But even in the hinterland there were extraordinary tales of triumph over the party apparatus. Kremenchug, in Ukraine, had the unenviable distinction of being one of the five most-polluted cities in the Soviet Union. In this wasteland, the local party had long ruled unchallenged. Now, showing its willingness to adjust to the new rules, it offered four local Communist officials, instead of one, for the voters to choose from.

But the party officials hadn't reckoned with Nikolai Kotsenko, a lawyer and a militant in the local environmental association. Invoking a clause in the new electoral law which required nominees to obtain at least 50 per cent of the votes at the election commission meeting to appear on the ballot, he urged the commission electors to cross all four names off their list. The electors followed his advice: the local party hierarchy found all its candidates rejected for the election.

The next day Kotsenko was arrested. He was taken by police to a secret location eighty kilometres from Kremenchug. The district chief psychiatrist came to examine him, and when he understood he was about to be interned in a psychiatric hospital he began a hunger strike.

His arrest and disappearance sparked a popular revolt. Within twenty-four hours, eight thousand automobile workers at the city's largest factory were on strike, demanding his release. The party hierarchy retreated. Kotsenko was freed, and his nomination as deputy proposed and endorsed at a jubilant meeting of voters. Three weeks later he was elected.

"It was fantastic publicity for me," he said later. "My majority was a huge protest vote, just like for Yeltsin in Moscow. People said, if the party hierarchy is against him, he must be doing something right."[10]

It was the triumph of his life. As he recounted it five years later, Kotsenko was still camped in the room allocated to him as a deputy in the Moskva Hotel, just outside the Kremlin gates. The Soviet Union had collapsed, his riding now belonged to another country, but in his lapel Kotsenko still wore the little red badge which proclaimed him a Soviet People's Deputy.

For others, victory was equally sweet. Boris Yeltsin had taken 89 per cent of the vote in Moscow, aided by huge demonstrations of supporters in the streets and the clumsy intimidation campaign of the party hierarchy. Late in the campaign it announced a commission had been set up to investigate his calls for discussion of multi-party democracy in the Soviet Union.

Andrei Sakharov had stormed the fortress of the Academy of Sciences. A national outcry had greeted the crude attempt of the Academy old guard to prevent his name being put forward as a nominee. As in Kremenchug, the scientists who voted blackened their ballots, forcing a new election, where Sakharov ran and won.

By 26 March the shape of the revolt had become clear. Soviet voters rejected thirty-four of the 157 Communist regional party leaders running. The mayors of Moscow, Kiev, and Leningrad were defeated. Indeed, in Leningrad, the voters said no to all five leaders of the local party hierarchy. In the most ignominious defeat of all, Yuri Solovyov, the Leningrad party chief and a non-voting member of the Politburo, lost even though he ran unopposed. A majority of voters took advantage of a clause in the election law requiring every successful candidate to obtain at least 50 per cent of the vote. They crossed Solovyov's name off the ballot.

In the Baltics, the Communist Party was routed. In Lithuania the nationalist movement Sajudis won thirty-two of forty-two seats. The first and second party secretaries of the republic were spared humiliation only because the Sajudis candidates running against them tactfully withdrew at the last minute.

The ironies of history were manifest in the returns. Political scientists discovered that a comparison of the 1989 vote with that of November 1917 for the Constituent Assembly, the only other relatively unfettered election in this century, showed that the strongholds of the Bolsheviks seventy-two years earlier – Moscow, Petrograd, and the major industrial cities of European Russia – were once again the strongholds of radical opposition to the old regime. But the old regime in 1989 was now the Communist Party itself.[11]

The Politburo meeting on 30 March, four days after the elections, was turbulent. The message had now begun to sink in; the reaction of several men seated at the table was one of panic.[12] Sensing the mood, Gorbachev broke with a longstanding Politburo tradition that the general secretary sum up the debate and today spoke first. According to one participant, he was smiling broadly. The elections, he said, had demonstrated the enormous authority of the party. Eighty-seven per cent of the newly elected deputies were card-carrying Communists.

That was too much for Prime Minister Nikolai Ryzhkov. The party, he told Gorbachev flatly, had lost the elections. A slew of regional secretaries had been humiliated, beaten by less experienced, but more convinced opponents.

"But they're also party members!" Gorbachev answered.

"They didn't win because of their membership in the party," Ryzhkov said. "On the contrary, they've never supported it." The election result, he concluded, wasn't a chance occurrence; it was a disaster.[13]

Others jumped in. Yuri Solovyov, the Leningrad party boss, shouted angrily that the Central Committee "had abandoned them all to the mercy of demagogues." Yegor Ligachev and Anatoli Luykanov echoed his anger.

Gorbachev's smile at the outset had been calculated. His advisers said he went into the meeting wanting to see, as Lenin put it, "who was who" – in other words, who would attack his electoral experiment. Now he counter-attacked.

"I've received thousands of letters from people about them [the regional secretaries who lost]. These fat cats have done nothing to fix even the most basic problems for the population. And the Central Committee is now supposed to support them? That's not the way it's going to be. They should draw their own conclusions. We'll certainly be drawing ours."[14]

The Politburo meeting was only a foretaste of things to come. Three weeks later the Central Committee met. All day, like wounded animals, its members bellowed in pain and fury. The Azerbaijan first secretary fulminated that talk now spreading of multi-party democracy was "ideological Aids." A Moscow party boss said that democratization had opened the door to anarchy, to permissiveness, and to a massive attack on the hearts and souls of people by dubious members of informal groups eager to imitate the West. Speaker after speaker howled that the mass media was out of control, the party under siege.[15]

The ferocity of their reaction forced Gorbachev to make concessions. Elections for parliaments in the republics, scheduled for the fall, were postponed until the spring of 1990. And his insistence that unsuccessful candidates in the elections should give up their party posts as well was now quietly forgotten.

But the Central Committee was fighting a losing battle. Already the balance of power was shifting. According to Georgi Shaknazarov, you could actually see it moving from Gorbachev's party office in the Central Committee complex on Staraya Ploschad to the Kremlin, where he presided as chairman of the Supreme Soviet. "Gorbachev was now spending nine-tenths of his time in the Kremlin office. The Politburo was still meeting regularly but the real decisions were been taken elsewhere. Power is a delicate thing. You can move it in attaché cases."[16]

Drive twenty minutes from the Kremlin in a fast car, turn left off Minsk Boulevard, and Moscow magically vanishes. The visitor finds himself in a quiet, wooded valley at the centre of which stands a compound guarded by soldiers. The gates open, the visitor is waved past ranks of comfortable dachas to the end of the road. Here squats a monstrous Soviet summer palace, all glass and cement. A plaque next to the main door proclaims, in large letters: Dr Gavriil Popov; and underneath, in smaller letters: International University.

In a drawing room as cold as death, the marble fireplace is immense and the paintings on the walls all of a style – a sort of hideous socialist surrealism. A short man, with a belly as big and round as a bowling ball, shuffles in. He is wearing a tattered blue sweater. He is Gavriil Popov and in early 1994, this is now his dacha. It was once, he admits with a smile, the dacha of Leonid Brezhnev, in fact his last dacha, built hurriedly after his crippling heart attack when his doctors feared for his life if he was too far from the Kremlin hospital.

Much has changed in Russia since Brezhnev last looked on his dacha. The quiet compound was being transformed into an imitation American campus to house students of economic management. Corporations such as Coca-Cola and McDonald's put up the money to pay the professors at Popov's International University.

Popov has been many things in his life: economist, editor, party man, politician, mayor of Moscow, and finally founder and fundraiser for a university. He was a man who navigated effortlessly within the old system and, as it was collapsing, scooped up one of its jewels for himself.

But in the spring of 1989 Popov was a newly elected People's Deputy from Moscow. He was about to launch an initiative which would frighten Mikhail Gorbachev, provide a platform for Boris Yeltsin, and hasten the collapse of the Soviet Union.

As the final results became known, Popov did some calculations. By his count, twenty-three of Moscow's thirty elected members were reformers. He decided to invite them to meet to plan a common strategy. Thus was born the Moscow Group. It would later expand and take a different name – the Interregional Group.

Reformers were a peculiar breed in the dying days of the Soviet Union. Popov, like Yeltsin, had long been a card-carrying Communist. He showed no inclination to give up his membership. Another future star of the group, law professor Anatoli Sobchak, had just joined the party. Even younger, more radical deputies, such as Arkadi Murashev and the historian Sergei Stankevich, carefully took out insurance as they attacked the concept of the one-party state and the arbitrary nature of the nomenklatura, the elite of the Communist Party bureaucracy. They had both applied to become members of the party.

None yet foresaw the cataclysm to come. Instead, as Popov put it, they saw change coming very slowly. "We thought the process would stretch out over twenty years, as was the case with the end of serfdom. Our job was to be present in parliament in this twenty-year period, to influence events and suggest alternatives."[17]

Like Gorbachev, Popov had studied Lenin, but unlike Gorbachev, he was chilled by the Leninist vision. His Lenin was the hard revolutionary who had dismissed parliamentary assemblies as "a phantom, a phrase, a lie," a contrivance to keep the bourgeois ruling class in power. The soviets Lenin envisioned were a revolutionary step forward, "a power of the same type as the Paris Commune of 1871" – a power whose source was "not a law previously discussed and passed by a parliament, but a direct initiative of the popular masses from below and on the spot, a direct 'usurpation,' to employ the current expression."[18]

This was not what Popov wanted at all. He and the reformers who gathered in April sought to propose another model for the Congress of People's Deputies, also lifted from Russian history. Their model was the Constituent Assembly of 1918 and, like Gorbachev's, it was haloed in myth. The provisional government which overthrew the czar in February 1917 promised to transform the myth into reality by holding elections for the Assembly. So powerful was its hold on the people's imagination that even Lenin could not challenge it. After seizing power in October, he dared not cancel the elections, which went ahead the following month. The Bolsheviks won 24 per cent of the vote, but the Socialist Revolutionaries won 40 per cent.

On the eve of the Assembly's first session in January 1918, Lenin remarked sarcastically, "Since we stupidly promised everyone that we would convene this word factory, we will have to open it, but history doesn't yet say when we will close it."

The majority of deputies preparing to gather at the Tauride Palace in Petrograd on 5 January saw their task as historic: to draft a constitution and fundamental laws for the new republic, and to establish governmental and parliamentary institutions which would represent the whole country. When they arrived, they found two hundred Marine guards, loyal to Lenin, stationed around the Assembly hall. Lenin was also present, carrying a revolver in his coat pocket. He was not a member, nor would he speak to a legislature he despised, but he would, from the sidelines, keep a watchful eye.

It quickly became apparent that the Constituent Assembly would not bend before Bolshevik demands that it transfer effective power to Lenin's men. The Bolshevik deputies retreated into unconstructive opposition, howling, haranguing, and shouting threats, while, ostentatiously, Lenin lay down on a bench and slept. At 10 p.m. he got up, wrote instructions on how to end the Assembly, and left. The Assembly was dispersed at gunpoint eleven hours after it had opened. In a country exhausted by war, revolution, and coups d'état, the event was greeted with indifference.

Three days later Lenin convened his hand-picked Congress of the Soviets. Here the Bolsheviks and their allies controlled 94 per cent of the one thousand seats. The Bolshevik Council of People's Commissars was declared the country's legitimate government. It was done surgically and quickly. And thereafter the Council of Commissars all but ignored the Congress of Soviets.[19]

Popov and the other reformers feared that the Congress of 1989 would meet the same fate. Their fears were well-founded. Gorbachev's intention at this point was to hold a three-day session which would elect him chairman of the Congress, choose deputies for the smaller, 542-member working parliament, the Supreme Soviet, hear reports from government ministers, and then adjourn.

Joined by Andrei Sakharov, the Moscow Group began drawing up an alternate agenda and rules of procedure. Their first goal was to have the Congress hold a general debate on economic and political conditions in the country *before* the elections for the chairman and the Supreme Soviet. They also proposed rules for competitive elections to the Supreme Soviet and for the creation of deputies' groups. Sakharov himself was writing a separate statement setting forth the need for the Congress to assume all legislative power.[20]

The Moscow Group's alternate agenda was published in the liberal magazine *Ogonyok* on the eve of the April plenum of the Central Committee. Gorbachev, according to Anatoli Chernayev, was shocked. Immediately after the plenum he called his advisers together and for six hours they discussed how best to counteract these proposals. Gorbachev saw himself facing not only the attacks of his own Central Committee but also a group proposing to form a faction, a loyal opposition in the Congress.

"Communists like Gorbachev, educated by Lenin, see red when they hear the word 'faction,'" Chernayev said. "Gorbachev always preferred words like 'friendship' and 'together.' And he never expected such divisions would appear right away."[21]

The tactic chosen to combat the reformers was that of the smiling semblance of cooperation and Anatoli Lukyanov became its agent.

He immediately invited representatives of the Moscow Group to come to the Kremlin and discuss their ideas. They were flattered by his attention. He listened carefully to their arguments and promised to help. But at the same time Lukyanov was drawing up the Kremlin agenda. It adhered closely to the original Gorbachev plan for the Congress. And it was kept a secret from the Moscow Group. When it was distributed on the eve of the Congress, they were the only deputies not to receive copies.

"They toyed with us," Arkadi Murashev remembered ruefully. "Lukyanov treated us like fools. They did it quite openly. It was the first example of really cheap politics in that period." Later Lukyanov would simply shrug: "They were young kids. They had difficulty grasping certain things."[22]

Another tactic employed with success was that of the secondary concession. Anatoli Sobchak travelled to Moscow on 23 May for a pre-Congress meeting of selected deputies with Gorbachev and the Politburo in the Kremlin. There he listened with excitement as the general secretary declared that the Congress would decide everything, that the party leadership would put no pressure on the deputies. He remembered: "At that time I was literally overwhelmed by the charm and the force of Gorbachev's personality." Within minutes, however, he was shocked to hear that the Central Committee had nominated two party stalwarts with little judicial experience to the posts of chief judge of the Supreme Court and chairman of the Constitutional Review Commission. Sobchak stood up and condemned the nominations as a mockery of the commitment to create a "law-based state." The members of the Politburo listened in grim silence. But, to Sobchak's amazement, the next day the nominations were withdrawn.[23] An easy concession but one which would help keep a man destined to become an influential deputy on Gorbachev's side in key battles for the next year.

By this time the Moscow Group had grown far beyond a collection of "kids." The group had sent a letter to all deputies outlining its ideas, and about two hundred new members from around the Soviet Union had expressed interest. Now the group was fighting another battle with the Kremlin which, for once, rallied a majority of all the new deputies to its side. It was arguing for gavel-to-gavel television coverage of the Congress as a way of protecting against the most obvious abuses of democracy.

But other deputies, Gavriil Popov remembered with a smile, had other reasons:

The Baltic representatives wanted to show their people how they were fighting for their rights in Moscow, the Armenians how they were defending Nagorno-Karabakh against Azerbaijan [an Armenian enclave in Azerbaijan over which the two republics had been fighting an open war for the previous year], and the Azeris wanted to proclaim publicly the righteousness of their position. And many deputies were pushing for televised coverage simply because of their egos. In the end the Kremlin just couldn't prevent it.[24]

Nevetheless, the old guard of the Politburo tried. It was Boris Yeltsin who finally secured this victory. A vague commitment had been offered to broadcast the sessions but when Yeltsin saw the television listings printed in a Moscow newspaper for the opening days of the Congress, he demanded a meeting in the Kremlin. Facing three Politburo members across the table, he flung down the paper in front of them and demanded to know what they were trying to do. The listings indicated that only excerpts of the Congress would be broadcast in the evenings, as had been the case for the Communist Party conference the previous June. He denounced it as a cheap trick and said those who had connived at it should be punished. The meeting ended in an angry shouting match.

The matter was finally settled in the VIP lounge at Moscow's Vnukovo airport. Gorbachev was returning from a one-week state visit to China. A Politburo delegation went out to meet him and to ask him to make the final decision. All right, he said, let's agree. Otherwise, they'll make things impossible for us![25]

The small group of reformers would lose almost every other battle in the Congress. It would not matter; they would fight and lose them before the whole country. Television would shake the ground of Soviet politics with the force of an earthquake.

Why had Gorbachev agreed? This was, after all, the man whose chief adviser had proclaimed in 1985 that "the television image is everything." Gorbachev himself oversaw the minutest details of his television appearances, frequently phoning to the head of Soviet television's news service and sometimes personally selecting the pictures which would make up the televised reports of his visits around the country.[26]

Part of the answer lies in the enormous success of the experiment of broadcasting excerpts from the 1988 party conference. These had shown Gorbachev at his best, fast on his feet, never at a loss for words, improvising artfully. The political reviewers had been fulsome in their praise. Now, almost one year later, he had even more faith in his ability to dominate the political landscape, to outwit his adversaries, to achieve victory. And Soviet viewers, naturally, should be given the opportunity to see this giant bestride the scene.

In April 1917 Vladimir Lenin had just returned from exile to the Finland Station in Petrograd. His vision of a forced march to revolution had set most of his Central Committee against him. The test of power and of his ability to control the forces he would unleash was still ahead. In these uncertain days, Viktor Chernov, a Menshevik, a man who saw much of him and would finally be struck down by him, wrote these lines: "Lenin could say of himself, 'I know not where I am going, but I am going there with determination.' Lenin is certainly devoted to the revolution, but with him this devotion is embodied in his own person: 'I am the State!'"[27]

Seventy two years later, writing in his diary in May 1989, on the eve of the first Congress of People's Deputies, Anatoli Chernayev would draw an eerily similar portrait of Mikhail Gorbachev, with this difference: the portrait didn't frighten him, it depressed him. The private thoughts of his closest confidant stand in stunning contrast to the reputation for far-sighted leadership Gorbachev enjoyed at this time around the world:

I have a growing feeling of dread and lassitude, a feeling we are entering the crisis period of the Gorbachev years. Gorbachev says he is ready to "march very far." But what does that mean? ... He has no conception of where he is going. He is constantly invoking "socialist values" and "the cleansing ideals of October." But as soon as he starts listing them, people react with ironic smiles. Because behind those slogans, there is nothing.[28]

CHAPTER FOUR

The Day of Discussion

The regime was dying but unaware of approaching death. At a deeper, subconscious level there seemed to be a recognition of danger and a will to affirm life. It took the form of a confused and symbolic equation. As the Soviet colossus shrank steadily into decrepitude, the statues of the founder grew proportionately more commanding.

The marble Lenin which greeted the new deputies in the vast hall of the Kremlin Palace of Congresses on 25 May 1989 was immense. Twelve metres high, he grimly faced the future. On the podium below, the heads of the Congress leaders barely rose above his ankles. The effect was of rodents scurrying about his shoes.

For two weeks the Cyclops of the old order would stand blindly above the spectacle. For these proceedings were both parliamentary and something more profound. They were part fairy tale, part morality play, an improvised drama dominated by two men: Mikhail Gorbachev, the good czar, and Andrei Sakharov, the prophet and martyr. Others would play lesser roles, attacking abuses of power and privilege, shattering the spell of the past. In the emotional climax, a furious chorus of Communist believers would howl for the head of Sakharov, while his colleagues waited, frozen in fear.

The spectacle would be watched by eight television cameras and by the whole country, transfixed as the mystery of power was stripped bare. In the end, power would not change hands here. Instead, something more important would take place: the transfer of legitimacy, from those unelected in the Kremlin to those who had won the right, and used it, to speak for the people.

The struggle for control and the improvisation were evident from the opening moments. A deputy from Latvia went to the podium uninvited and called for a minute of silence for the dead of Tbilisi, massacred in early April by Soviet Interior Ministry troops following orders to break up a nationalist demonstration. His goal was to dramatize the worry of Baltic representatives that Soviet troops would someday be used in their republics.[1]

The Latvian deputy had succeeded because Gorbachev was not presiding over the session at the outset. The Congress rules of procedure, drawn up under his guidance, stated that until the election of the new chairman, the chief of the electoral commission would preside. But rules and decisions, as Lenin had taught, are made to be broken. Within three minutes of the call for silence, Gorbachev was piloting the session. When, later in the morning, two deputies protested with growing boldness at this flouting of the rules, Gorbachev asked in puzzlement, "Is somebody suggesting my behaviour is somehow undemocratic?"[2]

In fact, in comparison with seven decades of Soviet history, his behaviour at this Congress would be astonishingly democratic. A Soviet commentator wrote in wonderment the next day: "What we saw at precisely 10 a.m. was … an empty presidium. Where were the ranks of Party and government leaders? Nobody leapt from his seat in thankful ecstasy. Where were the noisy ranks of young 'cheerleaders,' where was the prolonged and stormy applause which left palms pained and consciences deadened?"[3]

Indeed, where was the Politburo? Sitting, not on stage as in the past, but in a special section reserved for dignitaries at the side of the hall. Knowing that the Moscow Group threatened to walk out in protest if the party leaders were seated in their traditional place of command, Gorbachev had cajoled and convinced his colleagues to move to the side. A special room was set aside for them to retire to. There they could relax, and there special private lunches were served them. Aides fawned as they arrived and left in enormous black limousines. "He preserved some of their privileges and, above all, the appearance that they were continuing to run things," said Georgi Shaknazarov. "As Marx said, it's better to buy off the bourgeoisie than to expropriate it."[4]

Gorbachev's puzzlement about criticism of his conduct of the session was genuine. He had known about the plan of the Baltic deputies and let them get away with it. Only then did he take the chair.[5] But implicit in Gorbachev's question was the assumption that he would define the limits of democracy at this Congress. That assumption would quickly be challenged.

The first deputy he invited to speak was Andrei Sakharov. The two men would develop a prickly, almost symbiotic relationship at the podium throughout the two-week session. By recognizing Sakharov, he was signalling that the scientist and human rights campaigner was not a deputy like the others. Gorbachev would let him speak, seemingly whenever he wished, while dozens in the huge hall fumed in enforced silence. But Sakharov's words invariably infuriated Gorbachev. Like an angry schoolmaster he would inter-rupt, slam his hand repeatedly on a night porter's bell by his chair to indicate Sakharov had gone over time, even cut off his micro-phone. Imperturbable, Sakharov would carry on.

In his first speech, Sakharov elegantly challenged Gorbachev to live up to his revolutionary rhetoric, to be as bold as his political patron saint. He proposed the adoption of a "Decree" that would give the Congress the exclusive right to pass laws, and to make appointments to the highest posts in the Soviet Union. It would bury the concept of dual power – power shared between the government and the party. "We are living through a revolution – perestroika is a revolution – and 'Decree' seems the appropriate word in the circumstances."[6]

Sakharov was deliberately evoking the memory of the October Revolution of 1917. Lenin's first act on seizing power was to convene his Congress of Soviets and to submit to it three decrees: on peace, on land, and on power.

Sakharov then called, in the name of the Moscow Group, for a general debate on political and economic conditions in the country to be followed by a competitive election for the chairman of the Congress. The post, after all, was that of head of state. To proceed with elections first, as Gorbachev intended, would be to bring shame on the Congress before the whole country.

He challenged Gorbachev personally to offer, before the ballot, a "self-critical review" of his stewardship and, above all, to outline his plans for a country in crisis. Increasingly irritated, Gorbachev now cut in. "Let's agree that if anyone wants to speak to particular issues, the maximum time is five minutes. Finish up, Andrei Dmi-trievich!"[7] The signal had been given. Sakharov spent the last twenty seconds of his speech shouting over the tumult in the hall.

Other leaders of the Moscow Group followed Sakharov to the podium. But Gorbachev was not to be swayed by appeals to democracy or even Lenin. There would be no decree, there would be no change in the program. Confidently he put the question to a vote. Only 379 deputies voted against the Kremlin agenda. That was just slightly more than the 15 per cent of the deputies Gavriil Popov had earlier estimated supported his group.

For all his assurance, Gorbachev was anxious to have the weight of Andrei Sakharov's moral authority behind him. At the lunch break, Alexander Yakovlev was despatched to plead for it. He found Sakharov in a corridor and congratulated him on his first speech. But now, he said, everyone must help Mikhail Sergeivich. "He's taken on an enormous responsibility. It's very hard on him. In effect, he's turning the whole country around single-handedly. Electing him means guaranteeing perestroika." But Sakharov said he would wait to see how the election unfolded.[8]

It had been planned as a coronation, beginning with the inevitable chorus of praise, led by the Grand Mufti of Central Asia and deputy from Uzbekistan. But almost immediately criticism and questions sabotaged the scenario. A deputy from Gorki attacked the practice of combining the post of general secretary of the party and chairman of the Congress. It had always led in the past to the creation of a cult of personality. Six other deputies followed him to the podium with similar barbed comments. There was a question about Gorbachev's taste for lavish dachas, and his insistence on building a new one in the Crimea. He was accused of surrounding himself with syncophants, and of acting on bad advice, notably from his wife.

Once again it was Sakharov who mounted the key challenge. The election to the post of chairman of the Congress and head of state could not be a simple formality. There had to be open competition. "Otherwise, it won't be possible for me to vote."[9]

Gorbachev admitted the question was "fundamental" and indeed that it had been the principal subject of discussion behind the scenes for the past three days. Other candidacies were possible. We would have to discuss them, he said. The door to competition seemed to be open. It wasn't.

Half an hour later Alexander Obolensky, an engineer working at the Polar Geophysical Institute in the Soviet far north, stood up and nominated himself for the post of chairman. He then gave a carefully crafted speech outlining his program: a clear separation of legislative and executive powers, the creation of a Constitutional Court, a commitment to cut the yawning budget deficit, a realistic approach to land reform. He finished by admitting the obvious: "I understand perfectly that I have no chance against Mikhail Gorbachev. But

I want history to note that a precedent has been created here, with the holding of a real election. This was what my voters demanded and this is what I promised them."[10]

Immediately the acting chairman (while Gorbachev submitted himself for election) recognized an Uzbek deputy, who denounced Obolensky harshly. He was a "demagogue" wasting the time of the Congress. A few minutes later the chairman proposed a rule that hadn't applied to Gorbachev himself. The Congress would vote on whether to include Obolensky on the ballot. In the end, 1,415 deputies rejected it; only 689 voted for Obolensky's nomination.

The handling of this incident would set a pattern for the years to come: the careful selection of a deputy whose comments would send the appropriate signal to the majority, and the "invention" of a special rule to deal with the problem.

Gorbachev's speech, in answer to the questions posed to him, was short on details but, in one passage, very revealing.

I want to reassure deputies who complain that I don't know what's going in the country. On the contrary I know of the smallest incidents. I know about the bus in Moscow where war veterans carried portraits of Brezhnev decorated with medals, and portraits of Gorbachev decorated with ration tickets. I know everything. I know more than you, perhaps not as much as all of you combined, but far more than any one of you.[11]

In the circumstances, the outcome was hardly in doubt. Running alone, Mikhail Gorbachev received 2,133 votes. Eighty-seven deputies voted against him. Just minutes before the ballot, Andrei Sakharov had stood up and walked out of the hall.

Gorbachev had been endorsed by 95 per cent of the deputies but Sakharov's gesture gnawed at him. He sought out the scientist the next day. Why had he left, why hadn't he voted?

It was a matter of principle, Sakharov replied.

But there was a discussion!

Not what was called for, Sakharov said.[12]

The gulf between the two separate visions of political participation would yawn even wider the next day in the wake of voting to select deputies for the Supreme Soviet.

Gorbachev, against the wishes of most of his advisers, had insisted on a complicated two-tier parliamentary structure. Voters had elected 2,250 deputies to the Congress but it would sit only two weeks a year. From its ranks the deputies themselves would elect 542 members of the Supreme Soviet. The Supreme Soviet would be a working, permanent legislature sitting eight to ten months a year. It would have the power to adopt laws but fundamental legislation, such as constitutional changes and treaties, would have to be ratified by the Congress. Gorbachev defended this cumbersome system by saying it would better reflect the diversity of the Soviet Union and allow leaders of society who couldn't serve full-time in the Supreme Soviet to vote on key issues in the Congress.

The issue, as the Congress prepared to choose from its ranks the members of the Supreme Soviet, was, once again, competitive elections. The Kremlin had devised a quota system to allocate seats in the Supreme Soviet with each republic and each major region receiving a certain number. Moscow was given twenty-nine. The Moscow Group had earlier proposed to the Kremlin that each seat in the Supreme Soviet be assigned to four deputies in the Congress, thus assuring a rotation over four years which would accurately reflect its political composition. That idea was flatly rejected. Now, after a late-night caucus meeting, the Moscow delegation offered a new model. Gavriil Popov announced that the delegation would offer fifty-five candidates for the twenty-nine seats. "We ask every delegation here to follow our example. The idea is to offer a real choice and to defend our new democracy."[13]

His call was all but ignored by regional party bosses. The slates for the Central Asian republics, Ukraine, Belorussia, and most regions of Russia contained precisely one candidate for each post. In all, there were just six hundred candidates for 542 seats.

The Uzbek list suggested the flavour of the future Supreme Soviet. It contained the Uzbek Party first secretary, the chairman of the republic's Supreme Soviet, the deputy chairman, the first deputy prime minister, the chairman of the republic's central planning ministry, and the three regional first secretaries – in other words, the core of the local party hierarchy.

Far from rallying the Congress to the idea of greater democracy, the proposal of the Moscow Group became the pretext for resentful attacks from the provinces against the intellectuals of the capital. A trade union official from the coal-mining area of Donbass named Alexei Tkhor cast himself in the mould of defender of the proletariat. "You can't treat the working class as some grey mass which can't decide for itself. The interests of the miners and workers can't be defended by some professor from Moscow."[14]

Other strains which would grow and soon fracture the empire were also evident. The Lithuanian delegation threatened to boycott the vote because the list for each republic was subject to the approval of the entire Congress. The Lithuanians argued that only their deputies should vote on their representatives in the Supreme Soviet. The boycott was abandoned after intense pressure from the presidium, composed of party leaders from each republic, and from deputies from the Moscow Group with whom they were allied. It was merely a crisis postponed.

The result of the voting created an uproar. Offered the opportunity, the conservative majority took revenge on the upstart Moscow reformers. Gavriil Popov was rejected for the Supreme Soviet, as were his young lieutenants, Arkadi Murashev and Sergei Stankevich. But the most stunning rejection was that of Boris Yeltsin. Running for the upper house, he had been one of twelve candidates for eleven places on the Russian list. He came twelfth.

The election results were announced on the third day of the Congress. The first man to the podium was Moscow historian Yuri Afanasiev. To howls of anger from the hall, he shouted that the deputies – in his memorable phrase "the aggressively obedient majority" – had just voted to create a Stalinist-Brezhnevite Supreme Soviet with, he suggested, the active connivance or at least the tacit blessing of Mikhail Gorbachev.

He was followed by Gavriil Popov. More in hurt than in anger, he spoke of the naïve enthusiasm of the reformers, and of how the Kremlin had toyed with them. "The Presidium of the Supreme Soviet couldn't even find a room for us or paper for our work. Nothing we prepared was distributed to other deputies." Now, he said, the Moscow Group was forced to change its tactics. It would propose the creation of an interregional, independent group of deputies.[15]

Those two speeches led to a passionate all-day debate. One speaker compared the deputies to men and women waking from a long sleep, trying to come to grips with the concept of a loyal opposition in a Soviet legislature.

For Gorbachev, nurtured on Leninist doctrine, this was anathema. It was a "faction." This was the word he used in a short speech after Popov's announcement. Everyone in the hall knew that Lenin had expressly banned factions in the Communist Party. Gorbachev went even further. "Raising the question [of an interregional group] will lead to a schism in the Congress."

Yet his warning served only to stimulate debate, not to end it. But it was a debate which underlined the poverty of political thought after decades of Communist ideology. Blunt Leninist slogans predominated. One deputy described the discussion as "the infantile malady of democracy," consciously echoing Lenin's pamphlet on "the infantile malady of communism." Another declared, we can tolerate pluralism of opinions, but then we must have unity of action. It was Leninist democratic centralism seventy years on.

Supporters of the Moscow Group groped ineffectually for ways to express the legitimacy of opposition. One Estonian deputy resorted to a comparison with his parents' divorce when he was two years old. He couldn't choose between his mother and his father. In the same manner, he awkwardly concluded, he rejected the idea of having to choose between Gorbachev on the one hand, and Afanasiev and Popov on the other.

He wouldn't have to, at least at this Congress. At the end of the day Popov returned to the podium to announce that the Moscow Group was dropping the idea of forming an interregional group in the interests of Congressional unity.

But the idea of opposition, so long repressed, was now being openly discussed, and the debate was transforming the country. In a memorable metaphor, the writer and deputy Ales Adamovich described a drunk waking up, sobering up and asking, what happened to the czar? He was talking of the people of the Soviet Union.[16]

In phenomenal numbers, they were watching. By the end of the first week Soviet television estimated the Congress was attracting two hundred million viewers, 25 per cent more than any other previous program. In streets, in parks, in factories, people sat frozen for hours, watching and listening. Anatoli Lukyanov, the new vice-chairman of the Congress, announced later that industrial production had dropped 20 per cent during the two-week session.

The audience was active. Viewers bombarded their deputies with telegrams. Thousands travelled to Moscow and stood outside the Kremlin, waiting to talk directly to their representatives. On the third day of the Congress ten thousand Moscovites crowded into Luzhniki Park to denounce the exclusion of Boris Yeltsin from the Supreme Soviet. Radical deputies such as Arkadi Murashev watched the angry crowd from behind the stage of the rally, and saw defeat being transformed into a kind of victory. "Maybe if we had played by Gorbachev's rules, we would have got ten more reform deputies into the Supreme Soviet," he said. "This way we've exposed the reactionary nature of the Congress and maybe we can use that to change the system."

The rally was reported that night on television, along with an opinion poll that indicated widespread disapproval of the Supreme Soviet voting results. It was a startling departure for the heretofore very official newscast. Television producers in charge of broadcasting the debates reported that they'd received no directives on what or what not to cover.[17]

Public displeasure over the rejection of Yeltsin could not be ignored. On the fourth day of debates Alexei Kazannik, one of the eleven Russian deputies chosen for the Supreme Soviet in preference to Yeltsin, announced he would give up his seat, but only to Yeltsin. This was questionable but expeditious. Gorbachev quickly had the proposal ratified by a relieved Congress.[18]

The rulebook had been abandoned. It was the same in the corridors of the Palace of Congresses. At breaks during the sessions deputies found themselves, for the first time in history, mingling with voracious reporters allowed down from the press balcony. Huge journalistic barnacles attached themselves to passing politicians. The effect was chaotic – shouted questions, unheard answers, cursing cameramen, and bystanders leaping for safety as the volatile mass swept by. When asked why the Kremlin had opted for such anarchy, a Gorbachev adviser looked puzzled. "Isn't this the way you do it in the West?"

Gorbachev himself held a regular scrum, with a hand-picked Soviet Television cameraman recording every word. His favourite pose was that of the political headmaster. "We're still learning. We have to master the art of democracy, we have to learn to listen to each other."

Others had already mastered the technique of self-advertisement. The young Moscow deputy Sergei Stankevich would unobtusively drift out, pick a pillar to lean on, and wait. Within minutes he would be surrounded by journalists, and talking. His command of English and his ability to offer superficial and misleading parallels with American politics quickly made him a fixture on American television.

For a brief, golden period of a year, the Soviet elite was the most accessible on earth. There they stood, the stars of the Soviet state – poets, hockey players, cosmonauts, industrial commissars, scientists, surgeons, the patriarch of the Orthodox Church, virtually the entire general staff of the armed forces – all of them deputies and all of them bit players in a political pageant which left most distinctly uneasy. Even Raisa Gorbachev felt the need to make an appearance in the foyer after one deputy had publicly accused her of playing Josephine to Gorbachev's Napoleon. Displaying her own command of public relations, she told a knot of foreign reporters that the attack had sprung from sexist motives.

"It's the men," she said. "But the women are for me. Just look, here's a woman. Hello! Hello, my dears. Let's answer together. This is the foreign press, and they just came up to me and asked, 'How do you feel about the fact that one man deputy yesterday went into battle against you?'"

The women, all deputies, obediently played the game.

"All women are for you!" one said.

"Write that down!" a second ordered the reporters.[19]

It was an astounding spectacle which also left the country virtually unadministered for two weeks while the elite listened, like obedient pupils, to debate and denunciations of the Soviet past.

In this hall taboos were broken, icons smashed. A hero of Soviet sport and an Olympic gold-medal weightlifter, Yuri Vlasov, chose as his theme the KGB. His father had disappeared in 1953, after being arrested by the state security police. "The KGB is a real underground empire that hasn't yet divulged its secrets – except for some excavated graves," Vlasov said to a silent audience. For decades they tormented and tortured people – as a rule, the very pride and flower of the nation. "Despite such a history, this service retains its own, special status. It is the most powerful of all existing weapons of the party apparatus."

Never had such criticism been voiced publicly in the Soviet Union. When Vlasov finished, hundreds of deputies rose in a standing ovation. The members of the Politburo, including KGB chief Viktor Kryuchkov, sat silently, staring straight ahead. Mikhail Gorbachev, presiding onstage, applauded briefly.

He did not applaud when Boris Yeltsin criticized his steady accumulation of power, warned of a possible new dictatorship, and called for a referendum on Gorbachev's stewardship and for a law limiting the powers of the Communist Party.[20]

The greatest taboo remained any hostile reference to the corpse in the mausoleum on Red Square. This, too, was broken. A writer from Leningrad, Yuri Karyakin, stood before the country and said it was time to bury Lenin like any normal human being. "Tanks rumble across Red Square shaking his body, scientists and artists remodel his face," Karyakin said. "If he [Lenin] was a believer, and his soul immortal, his soul would thank you."

All of this was taking its toll on Gorbachev. The Congress was not following the scenario he had drawn up. It was all moving too fast. He sought out deputies such as Sergei Stankevich during the breaks, trying to persuade them, to caution them.

"Don't be so radical, don't be in such a hurry. You have to wait, and work with me. I know how to take the next step," Stankevich remembered him saying. The young deputy looked at a leader clothed in fatigue. "The tension of the Congresss was phenomenal. He was exhausted."[21]

Andrei Sakharov had arrived at the conclusion that Gorbachev was proceeding much too slowly. If he did not move dramatically, someone else would take the next step for him. On 1 June Sakharov asked to meet privately with him. He was told to wait after the end of the day's session. Finally, at eight in the evening, Gorbachev emerged from other talks. The unique private meeting between these two men took place in the darkened arena of their public confrontations. Sakharov described it in his memoirs:

I could see the enormous hall of the Palace of Congresses, dimly lit and deserted except for the guards at the distant doors. Gorbachev was accompanied by Lukyanov, which I hadn't anticipated, but there was nothing I could do about it. Gorbachev looked tired, as did I. We moved three chairs to the corner of the stage. Gorbachev was very serious throughout the conversation. His usual smile for me – half kindly, half condescending – never once appeared on his face.

Sakharov: "Mikhail Sergeyevich, there's no need for me to tell you how serious things are in the country ... There's a crisis of trust in the leadership and the Party. Your personal authority has dropped almost to zero. People can't wait any longer with nothing but promises to sustain them. A middle course in a situation like this is almost impossible. The country and you personally are at a crossroads – either accelerate the process of change to the maximum or try to retain the administrative-command system in all of its aspects. In the first case, you will have to rely on the left and you'll be able to count on the support of many brave and energetic people. In the second case, you know yourself whose support you'll have, but they will never forgive you for backing perestroika."

Gorbachev: "I'm against running around like a chicken with its head cut off. We've seen many 'great leaps forward' and the results have always been tragedy and backtracking. I know everything that's being said about me. But I'm convinced the people will understand my policies."[22]

It was not so much a disagreement as two distinct monologues. As Sakharov described it, Gorbachev listened but did not hear what he was saying. And yet the enormous self-confidence of the political pragmatist was misplaced; it was the analysis of the unworldly man sitting opposite him on the darkened stage which was to prove uncannily accurate.

Their conversation was an interlude before the jarring emotional climax of the Congress. It had been prepared with care and its target was Sakharov himself. He had become the symbol of reform at the Congress; he had to be crushed.

On 3 June, Sergei Chervonopisky, a provincial party official who had lost both legs in the Afghan war, made his way to the podium to accuse Sakharov of slandering the Soviet army by claiming in an interview published by a Canadian newspaper that Soviet helicopter pilots had fired on their own troops to prevent them being taken prisoners. He proclaimed: "There are three things we must all fight to protect: State power, our motherland, and Communism." He had outlined the program of the majority in the hall.

Gorbachev joined the standing ovation at the end of his speech. Sakharov was unrepentant, although he admitted he could offer no proof to support his statement. He said he had never wanted to insult the Soviet army, but the Soviet invasion of Afghanistan had been a criminal adventure. He was unable to finish. For several minutes pandemonium reigned as deputies whistled, clapped, and shouted insults at him. "Down with Sakharov!" they chanted. "I call universal contempt down on your head!" yelled a deputy from the balcony.

And then a procession of speakers came to the microphone to continue the ritual bloodletting in front of the country. "You have insulted the entire army, the entire nation, all our war dead," a teacher from Uzbekistan screamed at the Nobel Peace laureate. "I despise you! You must feel shame for what you have done!"

No friend or ally came to the podium to defend Sakharov. All in the hall knew what they were witnessing. This was the Communist Party technique of public humiliation and political execution. It froze lesser men than Sakharov. Anatoli Sobchak admitted that he was paralysed by fear: "In those minutes in that hall, we were breathing the air of 1937 [the year of Stalin's show trials]. We, as deputies, had ceased to exist. We had become blindly obedient members of a Stalinist crowd facing our victim. Sakharov was our leader. At the podium he stood, wavering. And we, his fearful pupils, cowered in our seats."[23]

At the end of this harrowing afternoon Sakharov intercepted Gorbachev at the podium. They had a brief exchange of words. The only emotion shown by the Soviet leader was irritation. "It's a shame you talked so much," he snapped at Sakharov.

Yet, as the country watched, Sakharov had wavered but hadn't broken under the wave of abuse. That, in itself, was a kind of deliverance.

A week later, the Congress would finish as it had begun, with Sakharov once again at the microphone. To viewers who had thought they had heard everything, he now offered one more surprise: the demand to end the one-party state and the constitutional primacy of the Communist Party. He called for the abolition of Article 6 of the Soviet constitution. He hadn't even consulted his colleagues from the Moscow Group before making the speech. They were astonished; Gorbachev was vastly irritated. Once again he would peremptorily demand that Sakharov cease speaking. He would not; Gorbachev repeatedly rang his bell. He turned off Sakharov's microphone. A wave of whistling, shouting, and clapping rose and rolled through the hall. Indifferent, Sakharov read his speech to the end.

In disarray, the deputies rose for the last time to sing the Soviet anthem. Nothing had been as they expected.

In retrospect, all agreed on the profound mutation wrought by this Congress. "On the day the Congress opened, we were one sort of people," Boris Yeltsin wrote. "On the day it closed we were different people."[24]

It had little to do with the actual decisions of the deputies. Instead, it was the act of speaking itself, of naming crimes, chronicling abuses, questioning leaders, calling for change. The tongues untied would led to revolutionary ferment. In his history of the French Revolution, British historian Thomas Carlyle wrote of "the flood of French speech." American journalist John Reed recalled the "frenzy of free expression" and the "spurting up of impromptu debate" on every corner in the Russian Revolution of 1917.

But the frenzy in Russia had been choked off by the Communists. The Soviet Union became again a nation of mutes, as it had been one hundred years earlier, when the French writer and traveller, the Marquis de Custine, had first coined the phrase.

In enforced silence, Russians invested words with an almost mystical power to transform the world. A young Russian poet wrote in the 1950s:

I know that men consist of words which
  have embraced them.
The word moves. Earth is on fire.[25]

And so, when the words were finally spoken, the country listened with religious intensity. De Custine had foretold it: "Nations are mutes only for a time. The day of discussion will arise: religion, policy, all speak and all explain themselves in the end. Thus, as soon as speech is restored to this muzzled people, one will hear so much dispute that an astonished world will think it has returned to the confusion of Babel."[26]

CHAPTER FIVE

The Swamp

The Moskva Hotel sits like a massive granite prison on Manege Square just outside the Kremlin walls. The eye cannot scan it; its shape seems somehow assymetrical. Like much of modern Moscow, its construction was decreed and approved by Josef Stalin. But when the dictator was shown the final two competing designs, he merely grunted in vague approval and left the room. In the terrible twilight of his reign, aides dared ask no questions. In desperation they ordered that the two designs be fused together.

From the spring of 1989 this misshapen monument to fear was home to hundreds of People's Deputies. Here they camped, often two to a room, meeting flocks of constituents in the dim and cavernous lobby below, while each day on the sidewalks outside hundreds of new petitioners pleaded with policemen to be allowed to approach their representatives.

The petitioners had come from across the Soviet Union to seek redress from the men and women who held out the first faint promise of justice in decades. Ismail Rozmatov travelled five thousand kilometres from Kirghizia that fall with his wife and baby to wait for a week in the street for a chance to approach his deputy. His mother had been murdered, their apartment sealed and then confiscated, and they had nowhere to live. His representative said he would try to help but there was little he could promise. The range of complaints was vast – from denunciations of unscrupulous party bosses to cries for help from whole nationalities, deported, decimated, and silenced under Stalin and his successors.

The Supreme Soviet, the working parliament of 542 members, quickly became the forum where these grievances were aired by activist deputies. Soviet citizens, watching the proceedings which were televised in full every evening, discovered abuses they had not even been aware of.

A deputy from Ishevsk named Nikolai Engver made his first speech in October 1989:

I want to raise a question that has never been addressed in the press, or by the government or the party. I'm talking of the children born in the gulag, in the camps. They started their sentences at birth.

I myself was born in the Potma camp, and the label *lagernik*, jailbird, has followed me all my life, even during the election campaign. I overcame it, but many others have not. All of us who were there continue to pay for it.[1]

The legitimacy conferred on the deputies by open elections empowered them to demand that officials, and ministers, even the head of state stand accountable for their conduct, their decisions, and their mistakes.

But legitimacy wasn't accompanied by organization. Attempts to create caucuses were, at best, partial successes, hobbled by infighting and the battle of egos among deputies and by the systematic attempts of the Kremlin leadership to derail these groups. But that would come later. In the beginning the deputies were discovering their power.

It manifested itself in spectacular fashion in the first month of the Supreme Soviet. Deputies demanded the right to question and confirm prospective ministers. (Government ministers were not members of the Supreme Soviet but had a special section in the chamber reserved for them. They were expected to give reports and answer questions.) For nine senior Soviet officials, several of them ministers already, it was an experience of almost total humiliation. After harsh questioning from deputies, their candidacies were rejected by the majority. On 27 June, after first announcing he would refuse to bow to the parliament's will, Prime Minister Nikolai Ryzhkov told the Supreme Soviet he would withdraw the nine rejected names. Among them were his choice for deputy prime minister, and for minister of culture.[2]

Mikhail Gorbachev was only able to save his minister of defence, Dmitri Yazov, by trampling on the rules he himself had approved. They stated that each minister had to receive the votes of an absolute majority of the Supreme Soviet's 542 members. Gorbachev insisted on a temporary amendment for Yazov. He would need the approval only of half the deputies present for the vote. Thus Yazov kept his job, with 256 votes, sixteen short of an absolute majority. Two years later he would repay his master by planning a putsch against him.

Already, at the First Congress of People's Deputies, the insistence on accountability had led to the creation of three investigatory commissions: on the violent confrontation in Tbilisi between Soviet Interior Ministry troops and Georgian demonstrators which had left twenty-one Georgians dead; on charges of corruption reaching into the highest reaches of the Communist Party; and on Baltic demands that the truth and the documents about the Molotov-Ribbentrop pact be revealed.

Under the chairmanship of Anatoli Sobchak, the commission on the violence in Tbilisi politely but persistently insisted until Politburo members, including Gorbachev himself, agreed to testify on their role in ordering the attack on civilian demonstrators. It was the first time members of the Soviet leadership had ever submitted to such questioning.[3]

Armed with documents he had received in an anonymous brown envelope at the third Congress of Deputies, Anatoli Sobchak also accused the prime minister, Nikolai Ryzhkov, of being implicated in an illegal scheme to sell army tanks and other equipment abroad through a shadowy joint venture called ANT. Ryzhkov protested his innocence before the Congress but he was so shaken that he finished his speech in tears. He was quickly, and derisively dubbed "the sobbing Bolshevik."[4]

The influence and legitimacy of the deputies were weapons which were quickly seized by anonymous men in the KGB. With deputies ready to make leaked documents public, they released a handful to warn some leaders and kept many back to frighten the rest.

However, the KGB's ability to manipulate the deputies and the parliament was nothing in comparison with that of Gorbachev. It was he who had forced his Politburo colleagues to testify before commission members looking into the Tbilisi massacre. He had just returned from a foreign trip and had not been involved in the decision-making which led to the slaughter. It had embarrassed him and stained his leadership. That was the message he wanted to convey to the commission in his own volunteered testimony. The commission's report was a damning indictment of senior Politburo members, the Georgian party leadership and, above all, of Igor Rodionov, the general in charge of the operation.

But, fearful of an angry backlash from the military, Gorbachev resorted to a last-minute tactic that completely undermined the commission's work. As soon as its chairman had announced the committee's conclusions to the Second Congress of Deputies in December 1989, Gorbachev offered the podium to Rodionov, who proceeded to give his version of events. He blamed the massacre on Georgian demonstrators who had provoked the Interior Ministry troops. This version was met with loud applause by many deputies. It outraged Edouard Shevardnadze. The Soviet foreign minister had promised his fellow Georgians the truth would be published and those responsible punished. "It wasn't just the 'series of proofs' [produced by Rodionov] which disturbed me. It was the atmosphere in which it took place. He was applauded so enthusiastically and with such open, vengeful pleasure. It was the same atmosphere as that which had greeted the public dishonour of Sakharov."

Shevardnadze went to Gorbachev and demanded to be allowed to speak to the Congress. Gorbachev refused. In a fury at what he saw as a betrayal, Shevardnadze left the hall and went to his office to draw up his letter of resignation. In it he talked of the rise of the forces of reaction. But he would make the dramatic announcement of his departure only one year later.[5]

Gorbachev's manipulation of the committee on the Molotov-Ribbentrop pact was even more blatant. Significantly, it was the one commission headed by a close adviser, Alexander Yakovlev. But when Yakovlev, at the urging of commission members, went to Gorbachev to ask for the originals of the treaty and the accompanying maps which divided Poland and the Baltics between Hitler and Stalin, he was told they had disappeared.

The draft report of the commission (which included Baltic representatives such as Vytautas Landsbergis, the future leader of Lithuania, and Edgar Savissar, the future prime minister of Estonia) contained a harsh condemnation of Stalin's repression of the Baltic states and a call to publish the original Molotov-Ribbentrop documents, but Yakovlev refused to sign it. Instead, at Gorbachev's urging, he published his own report in the name of the commission, which carefully avoided any comment on the legality of the Soviet annexation of the Baltics. The commision vice-chairman, Yuri Afanasiev, described Yakovlev's report as a "shameful comedy."[6]

Five years later Boris Yeltsin revealed that the "lost" Molotov-Ribbentrop documents had been found – in a safe in Gorbachev's office in the Kremlin which Yeltsin inherited with the collapse of the Soviet Union.[7]

Such manipulations were justified at the time by Gorbachev's advisers because of the growing atmosphere of crisis in the Soviet Union. In July the country's three hundred thousand miners had gone on strike. The catalyst was soap. In most mining regions it could no longer be found. Food, clothes – in state stores in the provinces these, too, were but memories. The miners demanded, not more money, but supplies of necessities. In August there were huge demonstrations in the Baltics to mark the fiftieth anniversary of the Molotov-Ribbentrop pact and to call for Baltic independence. In September Azerbaijan organized an economic boycott against neighbouring Armenia, in an escalation of the eighteen-month war over Nagorno-Karabakh, refusing to allow freight trains through its territory into Armenia.

In this atmosphere Kremlin officials argued that any concessions to these demands would lead to explosion or collapse. On the contrary, firm, even harsh measures were required. It was a logic which appealed to a large majority of Communist deputies in the new legislature. Thus, one of the first important laws passed by the Supreme Soviet in October was a ban on strikes in strategic sectors for fifteen months.

So eager was the majority to re-establish order that it even allowed Gorbachev to step in as the voice of moderation. The original proposal from his own deputy prime minister was so sweeping as to give him quasi-dictatorial powers to break any strike and jail any strikers, no matter how symbolic the strike or how serious the grievance. Gorbachev urged deputies not to pass the measure immediately but to spend the evening discussing it. After an all-night negotiating session, the more limited bill was agreed on and passed.[8]

Yet in its first eighteen months the Supreme Soviet was also the source of a dozen laws which signalled a symbolic rupture with the totalitarian past: on religious freedom, on free entry and exit from the country, on the presumption of innocence in criminal trials, on agricultural leasing for individual farmers, and on the right to create independent parties and associations. Many of these pieces of legislation were initiated or approved by the Kremlin, but some were pushed through despite the active resistance of Gorbachev and his advisers.

One of these was the law on freedom of the press. The members of the legislative committee which drew up the bill quickly agreed on the fundamental principle to be enshrined in the first article of the law: prior censorship of the press and publications was to be banned. This was not what Mikhail Gorbachev wanted at all. At the time there were still almost two thousand censors working for the Main Administration for Safeguarding State Secrets in the Press. Censors no longer sat in every editorial office in the land but they still had the duty to check everything.[9]

When the Kremlin learned of the legislative committee's commitment to abolish censorship, it began working furiously behind the scenes to preserve its editorial power. The chief censor was sent to testify before committee members. He argued that there was, in fact, no unnecessary censorship, that the measures in place were there only to protect state secrets. Members of the Central Committee testified before the committee. Others lobbied committee members in the corridors of the Kremlin. Gorbachev himself called several senior committee members into his office to plead for some continuing form of censorship.[10]

Gorbachev's relationship with the Soviet press was complex. He was proud of his policy of glasnost and of the atmosphere of free discussion it had fostered. But he viewed it not as a right, but as a tool, to be used in the causes he championed. He saw the senior editors of the most famous Soviet publications as his subordinates and many of them saw themselves the same way. Vitali Korotich, the editor of the liberal magazine *Ogonyok* and deputy in the Soviet Congress, boasted of his "redline," a hotline to Gorbachev's office. But more than once, Korotich admitted, the redline was used by Gorbachev to kill or delay articles which might cause him trouble.[11]

While the legislative committee was preparing its bill, Gorbachev called in senior editors for an off-the-record discussion. He demanded the resignation of Viktor Starkov, the editor-in-chief of *Argumenty i Fakty*, the largest circulation weekly in the Soviet Union with twenty-six million subscribers. Starkov's sin had been to publish a reader survey which showed that Gorbachev was less popular than Boris Yeltsin and Andrei Sakharov.

But forces unleashed by Gorbachev could now be used to counter his power. Starkov not only refused to resign, he leaked news of the confrontation to the *New York Times*. And he kept his job. The behind-the-scenes battle over the bill dragged on for a year.

On 12 June 1990 it was finally passed; censorship was formally abolished. This was a milestone in Soviet history.

Yet Gorbachev could not accept it. Seven months later, in the wake of severe press criticism of the killing crackdown by Soviet troops in Lithuania, he told the Supreme Soviet that the new law should be suspended and a new corps of censors created from the ranks of the Supreme Soviet. When deputies rose to protest, he amended his suggestion. With 275 deputies voting in favour and only thirty-two against, he pushed through a proposal to have the parliamentary committee on glasnost draw up, in conjunction with the Kremlin, "measures to ensure the objectivity of news coverage in the press, radio and television."[12]

The contradictions and incoherence in the conduct of the Soviet deputies are plain. Much of the explanation for their behaviour, and for the Kremlin's ability to persuade them to vote against measures they themselves had adopted earlier, lies in the political composition of the legislature. Mikhail Gorbachev regarded the parliamentary bodies he had created much like the Soviet press he had partially liberated: as an instrument to advance his cause and to reinforce his power. Therefore it fell to the small minority of radical deputies to try to define a wider role for the new legislature, indeed for Soviet democracy itself.

Gorbachev's fear of an organized opposition was palpable. He had reacted to Gavriil Popov's call to form such a group at the first Congress with apocalyptic talk of schism. Popov had withdrawn his call but in the corridors and rooms of the Moskva Hotel the Moscow Group continued to meet in the evening. Its ranks expanded. By 9 June 1989, the last day of the first Congress, 150 deputies had signed a vague declaration calling for more democracy and less Communist control in the legislature and more political and economic autonomy for the republics of the Soviet Union.[13]

In the expectation that Gorbachev would refuse to recognize one of its known Moscow leaders, the group chose a deputy from the Russian provinces, Vladimir Shapovalenko, to read out the manifesto on the final afternoon of the Congress.

Gorbachev reacted immediately by ordering an end to the live broadcast of the proceedings. Soviet Television was caught unprepared; without explanation, viewers suddenly found themselves watching the second half of a soccer match. Only when he realized that this was not the beginning of an organized opposition onslaught did Gorbachev order the cameras back on. Andrei Sakharov's judgment of this incident was that Gorbachev was "making plain his desire to keep 'glasnost' within definite limits."[14]

But less than two months later 319 deputies served notice that they planned systematically to challenge Gorbachev's limits. They met in Moscow on 29 July to formally launch the Interregional Group under the leadership of no fewer than five co-chairmen – Boris Yeltsin, Andrei Sakharov, Gavriil Popov, Yuri Afanasiev, and Victor Palm.

The name was unlovely and the structure unwieldy. There were reasons for both. By choosing to call themselves the Interregional Group, the deputies were dramatizing their defiance of the rules laid down by the Kremlin which stipulated that only groups of deputies organized regionally, and thus under the effective control of regional party bosses, would be officially recognized in the legislature. The choice of five co-chairmen reflected the forces and strains already apparent in the group. It was, according to Gavriil Popov, a loose coalition of three separate groups: intellectuals elected from so-called social organizations who had rallied to Andrei Sakharov; radical deputies who sought to create a counter-force to the Communist Party; and a group of deputies essentially loyal to Boris Yeltsin.

It was this last group which proposed that Yeltsin be elected sole chairman. The majority, led by the Sakharov intellectuals who feared that Yeltsin would use the position merely to advance his own ambitions, rejected the idea. Popov described Yeltsin as furious at this decision. "He never forgave the intellectuals. When the Soviet parliament was dissolved, he refused to take any of them into his government."[15]

Yeltsin was harsh in his criticism of the joint leadership. "As soon as things come around to organizational questions, our wheels start spinning," he said. "One co-chairman is afraid to show initiative, the third thinks that everything proceeds from the fourth, and the fourth …"[16]

Curiously, despite his wish to be the sole leader of the group, Yeltsin took almost no part in its deliberations. Other group leaders, as well as his advisers, describe this time as a strange and painful learning period for him. "Until then, Yeltsin was an apparatchik whose only experience was in the party hierarchy, and the party hierarchy is a huge machine which dries up and empties a man, and narrows his intellectual horizons," said Mikhail Poltoranin, a Yeltsin loyalist who was also a member of the Interregional Group. "Suddenly he was thrust into a milieu where he was dealing with first-rate intellectuals. Yeltsin is like a sponge: he started to absorb new ideas, he digested them and transformed them into his own opinions."[17]

The work of the group was further complicated by the sea of incomprehension which separated Yeltsin from the other dominant personality, Andrei Sakharov. In his memoirs, written that summer, Sakharov pointedly described Yeltsin as a lesser man than Gorbachev, whose faults he already considered enormous. "I respect him, but he is a person of different calibre than Gorbachev. Yeltsin's popularity is to a some extent dependent on Gorbachev's 'unpopularity,' since Yeltsin is regarded as the opposition to, and the victim of, the existing regime."

Faint praise, indeed. And Sakharov did not trouble to disguise his irritation with what he felt was Yeltsin's insistence on stealing the limelight at rallies where the two men appeared together.[18]

Gavriil Popov believed the scientist so often described as a saint suffered from a very human failing. "I had the impression Sakharov was very jealous of Yeltsin. He was offended by the idea that he, who had worked so hard and suffered so much for his ideals, was less popular with the voters than Yeltsin. And he tried to compensate by going to the podium and speaking constantly at the Congress." The man closest to Sakharov on the leadership committee, the historian Yuri Afanasiev, said there was no contact between the two men. "They had no relationship at all."

The nerve centre of the Interregional Group quickly became Sakharov's kitchen on Chkalova Street in central Moscow. Here Afanasiev and other group members would discuss strategy and tactics with the physicist late into the night. Yeltsin never once appeared in Sakharov's kitchen.

There were other strains in the group. For two months its members wrangled over the planks to include in their program. When finally published it was a smorgasbord of different ideas and laborious compromises. For example, it came out firmly for *every* form of property, from state-owned to private. It called for a new constitution with a president elected directed by the people where the sovereignty of each Soviet republic would be guaranteed. But Russian deputies, who made up 75 per cent of the membership, were uneasy with this idea.

It was Sakharov's insight that what bound this loose coalition together was not what it stood for, but what it stood against. And so he suggested the group forget its platform and concentrate on campaigning to abolish Article 6 of the Soviet constitution, which guaranteed the dominance of the Communist Party.

The group would win this battle in March 1990, but no other. Sakharov's last struggle was to transform the Interregional Group into a full-fledged opposition party. He failed. Yuri Afanasiev said most deputies were afraid to see themselves as a separate political force. It would mean leaving the Communist Party, and 90 per cent of the group were still party members. Indeed, they saw themselves not so much a caucus as a club, and a loose club at that. "It was totally unorganized, with no structure," Afanasiev said. "We couldn't even keep track of how many members we had ... it would vary somewhere between one hundred and four hundred at any given time."[19]

Afanasiev's epitaph for the group, pronounced five years later, in May 1994, at a conference to commemorate its formation, was short and sad. "We didn't believe in ourselves. We always wore a mask."

One deputy symbolized the political disarray in the Soviet parliament and in the Soviet Union itself as it lurched towards its death. His political transformation from Interregional "democrat" to the Interregional Group's greatest enemy was not an aberration, but rather a model for the stages of enthusiasm, confusion, deception, and betrayal that would later characterize the even more savage political wars in the Congress of the Russian Federation.

He was Viktor Alksnis, Colonel Viktor Alksnis, one of the infamous "black colonels" whose harsh denunciations of Gorbachev and dark predictions of chaos and coups to come would contribute to his frightening reputation both at home and abroad. Alksnis was the son and grandson of Communist standard-bearers. His grandfather had risen to become the head of the Soviet airforce. So faithful was he to the Stalinist regime that he had been chosen chief judge of the military tribunal which in June 1937 hastily condemned to death Marshal Tukhachevsky, the armed forces chief of staff. Six months later Alksnis's grandfather was condemned and eliminated in turn. His father grew up in an orphanage but never lost his Marxist faith. And Viktor joined the party at the age of twenty-three in 1973. In 1989 he was elected a people's deputy from a military institute in the Latvian capital, Riga. His platform called for Latvia to remain Soviet and for added legal protection for Russians living there.

Yet that spring Alksnis travelled to Moscow as a "democrat." Sakharov, Afanasiev, Popov – these men were his idols. Although a party member, he believed the economic structure of the country was rotten. It was time to create a market economy. He immediately became a member of the expanding Moscow Group. "I was a naïve man and I thought they were all true democrats. I remember how stunned I was when I first met Sakharov. When I told him about the situation in Latvia and about my fear that it would leave the Soviet Union, he answered that that was the way it should be. I was shocked and disappointed."[20]

But he remained in the group – soon renamed the Interregional Group – attending its founding convention and participating in the debates on its program.

By the fall of 1989, however, he was fed up. In the Moskva Hotel other like-minded deputies were gathering in the evenings to voice their fears and anger. They were Russians living in other republics and concerned at the growing wave of anti-Soviet nationalism and, above all, worried at Moscow's seeming indifference to the danger. One night in December their fear and anger crystallized into a decision to act. They would form a group of deputies to save the Soviet Union, and they would call themselves Soyuz (Union).

Alksnis himself typed up their manifesto in Riga and then, using the armed forces special postal service, mailed it to fifteen hundred deputies. By the end of 1990 it boasted it had the support of around seven hundred deputies, more than any other group in the Soviet Congress of People's Deputies.

It saw as its principal adversary the Interregional Group which, in its view, was undermining the very foundations of the Soviet Union. Yet ironically, it was the political mirror-image of its rival. Its leadership was just as cumbersome and just as quarrelsome. Five co-chairmen fought for the limelight and argued bitterly over tactics. Eventually Alksnis himself would be forced to resign from the directorate. Politically, its members shared little – only a common wish, the preservation of the Soviet Union, and a common tone, that of threats, ultimatums, and fear.

It was a tone established at the group's founding convention in February 1990, in the presence of Gorbachev's parliamentary lieutenant, Anatoli Lukyanov. As Lukyanov painted a frightening portrait of the dangers of democratization and of the Interregional group, delegates began shouting, "Hand out the guns! Give us weapons! We will deal with them!"

Lukyanov's presence was an unmistakable sign of the Kremlin's approval of Soyuz. The KGB also approved. One of its officers, Nikolai Leonov, told the founding convention: "Speaking on behalf of the majority of my colleagues, we join with you under one banner in this great cause – the defence of the Union of Soviet Socialist Republics."[21] Although the support of the KGB and of the armed forces wasn't official, as Alksnis remembered, "they allowed us access, in fact they arranged for us to receive all sorts of secret documents. For instance, the head of the KGB made sure we got their materials on the activities of the Interregional Group."

November and December 1990 were, in Alksnis's mind, the period of the group's greatest triumph. The targets in this battle were now Gorbachev's liberal lieutenants, such as Foreign Minister Edouard Shevardnadze and Interior Minister Vadim Bakatin. Soyuz had publicly issued ultimatums calling for their dismissal. Now, with ethnic violence and nationalist agitation rising, the Soyuz directorate decided on direct action. On 4 November eight of them stormed into Gorbachev's outer office in the Kremlin and demanded an audience with the president. They sat there for three hours, refusing to leave. Finally Gorbachev, flanked by Lukyanov and Prime Minister Nikolai Ryzhkov, received them in his office.

The meeting was stormy. The Soyuz deputies accused Bakatin of being too soft on separatist forces in recent clashes in Moldavia. He had to be fired. To Alksnis's surprise, Lukyanov and Ryzhkov appeared to agree. Gorbachev said nothing. And so the deputies turned on him.

"It was nasty," Alksnis said. "We went so far as to insult him personally. We called him a 'triapka,' a rag. He wouldn't even defend himself. I thought he was going to get up and walk out, or throw us out. Instead he just listened to all these insults, getting redder and redder. But he didn't say a thing."

Four weeks later Bakatin was dismissed, and at the end of December 1990 Shevardnadze announced his resignation, blaming the black colonels for their campaign of harassment and warning, in his turn, of an approaching coup. Alksnis was jubilant. In the strange new theatre of Soviet parliamentary politics, he had consciously sought a special role for himself, that of the swaggering, shocking officer who intimidated his enemies, unafraid to say what others only dared thought. "Naturally, I'm a reactionary. I'm a reactionary and an imperialist."[22]

He had wanted to be feared, and now he was. But the actor was acutely conscious of the reality beyond his public role. Soyuz was a hollow force. Like its Interregional counterpart, it had no organization and no discipline. None of its members were willing to do the hard work of analysing bills. The group initiated no legislation, and all its positions were the fruit of last-minute improvisation. It was the Supreme Soviet in miniature, and the Supreme Soviet was, in Alksnis's phrase, "a swamp."

"The great mass of deputies was completely passive," he said. "There was a handful of deputies, maybe three or four, who were never afraid to speak, and simply by the force of their argument they could often sway the assembly, one way or the other."

In this swamp, deputies of all camps agreed on one thing: they were constantly and easily manipulated by their parliamentary masters, Gorbachev and Lukyanov. Observers watched, bemused, as these two men forced deputies to vote, and vote again, until they got the majority they wanted. In the time-honoured manner of party and Komsomol meetings, they permitted amendments to bills which completely contradicted the sense of the vote in principle, taken earlier.[23]

Anatoli Lukyanov made no pretence of being the impartial arbiter of debates and legislation. Instead, he revelled openly in his role as behind-the-scenes manipulator. "I didn't present proposals to be adopted, the deputies did that. I just 'prepared' them so they put forward the right proposals, and then I would support them. It's true that often the proposal in question was my own, but on the floor of the Supreme Soviet it didn't come from me."[24]

With the vast resources of the Kremlin at his disposal, Lukyanov set about weakening the Interregional Group. A dacha, a foreign trip, a job for a member of the family, and gradually Gavriil Popov watched his troops melt from almost four hundred to just over one hundred. And when blandishments didn't work, Lukyanov blatantly broke the rules. In the spring of 1991, fed up with the persistent opposition of Interregional leader Arkadi Murashev, Lukyanov stage-managed a vote of the Supreme Soviet banning him from attending sessions of the legislature and its committees. His position no longer "conformed with that of the majority of the deputies."[25]

For those, like the leaders of Soyuz, who supported Lukyanov's initiatives, there were favours, like the chance to beat up a political enemy like Edouard Shevardnadze.

It was vicious, but still only posturing. Nevertheless, it was clear to many that this was a prologue to the violence that must result from such behaviour. After just six months in the Supreme Soviet, Nikolai Engver, the deputy born and raised in the gulag, could see the future and it resembled his past. "Our democracy," he said, "will be baptized in a throne of blood."

The violence came, blood was spilled, and the Soviet legislature was swept away. And in 1993 Viktor Alksnis, the black colonel who had dominated and intimidated the Supreme Soviet, who had sworn to keep his country intact, was living in a cottage outside Moscow, afraid to return to his native Riga, "retired" at forty-four, and repairing television sets in his home to augment his meagre pensioner's income.

CHAPTER SIX

An Unofficial Funeral

In life, Andrei Sakharov had stood alone, a man seldom followed and frequently reviled in his own country; in death, he would rally an army of mourners. His funeral, in December 1989, would become a major political event. His burial would help bury the hegemony of the Communist Party.

That weekend, in the bitter cold of winter, Moscow seemed to slow to a halt. Tens of thousands of people stood in the snow outside the Palace of Youth on Komsomolsky Prospekt, waiting to pass by the open coffin. They had come, they told reporters, from Moscow, from Siberia, the Baltics, and Armenia. They had come out of respect, and out of shame. "We are unworthy of him," one woman in the long line said. "He had called on us to demonstrate but we did nothing. We were cowards."

She was talking of Sakharov's last cause, the abolition of Article 6 of the Soviet constitution, enshrining the Communist Party's eternal right to govern. Two weeks before his death Sakharov had called for a two-hour national strike to protest against Article 6. His call had divided the Interregional Group; the strike had been a failure.

As darkness enclosed the city, the line of mourners grew longer, stretching three kilometres along the boulevard. Many people lit candles in the night. The next day a silent crowd walked through the centre of the city behind a cortège of three ancient school buses, the first one bearing Sakharov's coffin. Some mourners held up hand-lettered signs saying "forgive us." Mikhail Gorbachev emerged from the Kremlin to pay his respects.

The funeral service took place in the parking lot of the Luzhniki sports complex. Here the Interregional Group had held its rallies and Russians had often gathered to hear Sakharov speak. It was a choice which highlighted his political commitment. More than twenty intellectuals and politicians spoke. He was called a saint; he was called a martyr. Dmitri Likachev, eighty-three years old and himself a deputy, a scholar and a man who had spent years in the first camp in the gulag on Solovetsky Island, offered the most powerful tribute. "He was a prophet, a prophet in the ancient sense of the word. He was a man who summoned his contemporaries to moral renewal for the sake of the future. And like every prophet, he was not understood. He was driven from his own city." As he spoke, people wept.

The service itself became a political rally. Before the coffin, surmounted by Sakharov's photograph, many of the fifty-thousand mourners held pieces of paper aloft, each with the number 6 cancelled by an x. And when a speaker called for a vote, fifty thousand hands were raised in a silent plebiscite against the article offering constitutional protection to the party.

Seven weeks later Mikhail Gorbachev announced that the Soviet constitution would be modified, and the party's privileged position eliminated.

Sakharov became more powerful in death than in life. In that sense, he was the last of a long series of martyred prophets in Russian history whose unofficial funerals challenged the established order.

The tradition had begun in the tenth century, almost immediately after Prince Vladimir converted his people to Byzantine Christianity. His sons, Boris and Gleb, died as martyrs. In the eyes of the Russian Church, they accepted death in the political turmoil of the period in order to redeem their people through innocent, Christ-like suffering. They became Russia's first saints.[1] In the nineteenth century, great writers like Alexander Pushkin and Leo Tolstoy, by their temperament and their works, assumed the role of dissident-martyrs. Their deaths provoked fear in the imperial court. In the war of the czarist government against its people, their funerals were political events.

After Pushkin's death in a duel, the imperial minister of the interior ordered that his funeral be kept as secret as possible. There were to be no official honours. "A so-called public demonstration of the affliction felt by the people," he wrote, "risked being turned into an indecent triumph of the liberals." Still, large crowds came into the streets to accompany the coffin to the funeral service. The minister ordered the church locked and Pushkin's body removed, under police escort, in the dead of night from St Petersburg to be buried in secret, on his estate.[2]

Seventy-four years later, the news of Tolstoy's death again shook the czarist regime. "The most vociferous and most respected critic of the Russian government was silent," wrote one biographer.

In all the major universities throughout the Empire, there were student demonstrations to mark the death of the great rebel. In the two capitals, there were big rallies of protest against the death penalty. All over the Empire, hundreds of thousands of people waited at the news centres and the telegraph offices to hear the news that Tolstoy was dead. In the street demonstrations which took place all over Russia, the revolutionary movement felt itself revived.[3]

The Bolsheviks, on seizing power in 1917, banished God and the comforts of orthodox religion. But a messianic regime preaching the possibilities of an earthly paradise needed its own rites. The official ideology of paranoia invoked enemies on every side and the need for war, struggle, and sacrifice to achieve the ultimate triumph. And so the centrepiece of the Communist rites became the "martyr funeral."

Consider this description: "So they passed, hour after hour, day after day. It was as though there had been a sacramental need for his death, and he had answered the need, and therefore they were grateful to him. They honoured him more in death than they ever honoured him in life."[4]

This was Lenin's funeral, the first official political funeral, invented and orchestrated by Josef Stalin. The former seminarist reserved for himself the role of high priest. Standing before the coffin of the dead leader he chanted a liturgy he had written himself.

In departing from us, Comrade Lenin enjoined on us to guard and strengthen the dictatorship of the proletariat.

We vow to thee, Comrade Lenin, that we will not spare our strength to fulfill honorably this thy commandment.

In departing from us, Comrade Lenin enjoined on us to remain faithful to the principles of the Communist International.

We vow to thee, Comrade Lenin, that we will not spare our lives to strengthen and extend the union of the working people of the whole world – the Communist International.[5]

Thirty years later Stalin's own funeral would be attended by half a million people. It was a moment of dread and of liberation; it was a ritual heavily burdened with symbolism, and bad poetry.

He was, finally, only mortal,
Guide and Master of Workers everywhere,
Father of nations,
Great Genius of the ages,
Eagle of the Mountains,
Best friend of all children
Lenin's faithful friend in arms
The Lenin of our time.[6]

Father, demi-god, high priest of the state religion – Stalin symbolized all of this, and now the Soviet people had to cope with his disappearance. Just to be safe, the regime also officially designated him a martyr. "He gave his life with abnegation for the glorious cause of communism."

The paradox of Andrei Sakharov's power in death is thus rooted in the intertwined strands of Russian and Communist history. Both the official and unofficial burial rites had much in common: each had distinctly political overtones which mobilized tens of thousands of mourners; the dead man was eulogized as a martyr; the funeral itself became the occasion to outline a new political vision and to incite the mourners to follow it. With this crucial difference: the unofficial funeral was characterized by a spontaneous and thus far more powerful mobilization of mourners, drawn by the strength of the man and by the genuine change offered by the new political program he symbolized. For that reason, Sakharov's funeral, like those of Tolstoy and Pushkin, frightened the established order.

Anatoli Lukyanov spoke of the Kremlin's fear of "an explosion, of half-a-million people demonstrating in the streets" if the death of the scientist was not officially commemorated. He argued that the Soviet Congress "defused" this potential crisis by passing a resolution honouring his memory. A minute of silence was observed. Flowers were placed on his chair. The Kremlin took care of funeral arrangements "to avoid any confrontations."[7]

This was a self-serving reinterpretation of the role played by the Soviet leadership in the hours after Sakharov's death. Mikhail Gorbachev's attitude was particularly ambiguous. He could not bring himself to announce Sakharov's death or to praise the man before the Congress. Instead he delegated the task to a plodding Politburo colleague, Vitali Vorotnikov. When Interregional Group deputies demanded that the sitting be suspended to honour properly Sakharov's memory, the Kremlin leaders took refuge in Soviet protocol. Sakharov was not a senior government figure, merely a member of the Academy of Sciences. He could only be granted a minute of silence.

While this political fencing was playing itself out, the memory of Sakharov's last stand at the podium three days earlier was vivid in the mind of almost all in the hall. He had stood with sheaves of telegrams in his hand, sixty thousand of them, demanding the repeal of Article 6. Urging Mikhail Gorbachev to endorse this step, he had offered the telegrams to the Soviet leader. Like a furious headmaster dealing with a recalcitrant pupil, Gorbachev had pushed them aside. "I can show you my own, three folders of them with thousands," he said testily. "This won't do. Let's not manipulate public opinion."

And then, dismissal. Gorbachev's right hand came down on his bell, his left arm imperiously waved Sakharov back to his place. The final confrontation between the two men seemed to distil the essence of their relationship. Gorbachev had the power and the temper to silence the prophet for a time, but it was merely a defeat postponed. Even in death, the moral authority of Sakharov would triumph.

When the Interregional Group published its program in September 1989, two demands constituted its cornerstones. The first was the call to abolish Article 6 of the Soviet constitution. Just twelve years after its adoption, it read like a remnant from another era:

The Communist Party of the Soviet Union is the leading and guiding force of Soviet Society and the nucleus of its political system, of all state and public organizations. Armed with the Marxist-Leninist teachings, the Communist Party shall determine the general prospects of society's development and the line of creative activity of the soviet people, and place its struggle for the victory of Communism on a planned, scientific basis.

Linked to the demand to do away with Article 6 was the call to create an elected executive presidency. Together, these measures would pry the Communist Party hierarchy loose from power. Few Interregional members expected, however, to see these demands become reality for years.

The group faced, first of all, the unremitting hostility of Mikhail Gorbachev. Opening the second session of the Supreme Soviet on 25 September, he criticized reformers for making speeches with "too little content and too much harshness and simply a disrespectful attitude toward the Supreme Soviet." In his angry confrontation with senior Soviet editors in October he referred to Interregional members as "a gangster group."[8]

He reserved special fury for Yuri Afanasiev and Boris Yeltsin. He publicly asked why Afanasiev hadn't been thrown out of the party for his attacks on perestroika, thus unleashing a violent round of attacks against Afanasiev in the Communist press.[9]

His relationship with Yeltsin was even more difficult. Yeltsin was the only Interregional member on the Presidium of the Supreme Soviet. This was a committee composed of the speaker, the deputy speaker, committee chairmen, and leaders of factions which drew up the legislative agenda. His repeated interventions led to clashes with Gorbachev. "It reached a point where Comrade Gorbachev tried to shut me up: 'You, Comrade Yeltsin, calm down ...'" Yeltsin recounted later. "I had to respond: 'No, you, Comrade Gorbachev, calm down. Or do you get to do whatever you want?'"[10]

Gorbachev's fury with Yeltsin was such that he organized a day of humiliation for him in the Supreme Soviet. Referring to rumours flying around Moscow, Gorbachev called his Interior Minister Vadim Bakatin to the podium on 16 October 1989 to make a report on a recent mysterious incident when Yeltsin had emerged, dripping, bedraggled, and carrying a bouquet of flowers, from a river in the area near Moscow reserved for dachas of the party elite. According to Bakatin, he had announced to local police that he had been the victim of an assassination attempt. Bakatin told deputies that Yeltsin withdrew the accusation after police could find no evidence for it.

Yeltsin was ordered by Gorbachev to give his own version of events. It was, as Gorbachev had intended, an embarrassing moment. "There was no attack on me ... that's all I have to say," Yeltsin said. Amidst shouts and catcalls, he concluded truculently, "this is my private life."[11] But the effect on voters was the opposite of what Gorbachev sought. They saw Yeltsin as Gorbachev's victim, as a martyr of the political establishment. Yeltsin's popularity continued to rise.

The Soviet leader's hostility to the Interregional Group extended to the policies they proposed. On 23 October Gorbachev told the

Supreme Soviet that he rejected the idea of an elected executive president. The Soviet Union's democratic institutions were still too feeble, he said, to concentrate such power in the hands of one man. This would undermine efforts to build up the authority of the legislature and and divert energies from engaging people in grass-root politics.[12]

On 13 November he intervened forcefully to fight off an attempt by Andrei Sakharov and Interregional deputies to put the issue of Article 6 on the agenda for the upcoming Second Congress of People's Deputies. Gorbachev suggested to the Supreme Soviet that abolishing Article 6 would disturb what he described as the "normal process of constitutional change and introduce an artificial construction into our society." Those who saw a multi-party system as the basis of democracy were suffering from "a certain delusion." The key, as he saw it, was that "under cover of discussion of Article 6 attempts were being made to undermine the authority of the Communist Party, and – I say it openly – to deliver a blow to perestroika."[13] In other words, the idea had a whiff of treason about it.

Despite that, the deputies voted 198 to 173 with twenty-eight abstentions to include debate on Article 6 on the agenda. By the complicated rules of procedure it wasn't enough. To pass, the measure had needed a majority of all 542 members of the Supreme Soviet. Yet, in light of that vote, Gorbachev's ringing words three days later to a forum of students sounded defiant, even anachronistic: "I believe in the Communist ideal. This is the ideal, supported by the teachings of Marxist-Leninist thought and scientific socialism, which we proclaim as the highest value."[14]

Even in his own office he was being urged in different directions. After the Supreme Soviet vote Vadim Medvedev wrote him a memo urging that he take the initiative, and declare before the Soviet Congress in December that he was ready to abandon Article 6. Georgi Shaknazarov disagreed, but he renewed his attempts to convince Gorbachev to create an executive presidency and abandon his post as general secretary of the party.

Gorbachev hesitated. "He said, if I turn this monster loose [the Party], it's so powerful, it's better to keep it under my control," Shaknazarov remembered. "He dragged his feet. He was always waiting for the moment when it would become unavoidable."[15]

Gorbachev had another rendezvous with the monster on 9 December. This meeting of the Central Committee was the stormiest since he had come to power. The provincial party barons told him repeatedly they wanted to hear no talk of repealing Article 6. "The radical-democrats [of the Interregional Group] are scaling the parapets," one provincial first secretary cried, "and we're still sitting in the trenches!"[16]

The climax of this confrontation came when Alexander Melnikov, the first secretary from Kemerovo, where the nationwide miners' strike had begun in July, made an angry speech charging that decision-making had been hijacked by a small group of reformers in the Politburo intent on currying favour with the West. "At this critical point for our country, the whole bourgeois world is congratulating us, all our present and former adversaries. Even the Pope is blessing us."[17]

Gorbachev exploded. If the Central Committee thought he and the Politburo were no longer defending the Socialist order, but had chosen the Pope's order, then he would step down.

His threat of resignation beat back the attack but, in the circumstances, the carefully reasoned speech by the minister of the interior, Vadim Bakatin, fell on deaf ears. "We mustn't allow ourselves to take steps which could work against the authority of the Party. And the fight to preserve Article 6 is one of those steps. Tell me, why does the party, which believes in its strength and believes it's supported by the majority, need the protection of the Constitution which declares its leading role?"[18]

Bakatin even presented a resolution declaring that the Central Committee recognized the necessity of refusing the constitutional guarantee of the leading role of the Communist Party. Gorbachev simply ignored it. There was no debate and no vote on the motion.

On 12 December, in front of the Soviet Congress, Gorbachev once again offered an emotional defence of the political status quo. He was speaking on a new motion by the Interregional Group to include debate on the constitutional role of the party on the agenda. It was a speech in which logic played little part. The Communist Party, he said, didn't need Article 6; three Soviet constitutions before the present one had contained no such article. Yet to amend or abolish Article 6 now would be a grievous error. His voice rising and his finger wagging, he accused the Interregional Group of trying to manipulate political procedures by pushing through "hasty moves."

He then ruthlessly limited discussion on the question. The last of a handful of speakers was Andrei Sakharov, and Gorbachev cut him short. The tactic had succeeded once again; the vote of the Congress was 1,139 to 839 against including Article 6 on the agenda.

In the corridor after the vote Andrei Sakharov was unconcerned. Standing in a halo of television lights, he outlined the task before the opposition. "If necessary we must protect perestroika from the initiators of perestroika, if their position becomes reactionary or they drag their heels unjustifiably."[19]

Two days later he was dead.

Discussion of how to dismantle Article 6 began in the Politburo right after the close of the Second Congress of People's Deputies in December. As one Politburo member put it carefully, "After Sakharov's funeral, we understood that changes were necessary."[20]

Seen from the West, the fall of 1989 was the miraculous season of change in the East: the destruction of the Berlin Wall, the Velvet Revolution in Czechoslovakia, the bloody end of the Ceaucescu regime in Rumania. The Soviet empire was collapsing, the Communist rampart of the one-party state was breached; the leadership in Moscow would be forced to adjust or risk being swept away in turn. Yet almost none of the men in Moscow involved in the revolutionary rewriting of the Soviet constitution that winter even mentioned the events in Eastern Europe as a factor in their thinking.

For these men, Eastern Europe had always been another world, a lesser world – the outer empire. Now the satellite states had launched themselves on their own orbit. They were gone, and events there would have little effect on the political evolution in Moscow. The intellectual divorce was already evident in November. On 21 November after the breach in the Berlin Wall and with the Velvet Revolution in Czechoslovakia well launched, Gorbachev was asked whether he didn't fear that the pace of change in Eastern Europe was moving too fast. On the contrary, he replied, what was needed there was more and faster political and economic change. "We have to make up for lost time ... people want to create a more open, democratic society."[21] This was just five days after he had suggested that the belief that multi-party politics would help bring democracy to the Soviet Union was "a delusion."

Events in what Sakharov described as the "inner empire," on the other hand, were having a major psychological impact on the Kremlin. In early December both the Lithuanian and Estonian Supreme Soviets voted to open the way to a multi-party system.

Even more traumatic, the Lithuanian Communist Party voted to split from the Soviet monolith.

In early January 1990 Gorbachev went to Lithuania, hoping to persuade the Lithuanian party leadership to rescind its decision. The trip was a shock for him. He found a people quietly but resolutely opposed to his regime. It was during this trip that, for the first time, he opened the door to the possibility of change: "We should not be afraid of a multi-party system the way the devil is afraid of incense."

There were other shocks later in January. Ethnic tension in Azerbaijan between Azeris and Armenians exploded in the Azerbaijan capital, Baku, with Muslim Azeris hunting down and killing Christian Armenians. The local Communist government had lost control; the Azeri nationalist Popular Front seemed on the point of seizing power. Gorbachev sent in eleven thousand Soviet troops. Hundreds more were killed in the bloody crackdown. A week later, in Moscow, opposition deputies and intellectuals met and, declaring there was little hope of reforming the Communist Party, decided to found the Democratic Platform, in effect the embryo of a political party for disillusioned communists.

Gorbachev's advisers saw that Article 6 was already a dead letter. Other parties were springing up around the country. Gorbachev was now faced with the unavoidable. The key was to offer him a plan which would allow him to see himself, and not the detested Interregional Group, as the initiator of change. The answer lay in combining the end of Article 6 with the creation of an executive presidency.

At the end of January his key advisers sent him a memo outlining their proposal. In it they dwelt on what they called the growing paralysis of power in the Soviet executive. Gorbachev, as chairman of the Congress, was the head of state, but in order to send troops to Baku, he had had to consult with the forty-two members of the Presidium of the Supreme Soviet and obtain the permission of the Azeri government. He was presiding over a cumbersome collective presidency. He himself lamented that the constitution offered him little more power than that of a parliamentary speaker.

There was a further danger; the growing disaffection of the party hierarchy was now turning into active sabotage. "Faced with possibility of losing its power and privileges the hierarchy is terrified," they wrote. "It has abandoned all its principles. It is forging alliances with nationalist and chauvinist forces. It is beginning to play with ideas like imperialism and autocracy and to associate with fascist elements in order to prolong its life."[22] It was time to end the hierarchy's monopoly on power and to create a political counterbalance in a powerful presidency using France and the United States as the model.

Vadim Medvedev said plainly a few weeks later that the linking of the two steps was far from coincidental. "One the one hand, if we don't create a powerful presidency, and the party gives up its present leading role, it could lead to anarchy fraught with unpredictable consequences. On the other hand, any decision here touching on the powers of the President would be rendered meaningless if the Constitution continued to enshrine the leading role of the party."[23] In other words, the hierarchy would strangle Gorbachev unless stripped of its constitutional power.

Gorbachev was convinced. His job was now to convince his Central Committee and the Soviet legislature.

The Central Committee was to meet on 5 February. As rumours of coups and upheaval swept through Moscow, the democratic opposition decided to hold a rally on Sunday, 4 February, to demand the abolition of Article 6. Unexpectedly, the Kremlin intervened to help; Soviet Television carried a report the night before explaining the reasons for the rally, the Moscow press helpfully published a route map. The police were ordered to cooperate.

More than two hundred thousand people marched through the centre of the capital that Sunday carrying placards saying "Down with Article 6" and "Party Bureaucrats, Remember Rumania." It was the largest political demonstration since 1917. On Manege Square, just outside the Kremlin, Yuri Afanasiev shouted to the demonstrators: "All hail the peaceful February revolution of 1990!" This was a clear reference to the events which toppled the czar in 1917.

The next day Central Committee members found themselves running a gauntlet of reporters and cameramen as they entered the Kremlin for the first day of their meeting. This was all was very unsettling, but it was only a prelude to Gorbachev's dramatic suggestion that they create an executive presidency and abandon the constitutional rock of Article 6.

"The party," Gorbachev told the Central Committee members, "can exist and play its role as the vanguard – only as a democratically recognized force. This means that its status should not be imposed through constitutional endorsement."[24]

Once again the provincial barons snarled their disagreement. Gorbachev was taking them down the wrong path. Yegor Ligachev declared that such policies had already lost them Eastern Europe. They should not be stampeded by a handful of deputies and a few thousand demonstrators. But once again the inertia of discipline prevailed; the barons could not bring themselves to vote against the policy proposed by the general secretary and endorsed by the Politburo.

Gorbachev thrived on crisis; now he proceeded to manufacture one. One week after the Central Committee meeting, he rammed through a resolution of the leadership of the Supreme Soviet calling for an emergency session of Congress by the end of the month to transform the Soviet Union into a presidential republic. When the Supreme Soviet itself met on 15 February the deputies reacted angrily. They wanted to see the bill outlining the powers of the president. On 27 February they were shown it; the Interregional deputies, who had been calling for an elected presidency, were stunned. As written, the bill would give the new president virtually dictatorial powers, to rule by decree, to declare states of emergency in any republic without reference to parliament or local leaders. Speaker after speaker questioned the need for such sweeping powers. Interregional leaders talked of the return of the totalitarian tradition.

Then Gorbachev himself went to the podium. Employing the tactic which had always worked in the Central Committee, he turned the debate into a plebiscite, not on the presidency, but on Gorbachev versus the Interregional Group. "They [the Interregional Group] are trying to suggest that all this is being done just to please Gorbachev. That's just cheap demagoguery. It has nothing to do with Gorbachev's power when we speak of presidential power ... What does Gorbachev have to do with it? We must have a decision."[25]

Faced with that choice the Supreme Soviet voted – 347 to twenty-four with forty-three abstentions – to endorse the executive presidency and to send the bill on for final approval at a special Congress on 12 March.

Gorbachev's tactical triumph in the Supreme Soviet left the Interregional Group groping for a strategy. The strains the group had struggled to contain for almost a year now became public. On the weekend of 10 March, just before the opening of the Congress, some three hundred Interregional deputies and their supporters gathered in one of the six towering office buildings just off the Arbat in central Moscow. These angular glass and steel structures slice through one of the oldest residential areas of the capital. They were ordered built in a spurt of socialist urban renewal under Nikita Khrushchev. Perhaps because of their irregular facades and the wide gaps between them, they are known popularly as "Khrushchev's teeth."

In the lobby, earnest young men tried to give away political tracts and long letters to Gorbachev detailing his sins and those of his regime. The crowd of political activists ignored them, drawn instead, as to pornography, by the stacks of newly published books: a novel by Solzhenitzyn or Nabokov, the collected works of Mandelstam. By the beginning of the meeting the best books had been gobbled up.

The hall was full; people sat in the aisles. The spectacle itself was entirely predictable. Denunciation had become and would remain the most popular form of political opposition. It was the politics of purity; there could be no compromise with the enemy.

The most successful practitioner of the form in this period was Yuri Afanasiev, a stocky historian with grey hair and a commanding bass voice. Afanasiev was a contradictory product of his time. He had spent a generation – he was now fifty – studying the French revolution and lecturing on the virtues of Marxism-Leninism. Having loyally served the old Soviet regime, he had now transformed himself into the leading Jacobin of the perestroika period.

His speech to the group was a model of unbending virtue. "We do not accept strong executive power," he declared. "Gorbachev's choice is a tragedy of demagoguery." The Soviet constitution had to be completely rewritten. Gorbachev's insistence on having the first president elected by the Congress was unacceptable; he must be elected by the people. To do otherwise would be to open the door to a renewal of Stalinism and Russian imperialism.

At this meeting Afanasiev's principal opponent was Sergei Stankevich, a thirty-six-year-old deputy and an expert on American politics. In his own words, he was the representative of the constructive opposition to Gorbachev, while Afanasiev represented the aggressive opposition.

He bluntly told the group that Afanasiev's position was doomed to defeat. They should choose the politics of the possible and attempt to amend the more extreme aspects of Gorbachev's plan.

He announced that, in behind-the-scenes negotiations, he had already succeeded in persuading the Kremlin to limit the sweeping presidential power to declare a state of emergency. Thanks to his lobbying, the bill had been rewritten to ensure that the government of the republic concerned would have to give its prior consent before an emergency could be declared.[26] But the Interregional Group preferred Afanasiev's politics of purity. The meeting passed a resolution condemning Gorbachev's bill in words lifted directly from Afanasiev's speech.[27]

When the Congress convened on the morning of 12 March, a small band of Interregional deputies stood in the huge marble foyer of the Palace of Congresses, distributing leaflets to passing colleagues and journalists. "Everyone demands the direct election of the president," they read. "The procedure proposed by Gorbachev is anti-democratic." That was the beginning and the end of the group's strategy to persuade other deputies to join their camp. During breaks in the proceedings they joined the other members riding the escalators to the top floor where long tables of caviar and sturgeon sandwiches awaited. The food was consumed in concentrated silence.

The Interregional deputies were political neophytes; they had no experience of lobbying and arm-twisting. Even the idea of approaching other deputies seemed to disconcert Yuri Afanasiev. "We have no such plans," he said. "That would be useless."[28]

Indeed, Afanasiev carried the politics of purity to new heights in a blistering speech on the opening day of the Congress. In it, he mounted a frontal attack on Lenin himself. "If our founder laid the foundations of anything, it was the institutionalization of the state policy of mass violence and terror," he said.

The vast hall rumbled in disagreement. Afanasiev then proceeded to link Lenin's crimes with Gorbachev's plans. "He instituted the principle of lawlessness as a state policy ... And now it is suggested that we continue with this, according to our tradition."[29]

The reaction was stormy, in the hall and in the Interregional Group. Afanasiev's colleagues later accused him of ignoring the group's position, and of damaging its chances of blocking Gorbachev's plan by alienating other deputies. But Afanasiev had a highly unusual, not to say unique, view of caucus discipline. "I was against the idea that everything must be put on the table or put to a vote, that the majority would decide which ideas were right and which ideas were wrong. My conviction was that we should all express our opinions. That way the Interregional Group would remain lively and active."[30]

By contrast, Gorbachev had a carefully prepared strategy to win the support of the Congress. It was a strategy driven by the energy of desperation. The night before the opening session, the new parliament of Lithuania had unanimously adopted a declaration of independence. Lithuanian deputies told reporters in the lobby that they were attending the Congress only as foreign observers. Deputies from the other Baltic states were threatening to withdraw as well. That set the stage for the opening session.

It began with a parade of Kremlin lieutenants trooping to the podium to hammer home the arguments in favour of the presidency – the spectre of anarchy, the paralysis of executive power in a crumbling country, the need for a strong hand.

The logic offered by Sergei Alexeyev was typical. He was the head of the Constitutional Oversight Commission and had helped draft the bill on the presidency. Now, less than a year after something resembling a parliament had begun to function, and less than six months after Gorbachev had rejected the idea of an executive presidency because it would fatally weaken the newborn and still very feeble legislature, Alexeyev pointed to that same legislature as a source of great danger. "Power has not been functioning. A pure parliamentary structure leads to a political dead end. It can block all decisions and lead to dictatorship ... We need strong power, without which our system could explode and disintegrate."[31]

It was extreme rhetoric but it was very persuasive for a large body of deputies, including those from Soyuz, whose fear was of disorder and the breakup of the Soviet Union.

Gorbachev contributed to the atmosphere of crisis by ruthlessly herding the deputies, pushing the discussion forward, cutting off speakers, denying others the microphones, at times turning off all the microphones in the hall to deliver an impromptu lecture. He even urged the deputies to sit all night to pass the legislation as rapidly as possible. They refused.

His desperation was fuelled by the implacable logic of numbers. Only 2,087 deputies had registered for the Congress. The fifty-eight Lithuanian deputies had announced they would not vote. And Gorbachev needed the vote of at least 1,497 deputies (two-thirds of the 2,250 elected members) to pass the constitutional amendments creating a presidency.

In the end, he was forced to resort to old-fashioned political horse-trading. As he directed proceedings, his aide Georgi Shaknazarov sought out the leader of Estonia, Arnold Ruutel, and began an intense discussion. Estonian deputies later said that Shaknazarov, speaking in Gorbachev's name, had held out the promise of talks on Estonian independence if the republic's forty-two deputies would vote for the institution of the presidency.[32]

By the end of the second day the deputies were ready to vote. It was now that Gorbachev ripped up the rule book, duping the Congress in his quest for the presidency. The drafting commission had agreed to split the bill on the presidency into four blocks. The Congress voted on the first two – voted on principle, most deputies believed – and by margins of 1,817 to 133 and 1,771 to 164 approved the concept of the presidency and the powers of the office. Gorbachev congratulated the Congress, and immediately several liberal deputies stood up to present amendments to further restrict the powers of the president. Gorbachev calmly announced that the vote just held had been the final, binding vote on instituting the presidency. Any changes now debated would need a two-thirds majority because they would be amendments to the constitution.

It was a mockery of parliamentary rules and of the procedure established in the previous nine months by the new legislature: first a vote on principle, followed by votes on amendments which would need a simply majority to be adopted, and then a final binding vote on the amended package.

Arkadi Murashev, one of the young leaders of the Interregional Group, told Gorbachev the proceedings had turned into a circus. It would be highly irregular and unjust if the the deputies adopted a key constitutional amendment without understanding what they were doing. They would become the object of criticism and ridicule from their constituents.

Gorbachev: "Speak for yourself."

Murashev: "I find this shameful."

Gorbachev: "Here every deputy has the right to say whether he understands the procedure or not. Tell us, did you understand?"

Murashev: "I personally didn't understand and would have voted differently if I had..."

Gorbachev: "Then you should have raised the question and found out. This is standard practice in parliaments around the world. The matter is closed."[33]

There were still two major hurdles for Gorbachev to overcome. The first was a proposed amendment requiring the president to give up any other state or party posts upon assuming the presidency. This was aimed at forcing Gorbachev to give up his position as general secretary of the Communist Party. He now faced a coalition of unhappy Communists and radical-democrats ready to vote for this measure. Gorbachev wanted both jobs.

Thanks to his parliamentary shell game, he was able to remain general secretary. A total of 1,303 deputies voted for the amendment to split the posts. It was a solid majority, but not a two-thirds majority. The amendment didn't enter the constitution.

The second question was even more fundamental: should the first president be elected by the Congress or the people?

There was a break in the proceedings. Anatoli Sobchak went backstage where the drafting commission was working. Rumours were being retailed by advisers that Gorbachev had decided to step down if the president wasn't immediately elected by the Congress. The threat of resignation had always worked inside the party; now it would work inside the Congress. Sobchak, by his own account, panicked. If Gorbachev stepped down and there was a bitter election campaign for president, the Soviet Union would slide into chaos. He began urging other deputies to vote for an immediate congressional election, despite the resolution of the Interregional Group which bound him to support the concept of a general election. In a short speech from the floor, he, dramatically broke ranks with his caucus.[34]

He had also urged Dmitri Likhachev to speak. The oldest deputy in the Congress, a man respected by all, came to the microphone and raised the spectre of revolutionary chaos. "I remember perfectly well the February revolution of 1917," said Likhachev, who was eleven then. "I know what people's emotions are like, and I have to tell you that at the present time our country is swept with emotions. In these conditions the direct election of a president would lead to a civil war. Trust my experience. The election should be held here, and without delay."[35]

With that, the deputies voted. The measure to have the Congress elect the first president received 1,542 votes, forty-five more than the two-thirds necessary. The vote shattered the fragile unity of the Interregional Group. Sobchak, of course, voted for the amendment. Afanasiev voted against. Boris Yeltsin and Gavriil Popov weren't even in the hall.

The rest was anti-climactic. Gorbachev once again went on the ballot unopposed. Two other candidates, Prime Minister Nikolai Ryzkhov and Interior Minister Vadim Bakatin, were nominated but begged to be excused. Still, the vote on Gorbachev's presidency was sobering. He won the support of just 1,329 deputies, 59.5 per cent, a far cry from the 95 per cent who had supported him in the same Congress the previous May.

The next day he took the oath of office. The first act of his presidency was the adoption of a resolution prepared by his office condemning the Lithuanian declaration of independence. By some act of sleazy magic the legislature seemed to have suddenly reverted to the Brezhnev era. A stream of speakers came to the podium to denounce the actions of the nationalist clique which had somehow hijacked the Lithuanian elections. Telegrams were read demanding action to protect the rights of Soviet citizens in Lithuania. A Lithuanian deputy of Russian origin who tried to explain and defend the declaration finished to shouts of "Vrag Naroda" – "Enemy of the People," the Stalinist battle cry. The resolution was overwhelmingly endorsed. The spectacle was not encouraging.

Andrei Sakharov had warned of the danger a year earlier: "The construction of the state has started with the roof. This is clearly not the best way to go about it."

After the result of the vote to elect the first president of the Soviet Union was announced, Mikhail Gorbachev disappeared into a backroom. In his absence a table and a Soviet flag were placed centre stage. A few minutes later Gorbachev returned from the wings, carrying a red leather binder. This was the newly amended Soviet constitution. Placing it on the table and touching it with his fingertips, he proceeded to recite, haltingly, the oath of office he had just memorized.

He had just sworn himself in as president. The pin proclaiming him a deputy of the Congress was still in his lapel; he had forgotten to remove it.

The poverty of this improvised ceremony was telling. Gorbachev had proclaimed his desire to create a state of law, but he could not trust the people to vote for him. He could not trust the parliament he had created to obey his commands. And so he had torn up the parliamentary rules he had written and bypassed the people entirely. All these choices he justified by the uncertain temper of the times, but they were tragically wrong. In bludgeoning the Congress, he had demonstrated to the country that it was merely a toy, and not the repository of legitimacy. In refusing to face an election, he had denied himself a greater legitimacy.

The symbolism of the man standing at the table hesitating over the words he had memorized was apt. Gorbachev was now a man alone.

CHAPTER SEVEN

Miniature, Everyday Coups

For twenty months and ten days Mikhail Gorbachev was the first and only president of the Soviet Union. His period in office appears, at first glance, as a mad roller-coaster ride of policy, a wild lurching from reform to repression and back. Yet what is incomprehensible in terms of policy takes on a certain coherence if seen in the light of power and unity. These were the two concepts Gorbachev understood and clung to, and in his mind they were linked – power for himself to be used to preserve the unity of his country.

The method he would resort to most frequently was once analysed by Karl Marx. He called it the "miniature everyday coup," designed to give the illusion of leadership and to distract the public from the underlying political or economic crisis. For more than a year these coups would throw the country into turmoil, as Gorbachev strove to dominate his opponents and keep his regime from cracking up. Such was Gorbachev's obsession with and respect for power, however, that if an adversary, such as Boris Yeltsin, successfully resisted a coup attempt, Gorbachev was immediately ready to conclude a temporary alliance of convenience with him to pursue an entirely different policy.

There are two other factors which help explain the confusion of those days. Both have to do with the character of the new president. All of his colleagues, advisers, and opponents have tried to comprehend the complexity of the man. The less perspicacious, such as Yegor Ligachev, found him impenetrable. Ligachev was so mesmerized that he called his own memoirs *The Gorbachev Riddle*. Others offer less mysterious portrayals.

One of the most interesting came from Nikolai Ryzhkov, his prime minister for five years. In his memoirs, Ryzhkov described

Gorbachev as a parliamentary leader who saw politics almost exclusively as theatre, as role-playing. "He loved the sensation of power and strived for power, but it was for him, in large measure, a game."[1]

As the Soviet Congress prepared to install Gorbachev as president in March 1990, Boris Yeltsin, in his first book of memoirs, wrote the much-quoted aphorism, "If Gorbachev didn't have a Yeltsin, he would have had to invent one." The paragraph which followed developed Ryzhkov's idea of Gorbachev the actor.

He realizes he needs someone like me – prickly, sharp-tongued, the scourge of the overbureaucratized party apparat – and for this reason he keeps me near at hand. In this real-life production, the parts have been appropriately cast, as in a well-directed play. There is the conservative Ligachev, who plays the villain; there is Yeltsin, bully boy, the madcap radical; and the wise omniscient hero is Gorbachev himself. That, evidently, is how he sees it.[2]

The scene chosen for many of Gorbachev's so-called coups was the parliament he created. Indeed, under his presidency the Soviet legislature became, almost exclusively, the stage for political theatrics, directed first by Gorbachev and then against him.

The second aspect of Gorbachev's character has often been remarked on: he was a political actor who saw politics as performance and improvisation. Having proclaimed the urgent need for an executive presidency, having rammed his concept through a reluctant legislature, he gave little thought to how to use the instrument he had created.

"He devoted all of his attention to writing his inaugural speech," Anatoli Chernayev noted at the time. "And none to the new structures of power. What was he going to do the next day? Whom would he consult? Meanwhile, people were counting the days, waiting for the major changes he had promised."[3]

Pavel Bunich, a senior Interregional deputy, noted the propensity to substitute activity for action. "He talks a lot but accomplishes little. He's a man who every day goes to meet with everyone, talks with everyone – the ones he needs to and the ones he doesn't. He won't be an iron president. He's a very soft person, too soft – one compromise after another."[4]

As the new president, Gorbachev simply carried on as before. One week after his elevation he held his first strategy meeting. It was not with members of his presidential council or with the cabinet but with the Communist Party Politburo. The subject was Lithuania and its defiant declaration of independence. The Politburo members listened to a plan presented by General Valentin Varennikov, the commander-in-chief of Soviet land forces. It was a scaled-down version of the 1968 Soviet invasion of Czechoslovakia: the despatch of three Soviet regiments, the declaration of direct rule by Moscow, the "isolation" of Lithuanian leaders, and the creation of a puppet government answerable to the Soviet forces. Most Politburo members vigorously approved the plan. Gorbachev's liberal advisers, Alexander Yakovlev and Vadim Medvedev, kept silent.[5]

But Gorbachev was not Brezhnev and the Politburo no longer had the power to decide. Two days later, the first presidential decree on Lithuania was issued. The republic's borders were sealed and put under the control of the KGB. The new president wanted to preserve the unity of his country. He would try to squeeze the independence drive to death with an economic blockade. Like so many of his laborious compromises in this period, it would only hasten the result he sought to prevent. In retirement and exile from power, Gorbachev's advisers uttered again and again this lament: "He didn't see the danger, he was late in reacting."

Gorbachev's reaction to the attempt of Boris Yeltsin to create a new power base for himself illustrates their point. In March 1990 the second wave of competitive elections took place in the Soviet Union. These were to elect deputies to the legislatures of the fifteen republics which made up the country. The largest and most important of these was the Congress of the Russian Federation. Boris Yeltsin ran for a seat in this Congress and won in a landslide.[6] He quickly announced he was a candidate for the post of chairman of the Congress. Under the new parliamentary system introduced by Gorbachev, this would make him the head of the most powerful republic in the country. Gorbachev's men had tried to alert their chief to the threat during the general election campaign. He had to have a powerful lieutenant such as Prime Minister Nikolai Ryzhkov or Interior Minister Vadim Bakatin in the Russian Congress to block Yeltsin if he chose to run for the chairman's job.

There were talks with the two men but they showed little interest. Both shared the general view of the time that election to the Russian Congress was a step down to a junior legislature. Gorbachev made little attempt to persuade them; he seemed curiously indifferent to the potential danger of Yeltsin. Perhaps it was simply a problem which lay too far in the future. As Anatoli Lukyanov recalled, "he didn't like politicians who calculated fifteen moves ahead, he felt it was enough to be three moves ahead, no more."[7]

Gorbachev also had more pressing business: he was working feverishly on another speech. It was to mark the 120th anniversary of Lenin's birth on 21 April. Gorbachev told a Kremlin audience that Lenin was the greatest thinker the twentieth century had produced. "Philistine slander of Lenin as a man is immoral, and attempts to cast aspersions on his noble goals and aspirations are absurd."

Not surprisingly, Gorbachev's Lenin was not the man of murderous memoes ordering hundreds of peasants and intellectuals shot as an example to the others, but rather the serpentine politician of the New Economic Policy who, by allowing a relaxation of central planning and a return to low-level capitalism, saved the Soviet state.

Lenin not only had to struggle with himself and and his political opponents but had to withstand strong pressure from his comrades in the party who reproached him for "giving up the principles" of Marxism and even "deviating" from it ... For all his love of theory, Lenin changed his mind when life demanded, disregarded any postulates or dogmas which had seemed sacred, and relied on a specific analysis of a concrete situation, which he considered to be the living soul of Marxism.[8]

Gorbachev was, of course, describing himself.

One month later, in May, the problem of how to block Yeltsin's candidacy loomed up again before Gorbachev. Even then there was a strange air of unreality about the Kremlin's approach. Gorbachev listened and nodded as Georgi Rasumovsky, the Politburo member dealing with the Russian legislature, reported that there was no danger of Yeltsin being elected because 80 per cent of the Congress members were Communists and would follow party orders. This was more than naïve; it was schizophrenic. Gorbachev's relationship with the hierarchy of his party had deteriorated drastically and was now scarcely better than an armed truce. He had taken to referring to the party as "a vicious, mad dog." It seemed ludicrous to believe that these same men and women would meekly obey his commands in the Russian Congress.

The Yeltsin camp was far more realistic in its approach. Yeltsin had been nominated by Democratic Russia, the umbrella organization which claimed to represent approximately one-third of the one thousand deputies newly elected to the Russian legislature. An election group of seventy deputies would spearhead his drive. Its leaders were not intellectual democrats but deputies with backgrounds as factory managers or in the military-industrial sector. They would seek to win over the floating mass of undecided deputies, many of whom had similar backgrounds.

In the Kremlin hall which had once been the scene of Stalin's staged Communist congresses, the First Russian Congress of People's Deputies convened on 16 May 1990. From an ornate loge in the balcony to the right of the podium, Gorbachev and Politburo members, flanked by the Soviet flag, sat watching the proceedings like stern parents.

Yeltsin and his camp now put to use the lessons they had learned from the defeats at the hands of the Kremlin in the first Soviet Congress of the People's deputies one year earlier. They insisted on an agenda where the government of the Russian Federation would first deliver its report on the state of the economy. Only then would the election take place for the post of chairman of the Congress. The man who won would become the leader of the Russian Federation.

The report, delivered by Alexander Vlasov, the prime minister of the Russian Federation, was a disaster – a disjointed compendium of huge problems and tiny successes with no hint of how to proceed. It was all the more disastrous because Vlasov was the announced candidate of the Kremlin in the election for chairman.

On 22 May in the midst of the debate on Vlasov's report, Boris Yeltsin made his move. He demanded ten minutes at the podium as head of a committee drafting a resolution on Russian sovereignty. "The long imperial policy of the Centre [the new vernacular for the Soviet leadership] had led to complete confusion and lack of power in the republics," he began. "Russia has been the greatest victim of this policy. Today, for Russia, the Centre is a brutal exploiter."[9]

He then read out the thirteen-point resolution. Its heart was point four, which stated that the legislation and powers of Russia would take precedence over legislation of the Union on the territory of Russia. This didn't mean, Yeltsin said, that his group was looking for a confrontation with the Kremlin, but in the next breath he demanded that the treaty creating the Soviet Union in 1922 be completely renegotiated.

Yeltsin had unveiled his platform in his bid to win the post of chairman of the Congress. He would run against the Kremlin and against Gorbachev.

He was helped immeasurably by Gorbachev himself. The next day the Soviet president demanded to speak to the Russian Congress. He denounced as "political swindlers" politicians who said the Soviet Union was on the wrong path and who promised easy recipes to make Russia great. By the second half of his forty-minute speech he was attacking Yeltsin by name. His concept of Russian sovereignty was "corrosive acid ... an invitation to reject Socialism and the Soviet Union ... If we embrace his concept, we will destroy not only the Soviet Union, but also the Russian Federation."[10]

His inner circle had pleaded with him not to make this speech. They told him it would only create more sympathy for Yeltsin among wavering deputies: once again Gorbachev was trying to victimize him. But Gorbachev was supremely convinced of his power to dominate any parliamentary gathering. Anatoli Lukyanov summed up the situation sourly: "At this point, sober analysis was not something Gorbachev indulged in."[11]

On 26 May, helped undoubtedly by Gorbachev's attack, Yeltsin topped the first round of balloting for the job of chairman but he was still sixty votes short of an overall majority.

Once again, against his aides' advice, Gorbachev intervened. He summoned all Communist deputies to a closed-door evening meeting in the Kremlin. "Gorbachev feared Yeltsin like fire," said Leonid Ivanchenko, a deputy who attended. "He was literally yelling, 'we have to do everything to stop him!'"[12]

Gorbachev heaped abuse and scorn on his adversary, accusing him of drinking too much, of being erratic, of being a destroyer not a builder. He ordered the men and women in the room to vote for Ivan Polozkov, a squat little party secretary from Krasnodar. The irony was that Polozkov loathed Gorbachev and his policies with an intensity greater than Yeltsin's, with this difference: if Yeltsin wanted to destroy the Soviet monolith, Polozkov wanted to rebuild it. For each, Gorbachev was the man in the way.

Gorbachev failed. Many of the Communist deputies in the Kremlin room that evening disagreed with their leader's policies and resented his intervention. At least fifty of them rejected his instructions. On 29 May Yeltsin was elected chairman of the Russian Congress with 535 votes, four more than half the Congress.

Triumphantly, he marched through the Kremlin grounds and out through the Spassky Gate. A cheering crowd waited in the parking lot below St Basil's Cathedral. As he saluted the crowd with a clenched fist, old women held up photographs of him like icons and cried with tears in their eyes, "Yeltsin will save Russia!"

Gorbachev was halfway around the world, in Ottawa, on a state visit when Yeltsin's victory was announced. He had left Moscow that morning. For Georgi Shaknazarov, the result of the vote in the Russian Congress was the beginning of the end for his master. He was never again to have the initiative, although a series of spectacular announcements and manoeuvres would often give the illusion of Gorbachev's continuing dominance of the Soviet political scene.

Less than two months later Gorbachev was collaborating with Yeltsin to create the "500-day plan," a sort of forced march to a market economy cobbled together by two teams of economists, headed by Stanislav Shatalin, named by Gorbachev, and Grigori Yavlinsky, named by Yeltsin.

Different factors explain Gorbachev's complete turnabout. Yeltsin had shown himself to be a man of power and Gorbachev respected power. Fear also played a role. Yeltsin was now not only the chairman of the Russian Congress, he was armed with the sovereignty resolution he had helped draw up. In attacking that resolution Gorbachev had revealed his fear, that without Russia there would be no Soviet Union. He had to ally himself with his adversary. And there was another factor; the economic policy of the Kremlin had gone completely off the rails.

With an exquisite sense of bad timing, on 24 May 1990 the Soviet Prime Minister Nikolai Ryzhkov had stood before the USSR Supreme Soviet to unveil his new economic program. The Russian Congress was about to vote on its new chairman in another hall in the Kremlin. While Gorbachev looked on, Ryzhkov announced the first steps on the road to a market economy – massive price rises on essentials such as bread and milk, but not right away. The program would start on 1 July.

The result was predictable. A shock wave of Soviet shoppers emptied shelves of bread and milk in a panic-buying spree. Moscow city hall issued a decree banning out-of-town residents from entering the stores in the capital. Gorbachev went on national television to plead for an end to panic. On 14 June the program presented by Ryzhkov was defeated by an overwhelming majority of the Supreme Soviet.

Having decided to join forces with Yeltsin, Gorbachev showed the enthusiasm of a university student as the 500-day plan developed. He read the position papers avidly. He left on vacation in August for the Crimea but phoned several times a day to the dacha near Moscow where the teams were preparing the document. On returning to Moscow, he announced to foreign visitors that the march to the market was about to transform the Soviet Union. But in his mouth, the market was just a word, the 500-day plan was just a document, a prop to foster the illusion of movement and change.

Others were far more serious in their commitment or in their opposition. On 11 September the Russian legislature, guided by Yeltsin, passed a resolution officially endorsing the 500-day plan, which began by asserting that "property, in the hands of individuals, is the guarantee of social stability, and one of the great bulwarks against social and nationalist upheavals."[13] It laid out the timetable, day by day, for the transformation of the Soviet economy, and the transformation of the Soviet political structure. On Day One, it would require Gorbachev and all leaders of Soviet republics to guarantee by decree the right to private property. Central planning would end. There would be a major devolution of power from the centre to the republics.

The same day Prime Minister Nikolai Ryzhkov appeared before the USSR legislature to attack the 500-day plan as cruel and irresponsible. It would lead only to chaos. Between the government's approach – basically to continue as before – and the Shatalin-Yavlinsky plan, there could be no compromise. The parliament would have to make a clear choice. When Gorbachev then told the deputies he still favoured the Shatalin plan, Ryzhkov increased the political pressure. In the back room after the session, he told Gorbachev he and his whole cabinet would resign if the plan was adopted. Ironically, the deputies themselves were protesting that they still had not received the working papers and documentation about the plan promised by the Kremlin. Their role in this drama had already been decided; they were to be spectators.

The stage was set for what Alexander Yakovlev would later call "the first putsch – the economic putsch." The party hierarchy saw the plan, rightly, as an attempt to break its grip on power and it was determined to hold on.

Suddenly, there were unexplained shortages of bread in the Moscow region. In the week of 11–18 September there were press reports of troop movements around the capital. The first official explanation offered by the Defence Ministry – that the troops were being mobilized to help with the potato harvest – merely increased nervousness and fears of a putsch.

Behind the scenes, the pressure was being applied directly on Gorbachev. The KGB started providing him with reports of breakdown and imminent chaos. He was told that plots were afoot in the Russian legislature to topple him. His closest advisers were smeared. "It was right at this time," Alexander Yakovlev said, "that the head of the KGB, Vladimir Kryuchkov, wrote Gorbachev a memo that I was an American spy, an agent of influence. They were trying to compromise me."[14]

Gorbachev began wavering under the pressure. On 17 September, six days after publicly endorsing the 500-day plan, he suddenly told the Supreme Soviet of the USSR that the question of private property was too important to be decided by a vote of politicians. There should be a referendum on the question.[15]

The assault on the 500-day plan reached a climax on 20 September. On that day the Politburo met for almost twelve hours. The meeting was one long, furious tirade by regional party leaders against the plan which, they said, would destroy the system and the country.[16] The assault convinced Gorbachev that he had to abandon the plan. A compromise would have to be found. Anatoli Chernayev noted in his diary on 22 September that Gorbachev still didn't grasp that tactical compromises were no longer possible. "The revolution approaches which Gorbachev called forth," he wrote. "But he never expected it would be like this. In fact, for a long time he didn't see that it would lead to a fundamental shift of power. Even today he talks only of economic change. No. What is happening is the equivalent of 1917."[17]

The day after the confrontation with his Politburo, Gorbachev told the Supreme Soviet the 500-day plan had serious flaws. It would be better to combine it with the best elements of the government plan. Three days later he demanded, and got, special powers to implement the still-undefined hybrid. Finally, on 13 October, he swept into the Soviet legislature with what he called the presidential plan, which he said took the best from the 500-day plan and from the Ryzhkov proposals. Dutifully, the deputies adopted the plan. In fact, it was little more than a vague commitment to "the transition to the market"; there was no timetable and no talk of painful price increases.

"It was an economic putsch by the party nomenklatura and it was successful," Alexander Yakovlev said. "It was then, in the fall of 1990, that Gorbachev ceased to exercise power – not formally, but in fact."[18]

Curiously, Gorbachev seemed to take no notice. In the next three months he would launch other miniature coups, each designed, as he thought, to reduce the threat of an outright putsch against him by his party. This was no longer power but the illusion of power.

But in November, as the country slid deeper into economic crisis, with the Kremlin under attack from Boris Yeltsin and the Russian legislature for having betrayed its commitment to fundamental change, the Supreme Soviet of the USSR suddenly revolted. On 14 November its deputies declared a legislative strike, refusing to work until Gorbachev told them how he planned to wrench the Soviet Union out of the mess. Soyuz hardliners, led by Viktor Alksnis, called for the introduction of national emergency rule.

Two days later Gorbachev addressed the deputies. He gave a rambling speech in which he declared he shared their fears about chaos and instability, but he offered no plan. For the rest of the afternoon he was mercilessly attacked by the normally quiescent legislature. One deputy mockingly suggested that Gorbachev was behaving like a political exile who had just returned to the country instead of like a president who had responsibility for the state.[19] That evening the Politburo organized another onslaught against the president. In a meeting that went on past midnight, member after member demanded stern measures to restore order.

The next day Gorbachev was back before the legislature with another speech. Like some political magician, he now produced a dramatic plan to reorganize the executive branch. He demanded sweeping new powers, including the power to rule by emergency decree, bypassing the legislature. He announced that he was abolishing his Presidential Council and replacing it with a Security Council, dominated by the defence and interior ministers and the head of the KGB. The prime minister and the cabinet would be placed under the president's direct control. It was the third major overhaul of the executive branch in eighteen months.

The deputies voted overwhelmingly for this plan, which would give Gorbachev the powers of a virtual dictator. The question is, why did they so meekly accept this when, the previous day, they were so furiously criticizing the president? According to Ivan Laptev, the deputy speaker of the Supreme Soviet, such seemingly incomprehensible behaviour had its roots in the psychology of the Leninist administrative-command system, which had institutionalized paternalism – commands from above, obedience from below.

"There was another aspect, which I call the 'psychology of expectation'," Laptev said. "Everybody waited for orders but also expected to receive everything, not to have to do anything themselves. When the bells rang to call the deputies to debate or vote, they didn't know what to do. So they yelled for Gorbachev to come to speak, to explain, to point the way."[20] Gorbachev pointed the way. It was decisive action, or at least the semblance of action.

By now Gorbachev had totally repudiated his alliance with Boris Yeltsin. He had embraced the position of party hardliners and, once again, it was a position based on his respect for power. It was his calculation that the party hardliners now had the upper hand; therefore, he rallied to their camp.

He demonstrated his new loyalty to them in December 1990. He announced to the Soviet Congress of People's Deputies his choice to fill the new post of vice president – a party hack and new Politburo member named Gennadi Yanayev, a man who summed up his political philosophy in these words: "I'm a Communist to the depths of my soul." There were no other candidates. Even in party circles, Yanayev's only claim to fame was as a drunk and a womanizer. Before the nation he confirmed that reputation when answering a routine question from a deputy about his health. "My wife has no complaints," he answered with a leer. This was too much even for the normally docile majority. Gorbachev's choice could not scrape together a majority of votes.

Gorbachev was furious; he demanded a new vote. He invented a pretext; several dozen deputies had dropped their unmarked ballots in the ballot box as a sign of protest. This, claimed Gorbachev, was a violation of the Congress's established procedures. Grudgingly, the deputies prepared to vote again. On the second count, Yanayev was elected – barely.

In all this manoeuvring, Gorbachev operated alone, consulting none of his longtime political advisers. In November Alexander Yakovlev learned that his job as a member of the President's Council was about to be abolished along with the council itself only minutes before Gorbachev rose to speak. In December his closest aide, Anatoli Chernayev, learned of the choice of Yanayev as vice-president only when Gorbachev announced it to the Congress. "He wanted an obedient vice-president, a 'gofer,' a lackey. He imposed Yanayev on the Congress and he was very pleased with himself," Chernayev said. "He was convinced that nothing and no one could resist him. He left the Congress believing he had total control of the situation."[21]

In reality, his political isolation was growing; Yakovlev described an "eerie silence" around the president; he had stopped listening. The deputy Roy Medvedev recalled being called to his office to discuss a legislative question in this period. "He said, 'I need your advice. I have to choose one of three options. And then he talked for twenty minutes until an aide came in and whispered that he had another appointment. And he said, ah yes, I forgot. Thanks very much for your advice.' And I hadn't said a word!"

None of this was remotely comforting to the scattered remnants of the radical-democrats as they disconsolately discussed the future in the Palace of Congresses at the end of the 4th Congress of People's Deputies. Confident clumps of military deputies now strolled the halls as if they owned them once again. The KGB chief was publicly voicing paranoid claims of attempts by Western intelligence agencies to destabilize the Soviet Union by poisoning its grain supplies. Fifty-seven hardline deputies, civilian and military, had just published a petition calling on Gorbachev to suspend the constitution. The optimism of the spring of 1989 seemed a lifetime away.

The presidency of Mikhail Gorbachev reached a moral nadir in January 1991. On Sunday, 13 January – Bloody Sunday for Lithuanians – regiments of the Soviet Interior Ministry and the KGB attacked the television tower in Vilnius, killing thirteen people. The Authorized Version, as related to the Soviet legislature by the man nominated by Gorbachev to be interior minister, Boris Pugo, was that the troops had been called in by a mysterious Lithuanian National Salvation Front, set up to defend the rights of the Soviet majority against a handful of nationalist fanatics who were bent on separation. Who were the members of this Front and what was their authority for such actions? Pugo told the parliament it wouldn't be "correct" to name them; their lives were in danger.[22]

Soviet Television, now in its turn "aggressively obedient" to the wishes of the Kremlin, reported the Vilnius attack this way: "Owing to the aggressive behaviour of a group of militants, tear-gas grenades had to be used. In retaliation, stones were hurled and shots fired. An officer was killed ... Soldiers had to return fire."

The reality was far different. Thousands of Lithuanians, including families with small children and old-age pensioners, formed a human wall before the television tower. They linked arms and sang Lithuanian folk songs as the tanks approached. They stood their ground against tear-gas and smoke grenades. Then, just after 2 a.m., the tanks began firing and moving forward. Some of the victims were crushed to death under their treads.

For twelve hours after the attack, Gorbachev was not to be found. The Lithuanian leader, Vytautas Landsbergis, tried vainly to phone him as the attack was taking place. He was told Gorbachev was "unable to come to the phone." Even attempts by his longtime aides, who had been told nothing of the coming attack, to talk to the president were rebuffed.

When Gorbachev finally surfaced on Monday afternoon, it was to tell a group of Soviet journalists that he had only learned of the attack in the morning. He then parroted the official Moscow version: Lithuanian nationalists were trampling on the rights of the Russian minority. They had beaten up seventy members of the National Salvation Front who had tried to present their views to the Lithuanian parliament. He repeated the ultimatum contained in a presidential decree of 10 January: the Lithuanian parliament had to renounce its declaration of sovereignty and all laws passed after it.[23] Neither he nor any member of the government admitted responsibility or even foreknowledge of the attack, despite the fact that the scenario followed almost to the letter the one outlined to the Politburo nine months earlier.

The imperial leadership no longer had the will to bloody its hands directly. It preferred half-measures to lost reputations. But it still took Gorbachev's aides ten days to persuade him to make a televised speech "dissociating" himself from the mess.[24]

During these unsettling days the Supreme Soviet of the USSR was conspicuous by its passivity. Dominated by the Soyuz faction, who repeatedly demanded harsh measures to keep the Soviet Union from flying apart, it posed polite questions, listened without protest to the Kremlin cover stories, and then voted to confirm Boris Pugo as the new interior minister and, at Gorbachev's angry insistence, to draw up new rules limiting the freedom of the press.

Gorbachev would turn to new devices. On 17 March 1991 he organized a referendum on the future of the Soviet Union. Six

republics – the three Baltic states, Moldavia, Armenia, and Georgia
– refused to participate. Voters in the Russian Federation strongly
endorsed the Union but they also voted in favour of a proposal
Boris Yeltsin placed on the ballot in Russia. They agreed to the
idea of an elected presidency in the Russian Federation.

Ten days later, with the Russian Congress about to meet in
emergency session and Communist deputies in open revolt against
what they denounced as Boris Yeltsin's autocratic ways, Gorbachev
ordered fifty thousand troops into the streets of Moscow, the centre
of the city sealed off, and a ban on all demonstrations. His advisers
said later the Soviet president had been convinced by KGB reports
that crowds of "radical-democrats," at Yeltsin's urging, were about
to scale the Kremlin walls with ropes and grappling hooks and take
the Soviet seat of power by force. Gorbachev was also apparently
hoping that his show of military force would help the Communists
in the Russian Congress in their battle against Yeltsin, who, one
month earlier, had publicly demanded Gorbachev's resignation.

His machinations misfired. A huge crowd of Yeltsin supporters
defied his ban and faced down the soldiers. Gorbachev was forced
to withdraw the army and Yeltsin emerged from the Congress with
new executive powers.

And so in April, for the second time in six months, Gorbachev
suddenly reversed field. On 23 April he called the leaders of nine
republics to his presidential residence of Novo Ogarevo and
announced he was now ready to sign a new Union treaty which
would drastically reduce the powers of the Kremlin. This was the
beginning of the nine plus one process – the nine republics plus
Gorbachev – and it was a magisterial Gorbachevian coup. His goal,
once again, was tactical.

Two days later he had to face his own Central Committee. He
knew many of the party leaders would be demanding his head.
Armed with this new piece of paper, and the support of the
leaders of the republics, he faced them down. Angrily, he told the
barons he was ready to resign and walked out of the room. It
was a dramatic and political success. A hastily cobbled-together
Central Committee resolution begged him to stay on as general
secretary.

Gorbachev had abandoned the party hierarchy because he saw
the real centres of power to be in the republics, and notably in the
Russian Congress. He had to ally himself with them to save the
Union, even if the Union was only to be a weak shell encasing a

collection of sovereign states. Now the party hierarchy would abandon him.

The first to turn on him seemed a most unlikely Brutus. Valentin Pavlov was a short, tubby fifty-four-year-old Central Committee apparatchik who sported a brush cut, double-breasted suits, and loud silk ties. The image conjured up was that of the accountant in a mafia casino. He was, in fact, Gorbachev's prime minister, named to the post in January 1991 after two years as Soviet finance minister. On taking office and surveying the economic distress on every side, his first act was to identify the culprits. "The fault lies, not with our system," he announced, "but with our people."

Pavlov also had the instincts of a mafia accountant. In 1993 he revealed that, as finance minister and then as prime minister, he had presided over a vast deception of Western banks and creditors. He had systematically lied about the Soviet Union's gold reserves. They were not several thousand tons, as he had always told the Western bankers, but a mere two hundred tons by mid-1991. Moscow had secretly sold off its stocks to finance its huge deficit. This Pavlov happily described as "playing the market game."

On taking office, he suddenly decreed the withdrawal from circulation of all fifty and one hundred rouble notes, thus destroying the savings of millions of citizens who kept their money, not in banks, but in their houses. He said this measure had been necessary to defeat a shadowy plot by Austrian, Canadian, and French banks to flood the Soviet Union with roubles and destabilize the regime. Amid scenes of panic and hysteria at every Soviet bank branch, Pavlov announced that his fellow citizens "could now carry on in peace."

By the spring of 1991 Pavlov had adjusted his analysis of the system's woes: the fault lay not with the people, but with their leader. His memoirs reveal a man who had come to hate Gorbachev with a pathological intensity. "He was a man with two faces," Pavlov wrote. "He was a traitor to his people and a hero to the outside world, and above all to the United States, Germany and Israel. All that mattered to him was who paid. That's why Gorbachev rushed to give away everything – the State, the Party, the People."

This was, as Pavlov himself revealed, not a disinterested analysis. In early June he learned to his fury that Gorbachev was talking of replacing him. He decided to move first.

On 17 June, visibly nervous, Pavlov arrived at the Supreme Soviet to deliver a report on the economic condition of the Soviet Union.

In the visitors' tribune sat almost every minister in the government and the vice-president. Only Gorbachev himself was missing. He had preferred to attend the national convention of peasants. For eighty minutes Pavlov painted the expected gloomy economic portrait. But his conclusion was unexpected. He announced that the root of instability was political – ongoing battles between the centre and the republics, the so-called war of laws between the the Soviet parliament and the Russian legislature, and, above all, the disequilibrium of power between the president and the cabinet. Mikhail Gorbachev had too much power and not enough time. He was tired.

"All the problems land on his desk," Pavlov told the deputies. "To deal with them all he would have to work forty-eight hours a day and he still couldn't do it." The cabinet, on the other hand, had far too little power. To correct the situation, Pavlov called for a massive transfer of powers from the president to him as prime minister. He had even drawn up a five-point resolution for the legislature to consider.[25]

What followed was a strange slow-motion parliamentary rehearsal of the August putsch. Power was there to be plucked from Gorbachev's hands, yet both he and his adversaries approached the confrontation in a completely casual, disorganized fashion.

Right after Pavlov's speech, Soyuz deputies, led by Viktor Alksnis, leapt up to endorse his call. Alksnis saw it as the only way to stop passage of the new Union treaty, which in his mind would mean the end of the Soviet Union. "We must support Pavlov and the cabinet because it's the only state organ now trying to preserve the Union." But while Alksnis demanded an immediate vote, another Soyuz colleague demanded to hear first from the head of the KGB, and the ministers of defence and of the interior. Their confused response was due to surprise. "It wasn't a putsch," Alksnis said later. "It could have been if, the night before, Pavlov had consulted us. We were all in favour of his plan but we had to improvise everything."[26]

By the afternoon session on Monday, Soyuz faction leaders had decided on their strategy; they wanted an immediate vote on the transfer of powers to Pavlov. The man in the chair was now the deputy speaker, Ivan Laptev, a loyal Gorbachev lieutenant. The speaker, Anatoli Lukyanov, had left for Novo Ogarevo for a session of constitutional negotiation, promising to tell Gorbachev. But Laptev didn't trust Lukyanov and he himself had failed to get in touch with Gorbachev during the lunch break. Now he frantically tried to stall. He steered the Supreme Soviet into a closed session to hear from the KGB chief and the ministers of the interior and defence.

The three men painted a hair-raising picture of collapse. Kryuchkov offered a particularly paranoid vision of Western intelligence agencies orchestrating the end of the Soviet Union, buying off Russian intellectuals and planting agents of influence in the Kremlin. They were following a plan drawn up in the 1970s. To prove it, he read out a 1977 secret report on the plan, drawn up by Yuri Andropov, the KGB chief at the time. The Western powers were preparing "to demilitarize and even occupy the Soviet Union." Gorbachev knew all this and had ignored it.[27]

"I could feel that the mood was such that the deputies would immediately vote for Pavlov's motion," Laptev said. "The Soyuz deputies were yelling 'vote, vote!' I refused to cut off debate. I just kept giving the floor to deputies who wanted to speak. I even made my own speech, saying we didn't have the moral right to vote when the president hadn't been informed. As I spoke, the Soyuz deputies were screaming at me. And throughout all of this, the ministers sat over there on the side, like stones."[28]

Amazingly, Pavlov himself wasn't there. Having launched his bid for power, he had gone off to a scheduled meeting with aides. Even more amazing, throughout the whole day Gorbachev himself knew nothing of the events in the Supreme Soviet. Lukyanov finally informed him *after* the constitutional discussions at Novo Ogarevo. Later that evening, Alexander Yakovlev phoned Gorbachev. "He was very surprised. He said to me, 'but Pavlov and I agreed that he would only make a report on the state of the economy'."[29]

The next day the Soyuz deputies returned to the attack. Now Lukyanov was back in the chair, organizing a second secret session so the deputies could ask questions of the ministers who had addressed them the previous day. Once again the vote was put off until a committee could draw up a proper resolution. And once again Gorbachev did not bother to attend.

The operetta was far from over. On Thursday Gavriil Popov suddenly demanded an urgent meeting with the American ambassador, Jack Matlock. In a scene right out of a cheap spy thriller, he pointed at the ceiling to indicate hidden microphones and then scribbled out his message. Pavlov, with the help of Kryuchkov, Yazov, and Lukyanov, was trying to organize a coup d'état. This was now seventy-two hours after Pavlov and his ministers first spoke to the Supreme Soviet. Matlock consulted with Washington and was told to report this to Gorbachev. That evening, in the Kremlin, he warned the Soviet president of the possible coup attempt. Gorbachev seemed amused by the possibility.

It was only after this meeting that he became agitated, when Anatoli Chernayev casually mentioned reports of mysterious troop movements around Moscow.

"Why didn't you tell me this before?"

"Because I really didn't believe them."

With that, Gorbachev left for his dacha but later that evening he phoned Chernayev. He was angry and worried. Bitterly he talked of the "swine and scum" who were plotting against him.[30]

On 21 June, four days after Pavlov's speech, Gorbachev finally appeared in the legislature. He angrily denied there was any difference of opinion between himself and the cabinet. He blamed the crisis on Alksnis and his colleagues. They were cut off from reality, living like insects under a bell jar. He told the deputies not to plunge the country into hysterics.

After his speech, the Supreme Soviet took a thirty-minute break and Gorbachev retired to the so-called shoe room where the Politburo met during sessions around a table shaped like the sole of a shoe. There, facing Pavlov and the three offending ministers, he gave an enirely different speech. His face flushed with anger and pounding the table, he shouted, "If you ever try this again, you won't get away with it!" No one else said a word.[31]

Later that day, the "swamp," as Alksnis bitterly called it, voted by a large margin to refer Pavlov's request to Gorbachev, for further study.

Gorbachev now went out to meet reporters in the hall, trailing the four glum "conspirators" behind him. "The putsch is over," he announced with a grin.

Gorbachev, in this crucial period, was no longer leading, he was merely acting. And as he acted, power ebbed from him, to men with the will to use it.

Even Pavlov, the incompetent plotter, knew precisely what he planned to do if granted the power he sought. Among the papers found by investigators after the August putsch was a draft declaration, dated June 1991, waiting for his signature. It would immediately establish emergency rule across the Soviet Union and martial law, under the control of the minister of defence with the help the KGB and the Ministry of the Interior where deemed necessary. All laws passed by republics contravening Soviet legislation were declared null and void.

Yet Gorbachev thought a tongue-lashing was sufficient to deal with these "swine and scum." It was only political theatre, after all.

CHAPTER EIGHT

Another Country ... Another Man

A surgical coup d'état gave birth in blood to the Soviet Union in 1917; seventy-four years later a comic-opera putsch which failed laughably announced its end.

The putsch of August 1991 can be seen as a parable of the Gorbachev regime. It was highly theatrical, indeed it contained all the elements of a morality play where good swiftly triumphs over evil. Gorbachev, now in the role of imprisoned hero, was saved by his rival Yeltsin, cast as the avenging democrat facing down a cast of bumbling Communist villains, while the crowd in the streets – as in Pushkin's play *Boris Godunov* – was both chorus and actor. Its voice would proclaim the new czar and he, in turn, would ask its forgiveness.

Like so many episodes in the second half of the Gorbachev era, this confrontation would be the fruit of manipulation and betrayal. This was betrayal on the grand scale; all the leaders of the coup owed their exalted positions near the throne to Gorbachev himself.

And finally, it would crystallize the confrontation which Andrei Sakharov had once succinctly summed up in a question: was Russia to be a democracy or an empire? This was the question which had gnawed at the body politic of the Soviet Union since Gorbachev had created the first quasi-parliament in 1989. Fittingly, the confrontation would take place against the background of those parliamentary institutions. The prize and symbol of this battle would be the Russian parliament, which would celebrate its victory with a scene of public humiliation more astonishing and complete than any yet seen in the Soviet parliament.

After his miraculous midnight return from his three-day enforced exile from power, Gorbachev sought to cast the events and his new role in the most revolutionary light possible. "I have returned to another country," he told the Soviet parliament, "and I am now another man."[1]

Not to be outdone in the rhetoric of rupture, Boris Yeltsin wrote in his memoirs: "I believe the 20th century ended in August 1991. This has been a century of fear. In those three days, the old century ended and a new one began."[2]

The rupture was indeed dramatic, but, as with so many coups in the Gorbachev era, the rhetoric strained the reality. It was not yet a new century, it was not even a new country, although it soon would be; above all, as he was to reveal quickly, Gorbachev had not become a new man.

For all its apparent theatrical clarity, at the heart of this putsch is a mystery: why did the men who seized power by locking up their master not do the same with Yeltsin, the man they loathed and feared more than Gorbachev?

The role and personalities of three men help explain this mystery. The first of them is Vladimir Kryuchkov, the sixty-seven-year-old head of the KGB. Life seemed to have prepared him specially for this. As a junior diplomat in the Soviet embassy in Budapest in 1956, and as a colonel in the KGB on special mission in Prague in 1968, he had participated in similar operations to put out the fires of democracy at the edges of the empire. Like Gorbachev, Kryuchkov was a protégé of Yuri Andropov, the first man who went from being head of the KGB to head of the Soviet Union. Gorbachev had made Kryuchkov head of the KGB in 1987, thinking that he would be thus bound by a double loyalty. But as perestroika unfolded, and then unravelled, Kryuchkov began telling visitors that his leader "was responding negatively to what is happening." That was polite code for what he really thought. In prison after the coup, he told prosecutors that, by the spring of 1991, he had come to the conclusion that Gorbachev had lost his mind. "Gorbachev was destroying the system which guaranteed him everything – servile aides, the respect of his foes, and a comfortable, not to say luxurious life. How could a man in his right mind saw off the branch on which he was sitting?"[3]

Kryuchkov was supposed to assume the role of the Trotsky of this putsch, the organizer and the man who decided where and when to strike. He didn't look the part. A man of medium height and nondescript suits, with a round head covered by wispy strands of white hair, he had all the charisma of a bank clerk. Only the cold little blue eyes behind rimless glasses betrayed his intelligence. Psychologically he was not a conspirator, and still less a leader; he was a compulsive collector. When investigators searched his office after his arrest, they found, carefully stacked and annotated, the programs of every play, concert, and opera he had ever attended.

This compulsion had made him an excellent spy. He had to have information on everyone. As head of the KGB, he spun vast webs. The telephones of deputies were tapped. The walls of the sauna at the club where Yeltsin played tennis were stuffed with microphones. The phone of Raisa Gorbachev's hairdresser was tapped. It wasn't enough. Gorbachev himself became a target. An aide was "turned" and provided detailed reports on discussions in the president's office. The presidential villa at Novo Ogarevo was bugged.

Thus, Kryuchkov learned that the signature of the new Union treaty, scheduled for 20 August 1991, would mean not only the end of the Soviet Union, but also the end of his career. In a secret, all-day meeting between Gorbachev, Yeltsin, and the president of Kazakhstan, Nursultan Nazarbayev, on 29 July at Novo Ogarevo, Gorbachev agreed to demands from Yeltsin that the republics would have the right, under the new treaty, to determine how much tax revenue to turn over to the Centre. He also agreed to Yeltsin's suggestion that the first thing he would do after signing the treaty would be to fire his prime minister, Valentin Pavlov, his minister of defence, Dmitri Yazov, and Kryuchkov. In the wake of the failure of the coup, investigators found a transcript of this conversation in a safe belonging to Gorbachev's chief of staff, Valeri Boldin. He too had betrayed his master.[4]

Many things would go wrong with this putsch. One of the most damaging failures of the organizers occurred even before they launched their adventure. They could find no Lenin, no intellectual leader with the cold-blooded nerve to justify their illegal seizure of power and force the country to accept it.

Anatoli Lukyanov might have assumed the role. The speaker of the Soviet Congress was, like the head of the KGB, desperately alarmed at the prospect of the Union treaty. He had warned many times, publicly and privately, that the treaty would lead to the destruction of the Soviet Union and its institutions. He was organized, he was cunning, and, Gorbachev's aides had come to believe, he saw himself as Gorbachev's logical successor. But Anatoli Lukyanov wasn't Lenin – he was a Russian romantic. Russians learned with astonishment that this sad bloodhound of a man, this grey party bureaucrat with forty years experience in the Central Committee, this consummate manipulator of deputies in the Soviet Congress, was, in his soul, a poet. After the coup, he spent each day in his cell in the Prison of the Sailor's Rest writing verse. By the day of his release sixteen months after his arrest, he had created two hundred poems, each written in a small, even hand in a notebook which he proudly showed to visitors. They began with an ode to honour and truth:

> To live, to live, to achieve the Right
> To work unceasingly to spread the Light
>
> On page after page without fear
> You must declare the Truth
> So that all others will hear
>
> You cannot flinch, you cannot bend
> A man you must be – to the end.

There were poems to friendship ("a friend seeks neither gain nor flattery; a friend and conscience are as one") and there were poems of love, delicately dedicated to his wife.[5]

But what Lukyanov really loved was the institution he had helped create, the Soviet Congress. On the evening of 18 August when the conspirators gathered in the presidential council chamber in the Kremlin, eying the empty chair where Gorbachev usually sat and drinking heavily as they debated how to proceed, Lukyanov told them that he agreed with their goals but he couldn't sign as a member of the Emergency Committee. He was the speaker of the Soviet Congress and the constitution required that he oversee debate and ratification by the parliament of the decrees creating the emergency committee and stripping Gorbachev of power.[6] He would, however, provide them with a statement denouncing the Union treaty. It was broadcast the next morning at the same time as the first announcement of the takeover by the Emergency Committee.

Lukyanov would earn the title of "grey cardinal" of the coup, refusing to call into session the Supreme Soviet of the USSR in the hope that it would be presented with a fait accompli when it finally convened, while assiduously passing on all information he could gather to Kryuchkov. His calculation was clear: if the coup failed, he would still have his parliament and his position.

And so, by default, the role of Lenin fell to Gennadi Yanayev, the party hack chosen by Gorbachev as his vice-president. It was he who would be the titular leader of the coup, signing the documents and speaking on behalf of the committee. Yanayev was a limited man and a lazy man – he hadn't read an official document in three months; investigators found them in his office after the putsch, unopened and untouched – but he had one virtue. He knew his limitations. As the reality of what they were about to embark on sunk in, he paced the room, smoking cigarette after cigarette and downing glass after glass of whisky. ("I only had four or five shots," he said later, "that's not enough to get me drunk.") Earlier he had whined, "Why me? Why do I have to take on the duties of the president? Why can't Lukyanov do it?" And Lukyanov patiently explained that that was the way the constitution was written; Yanayev was the vice-president, he had to take over.

With that, the men who had agreed to form the committee signed the declaration announcing their coup and stumbled out into the night. It wasn't a good beginning and Kryuchkov knew it. Just to be safe he had ordered wiretaps on the phones of two more men: those of Anatoli Lukyanov and Gennadi Yanayev.

The most revealing exchange of that strange evening had taken place earlier when the three men sent to deliver the plotters' ultimatum to Gorbachev – Valeri Boldin, Yuri Plekanov, and Oleg Baklanov – returned from the Crimea, all of them quite drunk. Gorbachev was now a prisoner in his summer dacha, cut off from the outside world, but he had categorically refused to cooperate. "What's the plan now? Tell me your plan," Lukyanov asked the plotters.

"Anatoli Ivanovich, we have no plan," answered the minister of defence, Dmitri Yazov.

"What are you talking about? We do have a plan!" sputtered Kryuchkov.

Both men were, in a sense, right. The plan Kryuchkov talked of was to publish several decrees announcing the existence of the Emergency Committee and its powers, along with a declaration explaining the reasons for its decision to take power. Shortly afterwards, Soviet tanks would enter Moscow. There would be censorship but it would be limited. Travel to and communications with the outside world would not be affected.

This was "a massive show of force without any use of force."[7] It constituted an almost total rejection of the principle of the

successful coup d'état, as forged by Trotsky and Lenin and sum-
marized by the Italian journalist, Curzio Malaparte, in 1931 in his
famous handbook, *The Technique of the Coup d'État*. A relatively
small group of armed and trained men, working quickly and quietly, seizing key buildings and points of communication, arresting
key adversaries – this was the key to success.

But the plotters of August 1991 were the spiritual heirs not of
Lenin, but of Gorbachev. Their initiatives were almost entirely
rhetorical, and their approach was almost entirely improvised, their
action was limited to the capital, indeed to a few buildings and
squares in the capital. As Dmitri Yazov told prosecutors after his
arrest, "We thought we just had to make a declaration and the
people would say 'Carry on'."

The declaration – read on Soviet Television on the morning of
19 August – is worth quoting at length because it, too, is a product
of the Gorbachev era.

Fellow countrymen! Citizens of the Soviet Union! In a dark and critical
hour for the destiny of our Fatherland and of our peoples, we address
you! A mortal danger hangs over our great Motherland! The policy of
reform initiated by Mikhail Sergeyevich Gorbachev, conceived as a means
to ensure the dynamic development of the country and democratization
of the life of its society, has, for a number of reasons, come to a dead end.
Authority at all levels has lost the confidence of the population. Malicious
mockery of all the institutions of the state is being implanted. The country
has in effect become ungovernable. Taking advantage of the freedoms that
have been granted, trampling on the shoots of democracy, which have only
just appeared, extremist forces emerged which adopted a course of destroying the Soviet Union, seeking the collapse of the state and aiming to seize
power at all costs ...

Only yesterday the Soviet person who was abroad felt himself to be a
worthy citizen of an influential and respected state. Now, he is often a
second-class foreigner, who is treated with disdain or pity.

The pride and honour of the Soviet citizen must be restored in full
measure.

Without delay, we intend to restore legality, law and order, to put an
end to bloodshed, to declare a merciless war on the criminal world and
to root out shameful manifestations, which discredit our society and
humiliate Soviet citizens.

We stand for truly democratic processes, for a consistent policy of
reform, leading to a renewal of our Motherland, to its economic and social

prosperity, which will make it possible for it to occupy a worthy place in the world community of nations.

The appeal is notable, first, for the almost complete absence of communist vocabulary. The people addressed are fellow citizens, the goal defined is the rescue of the Motherland from collapse due to treason from within by extremists. Reinforcing this call to patriotic instincts is the theme of humiliation. The Soviet Union was once a great power; now it is a pathetic giant. Its citizens were once feared and respected; now they are the objects of pity and even scorn. The new regime will restore that former greatness.

This was the nationalist call to empire. Muted as it was, the committee had tapped a rich vein. It would be mined again and again, with increasing stridency, by the whole range of opposition groups in the coming years, culminating in the astonishing electoral breakthrough of Vladimir Zhirinovsky in December 1994.

Unfortunately for the Emergency Committee, the declaration also exposed its political confusion. Having just overthrown Gorbachev, it now appealed, in his name and in the name of his policies, for the support of the people. The repeated references to democracy and legality were a triumph, albeit a perverted one, of Gorbachev's announced quest to create a law-based state. They suggested a group of men haunted by the spectre of legitimacy.

Legitimacy took the large and bulky form of Boris Yeltsin. He had power none of the Emergency Committee members could lay claim to – electoral power. In June, just two months earlier, he had been elected by the people as president of the Russian Federation – the first Russian leader in a thousand years to be chosen this way. To drive the point home, on 10 July, he had organized his own coronation in the Kremlin. The ostentatious ceremony had featured heraldic trumpeters, an army orchestra playing the new Russian national anthem – lifted from Glinka's opera *A Life for the Czar* – and, in an echo of Gorbachev, Yeltsin swearing in himself. Great Russia, he had intoned, is rising from its knees. Then the Russian Orthodox Patriarch and Mikhail Gorbachev had appeared, to give him first spiritual and then political blessing.

The plotters knew what they had to do to ensure the success of the putsch – 250,000 handcuffs had been ordered from a factory in Pskov, blank arrest forms had been drawn up, a KGB strike force was lurking in the woods waiting to seize Yeltsin at his dacha near Moscow on the morning of 19 August – but they did not strike.

Instead they waited, perhaps out of confidence, perhaps out of inertia and even fear. Yeltsin and his advisers prepared their counter-declaration denouncing the putsch, then got in their cars and drove to Moscow and the Russian parliament. One of those advisers, Mikhail Poltoranin, remembered their surprise at discovering that the Emergency Committee had not sealed the building off.[8]

The plotters had left the democratic opposition intact, armed with two symbols of legitimacy: a leader who could mobilize his forces, and an institution which would constitute the site and locus of opposition.

Yeltsin, in his memoirs, says he quickly realized that the plotters' obsession was with legitimacy. Arrests and bloodshed would only make that quest more difficult for them. His years at the top of the Soviet power structure had given him another paradoxical intuition which would serve in the days to come. The Soviet authoritarian state was no longer ruled by authoritarian leaders. Indeed, he believed that for years no one had actually ruled at all. The state system of bureaucracy functioned on its own, more or less autonomously.[9] The men who had seized power were products of that environment. They were not men of power; they were men of the state machine.

If this was a theatrical coup in the Gorbachev tradition, Yeltsin proceeded to provide the most striking image of all; atop a tank in front of the Russian parliament, he denounced the men who despatched it and and condemned their action as illegitimate. It was a scene almost instantly relayed by television around the world.

The grey men in the Kremlin were no match for this. Their riposte was a news conference the same day. The tableau was unforgettable: the shaking hands and sweating face of Gennadi Yanayev as he tried to justify the Emergency Committee's actions.

Consciously, Yeltsin and his advisers underscored the theme of legitimacy, parliamentary legitimacy. A stream of decrees, in the name of the government and the parliament, flowed from the Russian White House, the home of the parliament, outlawing the Emergency Committeee and stripping large chunks of jurisdiction from the Soviet Centre and transferring them to Russia. Russian deputies were organized into small squads and sent out to talk to tanks crews in the streets to persuade them to pledge their allegiance to the legitimate parliamentary authority. Others were despatched to airports and train stations to give copies of the declarations and decrees of Yeltsin for distribution in the provinces.

The poet Yevgeny Yevtushenko was offered the microphone and the balcony of the White House to read his instant ode to parliamentary legitimacy:

Never again
Will Russia be on its knees.
With us are Pushkin, Tolstoy,
With us are the people awakened,
And the Russian parliament
Like a wounded marble swan of freedom
Swims into immortality.[10]

It was left to Yeltsin himself to reaffirm the ultimate source of legitimacy, that which flowed to him from the people. On Tuesday, 20 August, before a crowd of more than fifty thousand massed on the square behind the Russian parliament, he delivered a speech which was a masterpiece of populist principles and rhetoric.

"The shadows of darkness," he growled, "have descended on our country, on Europe and on the world. I have resolved to resist these men, these usurpers [*samozvantzy*] in the Kremlin. I have resolved this, and I call on you to do the same!"

From the crowd there was applause and cries, "We're with you, Boris!"

"Without your help, I can do nothing ... but together with you, and with the Russian people, we are capable of the greatest feats of heroism: we are capable of defeating these putschists and ensuring the triumph of democracy."[11]

The roar of approval was full-throated; nevertheless, that crowd represented only a fraction of the population of the capital – far smaller, in relative terms, than the crowd that had created a human barricade around the Lithuanian parliament eight months earlier. The vast majority of Moscovites still waited, sitting on the fence to see who would triumph in this struggle. The key was the quality of the people who formed this crowd: young people, Afghanistan veterans, middle-aged intellectuals, workers who believed that democracy was worth defending. That evening, in the dark, they stood quietly, waiting for the expected assault, ready, if need be, to sacrifice themselves against tanks.

This was an essential element in Yeltsin's strategy. If Gorbachev saw the parliament he had created as a stage where he could perform, Yeltsin saw the institution of parliament as a fortress to be taken and, once seized, to be held and used as a weapon.

If the poet saw the Russian White House as a marble swan of freedom, the president saw the building in military terms. "By 10 a.m. on August 19," he writes, "I realized that the White House would be the main battleground in the days to come."

Built in the late Brezhnevian age of paranoia, it had been conceived, as Yeltsin describes it, as an immense fortress, with an underground bunker, a maze of secret tunnels, and wings which could be sealed off. It would take more than a day to explore all its corridors. "The key was to remain inside the White House. And not to leave it. The longer the siege lasted, the greater would be the political scandal which they [the coup leaders] feared above all."[12]

Yeltsin had his fortress, his battleground, and, as the hours passed and the crowds got larger outside the White House, he had his army. Faced with growing resistance, the putsch leaders forgot their lessons. On Yanayev's desk was a document drawn up by the KGB. Entitled "Certain Axioms for the Extraordinary Situation," it read like a handbook of the perfect putsch:

1. We must not lose the initiative and enter into any kind of negotiations with the public. We have often ended up doing this in an attempt to preserve a democratic facade. As a result, society gradually becomes accustomed to the idea that they can argue with the authorities – and this is the first step toward the next battle.

2. One must not allow even the first manifestations of disloyalty: meetings, hunger strikes, petitions and information about them. On the contrary, they become, as it were, a permitted form of opposition, after which even more active forms will follow. If you want to proceed with a minimal amount of bloodshed, suppress contradictions at the very beginning ...[13]

And so on, through six points. Yet no arrests had been made, a giant permanent meeting was now taking place, opposition was massing. Faced with this, Kryuchkov's espionage instincts triumphed over the written instructions. He had to gather more information, he had to spin more webs. He began taking phone calls from Yeltsin and his advisers. He was disobeying the first axiom.

By the second day of the coup, armed forces commanders were defecting. One even marched in to explain to Yeltsin how to reinforce his claim to legitimacy; with Gorbachev, the Soviet commander-in-chief, neutralized, all he had to do was issue a decree taking command of all forces on Russian soil. Yeltsin quickly complied.

There remained the assault troops of the KGB, the Alpha group. The conspirators gave the order for Alpha to prepare for an attack on the White House. The troops revolted in the name of legitimacy. "We're trained for operations against a real enemy," one Alpha colonel said. "But who is our enemy here? Our fellow citizens? The deputies? The legitimate government of Russia and its president? The leaders of the coup want to pickle us in blood."[14]

The symbol of democracy besieged had triumphed. In the night of 20 August a tragic skirmish between White House defenders and confused and frightened soldiers in a tank patrol left three defenders dead. They would be the martyrs of this confrontation, their deaths as tragic as they were unnecessary. The putsch was already unravelling. The next day it would end in a plane chase to the Crimea as the putsch leaders hurried to beat a Russian government delegation in order to beg forgiveness from Gorbachev. That night he would return to "a new country."

As large crowds massed around the immense statue of Felix Dzerzhinsky, the founder of the KGB, and workmen prepared to winch it off its pedestal in the late afternoon of 22 August, Mikhail Gorbachev began his news conference at the Ministry of Foreign Affairs. A loudspeaker truck which had been used to broadcast stump speeches of triumphant Russian politicians now broadcast his words to the suddenly silent crowd.

Within minutes he had lost them. He had not changed. His answers were long-winded, full of self-congratulatory talk about "the new stages of perestroika." The muttering started early. When Gorbachev said he would still work to reform socialism and the Communist Party, it changed to whistling. Voices shouted "turn it off." Abruptly the loudspeaker truck cut off the broadcast of the press conference.

The crowd had played a key role in this confrontation. Now it had chosen a new leader, and rejected the old one. It was somehow fitting that Gorbachev was completely ignorant of this choice. His politics of miniature coups had always been aimed at another, more select audience – the party barons and deputies, often the same people, who had filled the Central Committee and peopled his parliament, the Soviet Congress. Now their time, and his, was coming to an end.

He was to discover this brutally the next day in front of the Russian parliament. Boris Yeltsin, having successfully transformed his parliament into a fortress and a symbol of resistance, was now to transform it once more – into a weapon with which to exact revenge on his rival.

At noon, Gorbachev appeared before the Russian deputies. The meeting was chaired by Yeltsin and broadcast live to the country. Gorbachev arrived unprepared and proceeded to improvise. His thanks to the deputies and their leaders were vague and perfunctory. He talked about his own role in his dacha in the Crimea. He said the idea of outlawing the Communist Party and ending socialism in the Soviet Union smacked of religious war and witch hunts. By this time the Russian deputies were in an uproar, shouting at him, some openly denouncing him. Yeltsin played the role of impartial, benign chairman, asking for calm, waiting for the opportune moment. It came when Gorbachev suggested that several Soviet ministers had supported him behind the scenes during the putsch.

Yeltsin stood up and walked to the podium where Gorbachev was speaking. He had a file which he gave him.

"Read it out, Mikhail Sergeyevich," he said.

Gorbachev tried to ignore this interruption.

"Mikhail Sergeyevich, read that document out," Yeltsin demanded. "It is the transcript of the cabinet session on August 19."

There followed a ten-minute litany of betrayal. As Gorbachev read out the minutes of the meeting, he seemed to grow smaller. Each minister had been asked by Prime Minister Valentin Pavlov whether he supported the putsch. Only one out of twenty had protested at the overthrow of the Soviet president.

The hall grew more raucous. There were more shouts, more insults. "It's not us who need you," one deputy yelled at Gorbachev, "but you who need us. Have you understood?"

Gorbachev's humiliation was profound, but his ordeal was only beginning. Hostile questions rained down on him. He tried to parry them as Yeltsin watched and waited. Seeking relief from the onslaught, Gorbachev said that everything the government of the Russian Federation had done had been dictated by necessity and was legitimate. The deputies applauded. Yeltsin pounced.

"I request that this should be officially registered by a decree by the country's president," he said. The deputies laughed delightedly.

"Boris Nikolayevich," Gorbachev complained, "we didn't agree to reveal all our secrets immediately."

"It's not a secret," Yeltsin said, "it's serious."

And so the country learned the price Gorbachev had paid for his political resurrection. In a ninety-minute meeting earlier in the day, he had bowed to Yeltsin's demand that he confirm all the decisions taken by the Russian government during the putsch. He had further agreed to name jointly with Yeltsin all new Soviet ministers. In effect, he had surrendered most of his power; he had become a figurehead. Yeltsin drove the point home cruelly as he offered details of new appointments to the Soviet cabinet.

Then, half an hour later, one last thrust of the knife. "Now, for some light relief, comrades," Yeltsin suddenly announced with a crooked smile, "allow me to sign a decree suspending the activities of the Russian Communist Party."

There was a storm of applause, while Gorbachev stuttered that he'd had no warning. "Be democrats to the end," he protested. "Then everyone will be behind you – genuine democrats and people with common sense."

"Second microphone," Yeltsin said, "next question."

After one and a half hours, even the speaker of the Russian parliament, Ruslan Khasbulatov, a man not known for his political charity, was embarrassed. "To be frank, I felt sorry for Gorbachev. So I whispered to Yeltsin: 'Time we ended this.' 'Why?' asked Yeltsin. 'I can't help feeling sorry for him.' Yeltsin smiled and nodded."[15] With that, Yeltsin stood up and ended the ordeal.

Few were in doubt as to what they had witnessed. A Russian deputy who was there described it as it as a brutal lesson in power. "The deputies wanted Gorbachev to pay for all his past errors."[16]

So searing was the experience that Gorbachev excised it from his memory. In his book about the August putsch, in which he devotes pages to his battles in the following days with the Soviet parliament, there is not a line about that dramatic afternoon.

It was, in Yeltsin's eyes, justifiable revenge for several similar humiliations at the hands of his rival. Nevertheless, in his memoirs, he admits he was frequently criticized for the melodramatic and cruel mise en scene. He offers no apology.

The following day was Saturday, the day the Russian Orthodox Church buries its dead. The coffins of the three martyrs of the putsch were followed through the streets of Moscow by a huge crowd of mourners. Marching in the cortège were deputies, Afghan veterans in combat gear, anarchists, monarchists holding aloft portraits of Czar Nicholas ii, Orthodox priests, members of Hare Krishna – a crowd which seemed to symbolize the wild profusion of currents of thought and belief in Russia long repressed under communism. This was a procession as large and as silent as that which accompanied Andrei Sakharov to his grave. At the White House, with the coffins of the three young men lying before him, Boris Yeltsin offered a moving apology to their parents: "Forgive me, your president, that I was unable to defend and save your sons."

It seemed a new beginning. "Forgiveness is what Russians ask of each other before they take communion, and what an earlier Boris had also asked of the Russian people with his dying breath in the greatest of all Russian operas, *Boris Godunov*. There was hardly a dry eye in Moscow. A new moral dimension was asserting itself in the leadership: someone who was not responsible was accepting responsibility in a society where traditionally no one in power had accepted blame for much of anything."[17]

The day was not over. Late in the afternoon, the Soviet president's office announced he would be making a major statement that evening. "I do not think it is possible to carry out my functions as general secretary of the Communist Party of the Soviet Union," it read, "and I am relinquishing these powers." Gorbachev called for the dissolution of the party's Central Committee, which had effectively acquiesced in the coup against him. He was burying the party, after two days of wrenching discussions with his aides. But he could not bring himself to tell the Soviet people directly. At the close of the evening newscast an announcer was suddenly handed a piece of paper with the declaration, which he proceeded to read out haltingly.

Even now, Mikhail Gorbachev had not mastered the ritual of Russian burials.

On Monday, 26 August, the Supreme Soviet of the Soviet Union met. Its first session was a day of bitter recriminations, windy rhetoric, and endless arguments about what to do next. Its behaviour, one Soviet commentator wrote, closely mirrored that of the country in the wake of the putsch.[18]

The following days demonstrated that the Soviet parliament and the Soviet presidency were seriously wounded institutions. The

Supreme Soviet had played no role in the coup. Now, in a fury its deputies turned on their speaker, Anatoli Lukyanov, accusing him in angry speeches of betraying them. And this despite the fact that the majority shared his view that the Union treaty would destroy the Soviet Union: Lukyanov's betrayal lay in exposing the deputies to the danger of extinction at the hands of the now triumphant government of Boris Yeltsin. Lukyanov would have to be sacrificed to placate the victors. He was first stripped of his post as speaker and then, on 30 August, with only two votes cast in his favour, of his parliamentary immunity. He was promptly arrested and taken to join the other leaders of the failed coup in prison. Significantly, however, the deputies refused even to vote on the one idea which might have renewed their legitimacy: the dissolution of parliament and early elections for a new Soviet legislature.

Instead, taking their cue from the Russian parliament, they turned on Mikhail Gorbachev. When, on the second day of the session, he came to the podium, the scene was one of pandemonium. He had come to demand a special session of the Soviet Congress to try to revive the Soviet Union, now lying in agony.

"To abandon the Union treaty now would be a profound mistake," he said. "Personally, I will do everything in my power not to allow the line to be crossed which leads to the breakup of the Union. I want to carry out the people's will, as expressed in the March referendum. Otherwise, I will leave the scene."[19]

Once again, despite their fears and misgivings, the deputies bowed to Gorbachev's demand. They voted to call a Special Congress of People's Deputies at the beginning of September.

The stage was set for Gorbachev's last coup. It would unfold, in the words of one participant, "like a bad novel," and it would destroy the Soviet parliament Gorbachev had created just two and a half years before.

CHAPTER NINE

The Final Coup

Boris Yeltsin had taken the measure of his man. Politically, Mikhail Gorbachev was diminished, but not yet dead. He could still be of use. Gorbachev so worshipped power and the trappings of power that he would, in the end, willingly serve as the grave-digger of one of the few remaining institutions which stood between the Soviet Union and extinction.

On Sunday, 1 September, exactly two weeks after the August plotters had gathered in the Kremlin to decide how to proceed after Gorbachev's refusal to bend to their ultimatum, another group of men met in the Kremlin. These ten men, all former Communist Party barons, were the leaders of the republics, which still paid lip service to the Soviet Union. They were led by Boris Yeltsin.

That evening they drew up a declaration calling on the Congress to approve new interim legislative and executive structures pending the adoption of a new constitution for the Soviet Union. The declaration then called on the Congress to dissolve itself.

According to Yeltsin, Gorbachev was a passive participant in this process. "Gorbachev accepted all of these compromises without protest. He had changed greatly since the month of August. In this new period, there was only one role for him to play, that of mediator among republics in disarray."[1]

The new speaker of the Congress, Ivan Laptev, had also been working hard. That same day no fewer than five groups of deputies were preparing proposals for the special session starting the next day. There were bills to strip Gorbachev of his emergency executive powers, and to set in motion economic changes to end central planning. A leader of the political organization Democratic Russia had spent an hour with Laptev, threatening to organize a demonstration of several hundred thousand people just outside the walls of the Kremlin if the Congress failed to act decisively to end the crisis now engulfing the state. Laptev remembered the end of that day:

Suddenly, at 11 p.m. my special phone rang. It was Gorbachev. "Come to my office right away." It was just 150 metres away.

He was sitting at his desk. He pushed a piece of paper toward me and told me to read it. This was the declaration, signed by the ten leaders and by him. And then he said: "All right, tomorrow, you'll open the Congress and then, right away, you'll give the floor to Nazarbayev [Nursultan Nazarbayev, the leader of Kazakhstan] so he can read the declaration. And then, you'll immediately have the Congress vote on it!"

He was giving me an ultimatum.

Laptev protested. The deputies would rebel. Gorbachev told him he had no choice; this was what he and the leaders of the republics had decided. Laptev said he would think about it overnight. They agreed to meet in the Palace of Congresses at 8:30 a.m.

At the heart of the seven-point declaration was the third paragraph. It announced a new central legislative body whose members would be delegated by the parliaments of each republic. Real power would be in the hands of a State Council chaired by the Soviet president with representatives from each republic. The declaration outlined not a federation but a confederation, where the central power would exist only at the pleasure of the republics.

The next morning, when Laptev and the parliamentary leadership filed in, they were met by Gorbachev and the leaders of all the republics. For good measure, Yeltsin had brought along his closest aides, Gennadi Burbulis and Sergei Shakhrai. While Gorbachev presided, the ultimatum was repeated, this time accompanied by shouted threats. Laptev would do exactly as the republican leaders ordered. "If the Congress protests or deputies start whistling or booing, then we'll get up and walk out with our delegations," he was told.

The final word was Yeltsin's. "The Russian deputies will walk out as well!"[2]

Laptev did as he was told. At 10 a.m. he opened the fifth Soviet Congress of People's Deputies. Nineteen hundred deputies from ten republics were present. There was a minute of silence for the dead of the putsch. The speaker called on Nazarbayev to read the declaration. Laptev then adjourned the opening session. It had lasted nine minutes.

As he had predicted, dozens of deputies protested furiously. Several accused Laptev of betraying them. Others rebelled at the order to meet as members of delegations from each republic to discuss the declaration. They should discuss it in their political factions. Gorbachev and republican leaders spent their time threatening, ordering, and cajoling. Significantly, Sergei Stankevich, one of the most active deputies in the Soviet Congress and a leader of the Interregional Group, now told the protesters that they had a responsibility as elected representatives to follow the choice made by the people of Russia. The people had elected Boris Yeltsin as president in July and then had renewed their support on the barricades in August. The deputies had to bow before his legitimacy and obey his command to meet as members of the Russian delegation.[3]

Within an hour the revolt was over. When the Congress resumed sitting in the afternoon, the deputies adopted the declaration as the basis for their work. The vote was 1,263 for, 125 against and sixty-seven abstentions. Of the 1,780 who registered for the session, 314 simply refused to vote as a last protest.[4]

The rest was anticlimax. With ruthless energy, Mikhail Gorbachev now worked to execute the orders of the new rulers of the dying empire, and once again, Laptev was a privileged witness to his activities. At 1 a.m. on Tuesday, 3 September, the special Kremlin line in his apartment rang. It was Gorbachev.

"Look, Rutskoi [Alexander Rutskoi, the Russian vice-president] has just phoned me. He says he and Shakhrai have just drawn up a very pretty version of the new bill on the interim institutions. Get copies made and distributed to the deputies so that they can vote for it tomorrow morning."

Laptev answered that a commission was already working on the bill and it would have to see the Rutskoi version first. Rules were rules. "All right, all right," Gorbachev said. "I know there are rules. Just make sure that tomorrow morning the parliamentary leadership has copies of the new version."

This pretty version was to be the bill the deputies finally adopted. As Laptev realized when he examined it, it further diluted the powers of the Soviet president. Control over the KGB and the armed forces had been transferred from him to the State Council, which would be composed of the leaders of each republic. Gorbachev simply pushed it through, describing it as "the best course at this precise moment. It will let us get on with the active work and the practical decisions which are now required in the country."

Others were far more apocalyptic. "What we've been seeing in this Congress for the past three days," said Viktor Alksnis, "is a repeat of January 1918, when the Constituent Assembly was broken up" and the Bolsheviks swept away the last parliamentary obstacle between them and absolute rule. Even some members of the Interregional Group echoed those fears, evoking the brutal dispersal of the Constituent Assembly and talking of the creation of a junta.[5]

Unlike Lenin, Gorbachev had no need of the marines to master this assembly. He relied on the bullying tactics which had served him well in previous congresses. At one point, as votes fell short of the two-thirds majority needed to adopt constitutional changes, he threatened to change the rules. "The mood of the majority dictates that we take this decision. If necessary, we'll alter the voting so that it takes only a simple majority to adopt these changes. Then we can move forward."

The ultimate threat came when, for the third time, the deputies refused to vote to create a new legislature whose members would be all be selected by the parliaments of the republics. "If we don't adopt this clause, then there's no point in continuing," Gorbachev announced angrily. "Then this Congress will be deemed to have finished its work. It will have shown itself incapable of taking the correct decisions."

As the deputies erupted in indignation, Gorbachev repeated his threat simply to send them home and find "other ways" of solving the problem. It worked. A few minutes later, two-thirds of the deputies voted for the new legislature.[6]

Earlier, Laptev had sat with Gorbachev in the back room reserved for the parliamentary leadership as the different delegations from the republics discussed this final version in their caucuses. On the internal loudspeaker they could hear Boris Yeltsin addressing the Russian deputies in the main hall, telling them that this law would consecrate Russia's victory and its new place in the new Union. Gorbachev sat quietly, listening, apparently undisturbed. Laptev said to Gorbachev: "Mikhail Sergeyevich, don't you realize what's happening? The last legal pillar which supports the institution of the Soviet presidency is about to disappear!"

"Don't worry," Gorbachev answered, "a little time will pass and then we'll unite again. Everyone will feel the need to have a relatively strong central power."[7]

Gorbachev's behaviour was inexplicable to Laptev; it wasn't to Boris Yeltsin. He had seen his adversary that spring working happily at Novo Ogarevo to weaken, even dismantle, all that he had repeatedly sworn to defend – the Soviet Union guided by a powerful central government. Yeltsin remembered these constitutional talks as calm and businesslike. There were no explosions of anger, and no clashes between Gorbachev and himself. Yeltsin felt Gorbachev was playing a new role, that of the paternal arbiter among squabbling republics. In all the changes being discussed only one function, that of president, remained untouched. "He found himself enjoying a role which had no precedent in world politics, that of the leader not of one but of several democratic states. It was an excellent launching pad for him in his quest to become a sort of 'world leader'."[8]

Gorbachev's last weeks in office were marked by frenetic activity in the service of an illusion. That he was an emperor unarmed was apparent to all except himself. His press secretary, Andrei Grachev, observed this with bemusement. "The state still had a president, but, as for the president, he no longer had a country."

He was now a man seized "with a mania to meet people." In the three months after the putsch, there were more than ninety meetings, all organized at the last minute, with kings, presidents, prime ministers, bankers, businessmen, journalists, almost all of them foreigners. It was, his aides believed, as if he needed these meetings to reassure himself that he was still the president.[9] And to almost everyone he met he repeated, like a mantra, one of his favourite phrases, "the process is moving forward."

He recounted to these visitors an adventure story in which he was the hero. After breaking the "blockade" of the putsch plotters, he had returned to Moscow to clear away the dead wood of the old regime and to begin building a new country. He told the British foreign minister, Douglas Hurd, "I would say that in the course of three days everything changed. A new life, a new epoch has begun!" The three days he was referring to were not those of the August putsch but those of the Soviet Congress in early September. Anatoli Chernayev, whom Gorbachev now called his "brother" after their mutual imprisonment in the Crimea, wrote later: "In this period, sincere self-delusion had replaced realistic policy as the basis of his political conduct."[10]

For Chernayev, Gorbachev's greatest delusion lay in his inability to take seriously the rise of nationalism. He had never understood the Baltics. He simply could not believe that the Ukrainian declaration of independence of 24 August was serious. Ukraine could never leave the Soviet Union. Ukrainians were Slav brothers. He himself spoke some Ukrainian. His personal driver was Ukrainian! (He would actually use this argument in a televised speech to Ukrainian voters on the eve of the Ukrainian referendum on independence on December 1. In that vote Ukrainians opted massively for independence.)

On 18 October a ceremony was held in the Kremlin to sign a new economic treaty linking eight republics of the disintegrating Union. Andrei Grachev described the details of the day:

Early in the morning, Gorbachev went to St George's Hall. His pretext was that he had to inform himself of the protocol requirements and the scenario for the ceremony.

He was shown the camera positions and those of the flags of each republic. He and his advisers chose the right angle so that the president would be seen framed by the Soviet flag behind him. There was a long discussion about whether the Soviet flag should be bigger than the flags of the republics.

There was another long debate about whether champagne should be served in front of the guests and the cameras. Eventually the president was persuaded ...[11]

Flags, cameras, champagne ... As his power melted away, Gorbachev became obsessed with the trappings of power. Should he rearrange his Kremlin office? How should the presidential plane be painted? It was essential that the words "Soviet Union" be just as prominent as the words "United States of America" painted on the plane of the American president. In the midst of these reveries, Gorbachev would occasionally stop and demand a plan to reorganize and reinforce his political chain of command.

These were just impulsive efforts [Grachev wrote]. Gorbachev knew subconsciously that they would achieve nothing. To have any chance of success, they would have required a systematic, organized mind and tenacity, in other words, qualities which were foreign to his nature. And so he seized any occasion "to put himself on display." The idea of abandoning the heights – his grand plans for the historic transformation of his country – to deal with the nuts-and-bolts of life bored him.[12]

Reality brutally intervened on 8 December 1991. That evening, in a dacha in the snow an hour from Minsk, the presidents of Russia, Ukraine, and Belarus unilaterally put an end to the Soviet Union with the signature of the Minsk Accord, declaring their republics to be independent states which would, from now on, form a Commonwealth.

Even then Gorbachev seemed frozen in illusion. On 10 December he issued a statement protesting that the move was illegal. Cancelling Soviet legislation would lead to anarchy. Such a decision could only be taken by constitutional means. "The Congress of People's Deputies of the USSR must be convened. As well, I don't exclude the possibility of organizing a referendum on this question."

But the Congress had been put to death three months earlier; Gorbachev had presided at its execution. A corpse could not be brought back to life.

There remained the rump Soviet parliament with delegations named by each republic. It was the subject of an acrimonious exchange between Gorbachev and Boris Yeltsin in the days following the Minsk Accord. "I begged Yeltsin: don't dissolve the Union parliament," Gorbachev told visitors. "This sin will weigh on you, as it did on the Bolsheviks who dissolved the Constituent Assembly in 1918. Give the deputies a chance to hold a final session: they understand and will take the necessary decisions themselves because the majority have been named by the republics. Think of our reputation in the world!"[13]

There is an irony in Mikhail Gorbachev denouncing the Bolsheviks for dissolving the Constituent Assembly. It was precisely this sin which deputies had begged Gorbachev himself not to commit three months earlier. But such ironies were lost on Gorbachev. He was already busy playing his final role: that of the lonely defender of democratic institutions betrayed by the ambitions of treacherous politicians from the republics.

For the next two weeks, he clung to office, giving dozens of interviews, even participating in a Soviet-American television documentary on the last days of the Soviet Union. In one interview he said, when asked if he had ever been happy, "I don't know any happy reformers."

On 24 December, Arkadi Murashev, a leader of the Interregional Group, phoned Gorbachev's office. He had had no personal contact with the Soviet president since 1989 but now he wanted to express his sympathy and best wishes. To his surprise, he was invited to see Gorbachev in the Kremlin that evening.

He found the president alone. On the eve of his resignation, all had deserted him, except a corporal's guard of advisers. "We talked about everything. On the table, an arm's length away, was the 'little atomic suitcase' (with the codes to launch Soviet nuclear missiles). He seemed quite relaxed. He was convinced he had made no mistakes, not concerning us [the Interregional group], not concerning the USSR – none. He was absolutely sure he had always been right."[14]

The president's farewell address to the Soviet Union the next evening embroidered on the theme of blamelessness. He began with a vigorous defence of his decision to try to transform his country:

I have never once regretted my refusal to sit in the general secretary's chair and simply "reign" for a few years. I would have considered that irresponsible and immoral.

I understood that to undertake such vast reforms in a society like ours was a task of the utmost difficulty, containing a certain measure of risk. But there was no other choice. Even today, I am convinced of the historical rightness of the democratic reforms undertaken in 1985.

He then proceeded to list the "accomplishments of historical importance" which had flowed from his decision: the liquidation of the totalitarian system, the creation of democratic institutions, and the end of the Cold War. These, indeed, were huge accomplishments and Gorbachev rightly took much credit for them. But, as he approached the period of crisis and collapse, the Gorbachevian "I" became invisible. The voice was now impersonal.

All these changes created enormous tension. They took place in conditions of ferocious struggle, against a background of growing opposition from the forces representing the moribund and reactionary past, and from the former structures of the party and the state.

These changes ran up against intolerance, the feeble level of political culture and the fear of change. The old system collapsed before the new one could be put in place. And the crisis affecting society was aggravated even further.

In the last eight paragraphs of his speech he bestowed thanks on his supporters and on foreign leaders who had understood his policies. He offered warnings and encouragement to the citizens of the state that was about to die. In only one sentence did he admit the possibility of error: "Without doubt, some mistakes could have been avoided and many things could have been done better." But the real culprit was not Gorbachev: it was "the feeble level of political culture and the fear of change." In other words, the Soviet people hadn't been up to the task set by their leader.

On the afternoon of 26 December, as Mikhail Gorbachev prepared for his farewell cocktail party, a strange gathering was taking place in the Kremlin room once reserved for meetings of the Communist Party Central Committee. The Supreme Soviet was holding its final session. The upper house, the Council of the Republics, had been convened. Only two dozen of the 374 deputies were present. The recently appointed deputy speaker, Anuarbek Alimzhanov, addressed rows of empty seats as he protested that officials had broken the law by dismantling the Soviet Union without prior legislative approval. But what was done was done.

"Now that the president has resigned and now that the red flag has been lowered over the Kremlin, it is time for us to take our leave. Until we meet again, wherever that might be ..." With that, the rump group of deputies raised their hands in approval of a resolution declaring the Soviet Union dead.

Outside, Kremlin workers hadn't bothered to wait. They had already unscrewed and carted off the bronze plaque which proclaimed "Supreme Soviet of the Union of Soviet Socialist Republics."

The whimpering end of the first functioning legislature in Soviet history went largely unlamented. For activist deputies like Gavriil Popov and Roy Medvedev, it had been no more than a quasi-parliament.

"It played a necessary role," Popov said. "It demonstrated to people that an elected body could represent their interests. It also fulfilled its role by taking certain key decisions: adopting a constitution which abolished the leading role of the Communist Party, choosing a president and deciding on his powers. But for the most part, its activities were symbolic."[15]

As for the Soviet president and his advisers, their attitude towards the institution they had created and then destroyed was one of pride mixed with intense irritation. In August and September 1991, by venting their anger on Gorbachev, wrote Anatoli Chernayev, "the deputies demonstrated for the final time their deep lack of culture, their political nihilism, and the moral infantilism of our democracy."[16]

In other words, the legislature, like the people, hadn't lived up to the task set by the Soviet leader.

Curiously, Gorbachev's departure was also little lamented, even by his own aides. To them, he was a leader now heavily burdened by tragic flaws: his overweening belief in himself which had led to his fatal misjudgment of party leaders and ministers who betrayed him, and his inability to "seize the hour," to take decisive steps at the right time. The final manifestation of this flaw, they said, was his refusal to leave the political stage until he was literally pushed off.

CHAPTER TEN

The Rebel

I could not believe my eyes. It can't be true, I thought: this type of person doesn't exist any longer. For looking straight into the camera was a typical Bolshevik, a Bolshevik straight out of central casting. Stubborn, overbearing, self-assured, honest, irresistible, a human engine without brakes – he must have jumped from an armored car just a few minutes ago. We have all seen such faces in the old photographs, except that they were usually dressed in leather jackets, they usually dangled a huge Mauser from their belts, and they were usually executed by Stalin. Where did they find this man?[1]

This man, this Bolshevik from central casting, was Boris Yeltsin in the wake of his election as chairman of the Russian parliament in 1990, as described by the Soviet dissident in exile, Vladimir Bukovsky. His sheer physical presence crowded out any other perception, even among many fellow Russians. So powerful was this image that even the publication, a few months earlier, of an astonishing autobiography by Yeltsin could not alter it.

Yet the book revealed a man who had created out of his life a vast and troubling personal myth, a man who saw himself as a child of destiny who would grow up to be a persecuted Russian rebel in the pre-Communist tradition, a *yurodivy*, a sort of holy fool.[2] Yuri Afanasiev, a close colleague of Yeltsin in 1989, glimpsed this side of the man. In his memoirs, he described Yeltsin as a populist, a man who "embodied an impulsive and irrational Russian identity which, after seventy years of dictatorship and Marxist 'rigour', demanded to express itself."[3]

This populist would touch a chord among Russians, portrayed by the philosopher Nikolai Berdyaev as a people stirred by martyrs and drawn to rebels, seeing in them a reflection of themselves. "The Russians are fugitives and bandits: the Russians are also pilgrims in search of divine truth and justice."[4]

In his artful autobiography (entitled, in Russian, *Confession on an Imposed Theme*) Yeltsin presented his life as nothing less than a political passion play in which he consciously assumed the role of the martyr who was "betrayed and hounded," only to be "born again" on the day of his election as a Soviet People's Deputy in 1989.

From the day of his baptism, when he was almost drowned in the baptismal font, his memoirs depict him as an individual mysteriously protected by fate. Death again and again reached out for Yeltsin – as he played with a grenade having sneaked into an army munitions depot and, in the explosion, lost two fingers of one hand, in a stalled truck on the railway tracks as a freight train bore down upon him, in a dramatic card game with convicts on the run where the penalty for losing was death. He always escaped.

Rebellion was the second theme, and once again it began in childhood with a dramatic revolt against a hated teacher on the occasion of his graduation from primary school. He stood up and attacked her persecution of pupils. The ceremony was ruined; he was expelled. But, as he recounts it, he singlehandedly forced the school board to review its decision and fire the teacher.

This saga serves a dramatic purpose by foreshadowing exactly his revolt in 1987 against Mikhail Gorbachev and the Communist party establishment.

But that was much later. Yeltsin's career until that decisive moment would be little different from that of dozens of other successful and unremembered party bureaucrats. Armed with a construction engineer's diploma and his new Communist Party card, he progressed steadily up the ladder – factory manager, regional boss, first secretary of Sverdlovsk province. Then, in 1985, came the call from Moscow. He was invited to become a section head of the Central Committee in charge of construction.

Yeltsin refused. Here we first glimpse the pride and ambition of the rebel, as well as the other emotion which was to drive him in the years to come – jealousy. He refused the post because it was unworthy of a party secretary of his seniority and experience. Other provincial bosses had been directly elevated to posts as Central Committee secretaries. One of them had been Mikhail Gorbachev.

Yeltsin's refusal was symbolic. When the offer was repeated with the injunction to obey party discipline, he submitted and came to

Moscow. Mikhail Gorbachev was now the general secretary and Yeltsin waited for an invitation to meet from the man who had been his equal when they had worked in the provinces. It didn't come.

In December 1985 Gorbachev invited him to become an alternate (non-voting) member of the Politburo and head of the Moscow region. Once again Yeltsin began by refusing, this time because he felt he was being used as a pawn by Gorbachev in his manoeuvres to rid himself of an old Brezhnev crony, Viktor Grishin. But once again Yeltsin bowed to party discipline and took the job.

Looking back on this period in his memoirs, Yeltsin describes himself as a unique figure in the annals of the Soviet leadership. "Why is it that a system perfected over the years and specifically designed to select only people of a certain type should have suddenly failed so badly as to choose Yeltsin. True, I didn't last long among them, and I bolted like an uncaged animal when I could stand it no longer, but an appointment like mine had never happened over seven decades."[5] His unique character was not nearly so apparent to Yeltsin's colleagues. Their recollection places Yeltsin at the junior end of the Politburo table where he sat uncomfortably and, for the most part, silently. He seldom took part in policy discussions.[6]

Yeltsin's own chronicle is far more dramatic. In early September 1987 Gorbachev had distributed a draft of the speech he proposed to make to mark the seventieth anniversary of the Bolshevik revolution. Yeltsin raised a number of criticisms of how the Communist Party was running the Soviet Union, and asked how the speech would address these questions.

Gorbachev abruptly adjourned the meeting for half an hour. When he returned, Yeltsin writes, he launched into a personal tirade against him. "There can be no doubt that at that moment Gorbachev simply hated me."[7]

This tirade was the catalyst which led to an act unprecedented in Soviet history. Yeltsin wrote Gorbachev a letter announcing he wanted to resign from the Politburo for reasons of policy. His letter criticized the party's style of work, accusing the hierarchy of reducing perestroika to an empty slogan. The principal target was Yegor Ligachev, the number two figure in the party and the man in charge of its day-to-day administration. Since arriving in Moscow, Yeltsin had clashed repeatedly with Ligachev in the Politburo and at Central Committee meetings. Now he urged Gorbachev to replace him and to reduce the bloated party bureaucracy by half.

Yeltsin presents this act as the point of no return. "My bridges were burned," he says. A closer reading suggests otherwise. Nowhere in the letter does he criticize Gorbachev. On the contrary, he writes of his "incredible efforts" which have led to "the splendid events" of perestroika. It is this work that is being sabotaged by a silent conspiracy from within, led by Ligachev. Yeltsin's accusations are powerful, and he knows it. "Great harm would be done to the party if all this were to be said publicly. Only you personally can change this state of affairs, in the interests of the party."[8]

Yeltsin describes himself in the letter as "an awkward person" whose style and frankness left him untrained for work in the Politburo. "I realize that it is difficult for you to decide what to do about me." That sounds more like a plea for encouragement and praise rather than an irrevocable slamming of the door.

Gorbachev returned from his Crimea vacation and phoned Yeltsin to acknowledge the letter. He suggested they meet later. But no meeting was arranged. To all intents and purposes Gorbachev simply ignored Yeltsin's dramatic gesture.

It seems clear Yeltsin was mortally offended. This was too much for the man who saw himself as the moral equal of the party leader. Now he prepared truly to burn his bridges with a speech at the October meeting of the Central Committee.

His speech was like a grenade exploding in the Kremlin hall. As in his letter to Gorbachev, he criticized the bloated and smug party bureaucracy. But his conclusion was crucially different. He was no longer attacking Yegor Ligachev as the author of the party's ills: he was attacking Gorbachev himself. "Recently ... there has been a noticeable increase in what I can only call adulation of the general secretary by certain full members of the Politburo. This is absolutely unacceptable ... It can become a 'cult of personality.' It must not be allowed."[9]

Yeltsin writes that he knew that his speech would doom him. In the space of a dozen pages the metaphors of martyrdom pile up. "I knew what would happen next. I would be slaughtered in a methodical, organized manner ... They were like a pack of hounds ready to tear me to pieces. What do you call it when a person is murdered with words? Because what followed was like a real murder."

Presiding over all of this, playing the role of dispassionate judge, selecting speakers, summing up the arguments, was Mikhail Gorbachev. Immediately after Yeltsin's speech, he suspended the session.

"I could see that he was struggling to contain his anger," Valeri Boldin, a Gorbachev adviser, recalled.

But [Yeltsin's] suggestion that he aspired to greatness had touched a raw nerve. Had it not been for that, he would probably not have felt compelled to send all the king's men to the podium in his defence. The entire Politburo and all the members of the Central Committee girded themselves for combat. They hastily jotted down the main points they intended to make and I could see that Gorbachev was deciding the order in which the Politburo would address the assembly ... Now it was as if a dam had burst, loosing upon the hall an outpouring of disjointed, rabid expressions of hostility. Gorbachev no longer tried to preserve decorum."[10]

Three weeks later the process was repeated. By this time Yeltsin was in hospital, suffering, he said, from a general nervous collapse. Gorbachev phoned him and insisted he attend a meeting of the Moscow party committee, which Yeltsin headed. Sick and sedated, he was carried into the room. Once again he was denounced by speaker after speaker, this time for mismanagement of the capital, until at last he confessed his "guilt." Then he was fired.[11]

One by one, a Yeltsin adviser remembered, the party leaders left the room. Yeltsin was now alone, defeated, slumped in a chair. Then Gorbachev himself returned to help him up and lead him out. Having orchestrated and presided over the show-trial proceedings, Gorbachev's final gesture was a bizarre mixture of pity and the coup de grâce.[12] It would not be forgotten.

Yeltsin's writes of his political "death" and his period in purgatory in striking language. "I looked inside and there was no one there. A kind of void, a vacuum had been created – a human vacuum ... Politically I was a corpse ... All that was left where my heart had been was a burned-out cinder. Everything around me was burnt out, everything within me was burned out."[13]

At the Nineteenth Communist Party Conference eight months later he asked for political rehabilitation. It was refused by the party. "Rebirth" came only in March 1989 when he was elected to the Soviet Congress by 89 per cent of the voters in Moscow. But the martyr continued to carry the stigmata of his ordeal. "Even now, a rusty nail is still lodged in my heart and I have not pulled it out. It protrudes and bleeds."[14]

The image of the rebel, the outsider and alien at the Politburo table, the man so disgusted by the network of privileges that Yeltsin is at pains to create, strays considerably from the reality of those days. Valeri Boldin writes that Yeltsin, in offering his resignation from the Politburo in 1987, had no intention of quitting the ranks of the powerful. Astonishingly, even after his bitter attack on Gorbachev himself, he thought he could keep his job as Moscow party chief and even wrote Gorbachev a letter with that request after the Central Committee meeting in October 1987.[15] His request was ignored. And a loyal Yeltsin aide wrote that when Yeltsin was stripped of his seat in the Politburo and overnight his bodyguards and his giant Zil limousine disappeared, he was crushed.

"It was as if two Yeltsins lived inside him," recalled Lev Sukhanov. "One Yeltsin was the senior party leader, accustomed to power and honours, and they were stripping him of that – the other Yeltsin was the rebel, the man who refused, or rather who was learning to refuse to play by the rules of the game. These two Yeltsins were struggling for supremacy. It was a hard struggle and the victory of the rebel was by no means assured."[16]

Whatever the facts of his evolution, Yeltsin had, by the spring of 1990, transformed his life into a chronicle almost biblical in its scope. As the Soviet order collapsed, the man and his myth would emerge to exercise a powerful hold on the Russian soul.

"The issue of primary importance is the spiritual, national and economic rebirth of Russia."[17] This was Boris Yeltsin in May 1990, at the First Congress of Deputies of the Russian Federation. Once again he was talking of resurrection, this time of a whole country. The rebel had found his cause.

In September 1989, according to Lev Sukhanov, Yeltsin made up his mind to lead the charge to overthrow the existing Soviet order. The catalyst was a visit to a Houston supermarket on his first trip to the United States. Stunned by a vision of plenty unavailable even to a privileged member of the Politburo, Yeltsin lost his last Bolshevik illusions. He would try to seize the leadership of the Russian Federation. His motives had little to do with Russian nationalism; he simply needed his own power base.

Elections for the new Russian legislature were to take place in March 1990. Voters in Russia would elect one thousand deputies to the Russian Congress of Deputies which in turn would elect a Supreme Soviet of 270 members from its ranks. The Supreme Soviet would sit eight months a year but, like in the Soviet legislature, the

Congress would have to ratify major legislation and changes to the constitution of the Russian Federation. In his election campaign Yeltsin continued to denounce the Soviet system of privilege and to call for deep cuts in the Communist bureaucracy and radical reform of the Communist Party. But of the renaissance of Russia there was little mention. Indeed, in his biographical "confession," published across Europe one week before the elections in March, there was no mention of Russia at all.

Yeltsin won another overwhelming victory, this time in his home base of Sverdlovsk. At the same time candidates backed by an umbrella organization called Democratic Russia won one-third of the seats in the thousand-seat Russian Congress. It was a major breakthrough, all the more so since in this new legislature, unlike the Soviet Congress, there were no reserved seats for the Communist Party and its subordinate organizations. The alliance between Yeltsin and Democratic Russia would provide the man with the weapon and the organization with the leader to proclaim Russia's sovereignty.

The Russian political commentator Alexander Golz has pointed out that the elections of 1989 and 1990 were, above all, plebiscites *against* something – in the first campaign, against the Communist Party establishment and in the second, against the "Centre" and Mikhail Gorbachev himself.[18] In 1990 Democratic Russia was an ideal vehicle of protest. "Democracy" was defined simply as opposition to the autocratic ways of the Communist Party and "Russia" as the negation of the rigidly centralized Soviet Union.

Such a vague, catch-all program drew into Democratic Russia's ranks newly elected deputies such as Ruslan Khasbulatov, Sergei Baburin, and Mikhail Astafiev. That they would, less than three years later, become the most visible and most ferocious political adversaries of Boris Yeltsin underlines the extraordinarily amorphous nature of this alliance.

It was at the meetings of Democratic Russia in April 1990 that the idea was born to draw up a resolution on Russian sovereignty and a draft Russian constitution to affirm the will of its new legislature. Two men, both newly minted deputies, played a key role in this. The first was Anatoli Shabad. In 1990 he was a fifty-year-old physicist from the Academy of Sciences, a bantam-rooster of a man with an ill-cut mop of thick grey hair. Shabad had been drawn into politics to help his patron, Andrei Sakharov. He had organized the campaign of scientists which had led to Sakharov's election as a deputy in 1989 in the Soviet Congress of People's Deputies.

Shabad shared his late mentor's view of the Soviet Union: it was the last, classic colonial empire left on earth and its breakup was imperative if democracy was ever to flourish in the region. Now Shabad drew up the first draft resolution on Russian sovereignty and presented it to a meeting of Democratic Russia deputies in April. He was well aware that the resolution constituted a fundamental, even unconstitutional challenge to the existing Soviet order. "Strictly speaking, the sovereignty declaration was illegal. It was a legal time-bomb."[19]

Oleg Rumyantsev was twenty-nine, a sociologist, thin and elegant, with a black beard and dark eyes. He looked like a young Mephistopheles. He was, in fact, a political romantic who preferred to believe that the resolution on Russian sovereignty was the first step in the process of building a more democratic Soviet Union. His introduction to Soviet public life had been in 1980 when he organized a public commemoration of the death of John Lennon. The KGB brutally broke it up. Clutching a cover of the Beatles "White Album," Rumyantsev managed to escape.

In 1987 he set up a political discussion club called Democratic Perestroika. That same year he helped organize his second demonstration, this time to protest the expulsion of Boris Yeltsin from the Politburo. Once again he ran up against the KGB. In 1990 he ran in a Moscow constituency for the Russian Congress. His opponent in the second, runoff round was, fittingly enough, a KGB colonel. He beat him handily.

Rumyantsev joined Shabad in April 1990 on the small drafting committee polishing Democratic Russia's resolution on Russian sovereignty. He also preached the necessity of drawing up a radically new Russian constitution. After one such plea to Democratic Russia deputies Boris Yeltsin approached him and suggested they discuss the idea. Two months later the Russian Constitutional Commission was born, with Yeltsin as chairman and Rumyantsev as secretary. For several months the two men talked almost every day.

By the time the First Congress of Russian Deputies opened in May 1990 sovereignty had become a symbol so vague and powerful that even Vitali Vorotnikov, the outgoing head of the Russian Federation and a Politburo member appointed by Mikhail Gorbachev, was obliged to endorse the idea in the new legislature.[20]

Mikhail Gorbachev only strengthened support for the declaration when he insisted on denouncing it, and Yeltsin, in an angry speech to the new Congress. Together, he said, the declaration and the man could help destroy the Soviet Union. His fear was justifiable. Article 5 of the draft stated plainly that Russian legislation would take precedence over Soviet law on Russian territory.

Boris Yeltsin consciously cast his approach in contrast to that of Gorbachev. "We're not aiming for confrontation with the Centre," he told the Congress. "The main aim is the strengthening of the Union."[21] The tactic of seeming to seek consensus was successful; Yeltsin won both the resolution and the job. Later, however, a close adviser admitted the goal had been clear from the beginning. "Russia's declaration of sovereignty was adopted in order to bring down the Centre," Yuri Skokov, the secretary of Yeltsin's Security Council, said in 1993.[22]

But in the heady days of June 1990 members of the loose democratic alliance saw in the resolution whatever they wanted to see. Oleg Rumyantsev was convinced that the declaration "created the basis for constitutional order" and "laid the foundation for a new union." After all, he told the Congress, he and the other authors had written in thirteen references to "the Union" in the fourth and final version![23]

Anatoli Shabad, his fellow democrat and drafter, had a completely different vision. In his speech to the Congress, he addressed the question asked by adversaries of the declaration: Why, when the world was moving toward integration, were the authors of this document talking of the breakup of the Soviet Union? "Because the integration we're talking about was brought about artificially … If today we don't move toward *disintegration*, we will never achieve further integration."[24]

The declaration was adopted on 12 June. On the key vote for Article 5, declaring that Russian legislation would have precedence over Soviet law on the territory of Russia, the vote was 544 to 271.

Shabad's analysis was both harsher and clearer. Three years later, disillusioned, Rumyantsev would describe this time as his period of "democratic naïveté." "We all knew what the Communist Party was capable of. No one knew what 'democracy' would bring. And so, for two years, in 1990 and 1991, I took part in the madness of the struggle against the Soviet Union. By eliminating the Communist Party we destroyed the Soviet Union. For me, this is a tragedy."[25]

In the months after Boris Yeltsin's election in May 1990 as chairman of the Russian parliament, political developments conspired to allow him to play the role for which his personality had destined him – that of the lone rebel challenging the established power to trial by combat.

The battle began on 9 August. The Presidium of the Russian Parliament – the executive committee composed of deputy speakers, chairmen of committees, and faction leaders and headed by Yeltsin – issued a resolution which barred the central government from exporting Russian natural resources without Russian consent. Two weeks later Gorbachev reacted. He published a decree declaring the Russian resolution invalid. Thus the so-called war of laws was launched. The conflict reached a climax of absurdity in October when the Russian Supreme Soviet passed a law making it a criminal offence for Soviet officials to carry out measures which contravened Russian legislation.

However absurd some of its manifestations appeared, this was a war for power; it was also a personal struggle. Yeltsin publicly reminded his adversary of that in December when he attacked the decision of the Soviet Congress to grant sweeping emergency powers to Mikhail Gorbachev.

The botched crackdown in the Baltics was the next battleground. The harsh light of crisis revealed the two adversaries in their primary colours: Gorbachev pirouetting, neither taking responsibility for the use of troops in Lithuania nor condemning the action; Yeltsin acting dramatically, and alone.

On 12 January 1991, just hours after the attack by Soviet Interior Ministry troops on the Lithuanian television tower and with Gorbachev still out of sight, Yeltsin issued a harsh condemnation of this action in the name of the Presidium of the Russian Supreme Soviet. It demanded an end to the violence and said the use of Russian conscripts on Baltic soil was illegal and unconstitutional. A Yeltsin biographer concluded that Yeltsin had hastily convened the Presidium and "won their backing for the blistering statement."[26] In fact, Presidium members said that Yeltsin acted alone, consulting no one, then and later when he flew to the Baltics.[27] There he issued a direct appeal to Russian soldiers, urging them, in effect, not to obey orders to attack civilians in the Baltics. Upon his return to Moscow, he raised the possibility of forming an independent Russian army. It was dramatic and it undoubtedly forced the Kremlin onto the defensive in the Baltics. But it also angered several of the members of the Presidium of the Russian parliament, some of them members of Democratic Russia, in whose name he was acting.

In February Yeltsin pushed his penchant for confrontation to a new level. At the end of a long, and rare, interview on Soviet television he unleashed a bitter attack on Mikhail Gorbachev. His policy of perestroika had resulted in economic chaos, higher prices, bloody clashes in the republics, and the use of the army against civilians. He had pursued "an active policy ... of deceiving the people. He has brought the country to dictatorship, eloquently terming this 'presidential rule'." With that, Yeltsin publicly demanded Gorbachev's resignation as Soviet president. Power should be handed over to the Council of the Federation, comprised of the leaders of the republics. Once again he had consulted no one before dropping this bombshell.[28]

What Yeltsin was proposing, at a time of extreme political uncertainty and great economic hardship, was a constitutional coup d'état. In effect, he was saying that Gorbachev had already forfeited the legitimacy conferred upon him by the Soviet parliament just one year earlier. In so doing, Yeltsin opened the door to his own opponents in the Russian parliament to use the same tactic against him.

His opponents wasted no time. On 21 February, just two days after his televised call for Gorbachev's resignation, six deputy speakers of the Russian parliament published an open letter calling for a special Congress to "evaluate" the work of Yeltsin as chairman. The letter was a catalogue of accusation:

Authoritarianism, confrontation and a tendency to make solo decisions on internal and external policy, as well as contempt for the laws and views of constitutional bodies have started to show more and more clearly through the initial progressive approach of Boris Yeltsin.

Many of the mistakes and miscalculations of the chairman of the Russian Congress flow from his desire to limit power to a small group of personal advisers – in effect a parallel power structure – while refusing to consult or seek the agreement of the Russian parliament.

Boris Yeltsin doesn't want to see that such a policy will lead not only to the collapse of the Soviet Union but also to the collapse of the Russian Federation.[29]

The criticisms would not change with the years, and they drew an essentially accurate picture of Yeltsin's leadership style. In his defence, Yeltsin and his camp said he was the object of an organized offensive, planned by the Kremlin and the Communist Party, to unseat him. This, too, was essentially accurate. A petition signed by 270 members of the Russian parliament, almost all Communist Party members, demanded a special session of the Russian Congress to review Yeltsin's leadership. The Communist faction in the Congress drew up a five-page secret plan, Action Plan 28, and distributed it to key members. It was a detailed strategy to dominate the parliamentary session with a relentless round of speeches and questions denouncing Yeltsin's style of leadership. The goal was to force Yeltsin onto the defensive and then to introduce a motion to impeach him.[30]

But the weakness of the Communists was apparent. They could persuade only a quarter of the Russian deputies to sign their petition. They did not dare announce publicly that they were seeking to impeach Yeltsin; he was too popular among Russian voters. And in the Congress itself, just as in May 1990, up to 40 per cent of the deputies belonged neither to the pro-Yeltsin nor to the anti-Yeltsin camp. They could be won over to either side.

Yeltsin was in no mood for compromise. On 9 March he told a meeting of Democratic Russia that it was time to think of forming a party to fight the Communists. Then, casting aside his prepared speech, he launched into a brutal attack on the "six" who had signed the open letter calling his leadership into question. They were "traitors," "enemies." Democrats should take the offensive against them; they should "declare war" against the Kremlin leadership. This was Bolshevik political rhetoric and his advisers, who once again had had no advance warning, were strongly critical of his language. Two days later Yeltsin conceded his words had been too harsh.

The special Congress was set for 28 March. The deputies of Democratic Russia opted for the tactics which had served them so well for the previous year: they called on Moscovites to demonstrate massively for Yeltsin on the opening day of the Congress. And once again Mikhail Gorbachev blundered. As president he signed a decree taking personal responsibility for order in the capital. Then he banned all demonstrations for two weeks and called the troops onto the streets of Moscow. The goal was to strip Yeltsin of his most potent political weapon – the support of the people. Riot police waited with shields and truncheons at key intersections. But tens of thousands of Yeltsin's supporters defied

the ban and peacefully challenged the soldiers. And, in the opening
moments of the Congress, Yeltsin's lieutenants seized the initiative.
They were no longer legislators, they were prisoners of the Kremlin,
shouted Anatoli Shabad. Citing the emergency situation, they
brushed aside the rules of order and introduced a resolution to
suspend Gorbachev's decree in Moscow. It rallied 532 votes, one
more than the 50 per cent majority of the Congress needed for
passage. With that the Congress adjourned for the day and despatched Yeltsin's deputy chairman, Ruslan Khasbulatov, to demand
that Gorbachev withdraw the troops. Yeltsin had won a key round;
the drive to remove him from office had been severely weakened.

The next day the soldiers were gone and Khasbulatov was in the
chair as the Congress began discussion. With ruthless determination, and with Yeltsin's approval, he herded the deputies along.
"Finish. Turn off that deputy's microphone. Leave the podium!"
These orders, and they were frequent, were accompanied by what
the official proceedings of debates described as "noise in the hall."[31]
The noise was, in fact, pandemonium as deputies shouted, cursed,
and gesticulated at each other and at the rostrum where Yeltsin
watched impassively as Khasbulatov did his bidding.

At stake was control of the agenda. Yeltsin's forces wanted to
include a debate on the creation of the post of executive president
of Russia, to be elected by the people. They did not succeed, even
with Khasbulatov throttling discussion. The Communists and their
allies would only accept a more general discussion on the results
of the 17 March referendum question on the Russian presidency.
Voters had indicated support for the creation of such a post by a
margin of more than three to one.

With that, Yeltsin rose to speak. For an hour he developed a
familiar theme – the stark choice facing the deputies. They could
opt for radical reform or the old Soviet system dressed in new
clothes. Even if the Soviet constitution had been altered to strip the
Communist Party of its right to govern eternally, 555 laws were
still on the books which buttressed the concept of one-party rule.
Despite the Russian declaration of sovereignty, the Centre still
controlled 85 per cent of the Russian economy. Radical reform, as
he outlined it, meant the creation of the office of Russian president,
"a new and key factor in the renewal of Russia as a state of law."

His vision was a model of the separation of powers: "On the
one hand, the president mustn't have the power to replace the
legislature or to put pressure on it. On the other hand, he must

have specific constitutional powers to influence the legal system, to name candidates to the courts and to address the parliament with the program of the executive branch."[32] Within six months his actions would bury those words.

Such was the division in this Congress that Yeltsin was only allowed to make his report on condition that it be followed by a co-report by a deputy speaker, Vladimir Isakov, once a Yeltsin supporter and now a strident critic and one of the six who had signed the open letter denouncing his leadership style. Now, he repeated his attacks. "Under the pounding of the drums of demagoguery, a new dictatorship is being prepared!"[33]

For six days the overblown, hysterical rhetoric by Yeltsin's adversaries ran up against the brusque, strong-arm tactics of deputy chairman Khasbulatov. The Communist faction could not muster enough votes to censure Yeltsin but found enough support to block attempts to create the machinery for a presidential election in the coming months.

The logjam was broken unexpectedly when an unknown Communist deputy – an airforce colonel with a walrus mustache named Alexander Rutskoi – came to the podium to make an announcement at the end of another day of recriminations and deadlock.

"The work of three Congresses of Russian deputies shows the destructiveness, the conservatism and the rigidity of the position of a portion of the faction of the Communists of Russia," he said. He then declared he was creating a new faction, Communists for Democracy, which would support Russia's course of renewal and strengthen its sovereignty. In other words, they would support Yeltsin.[34] By the end of the Congress his faction had gathered 170 deputies. With that, opposition to Yeltsin melted. The next day the head of the Communist faction stunned his troops by telling the Congress that this was not the time to change the Russian leadership.

Then Yeltsin sprang one more surprise. Arguing that a "paralysis of power" created by the struggle between the Russian Federation and the centre threatened society, he asked the Congress to grant him special, emergency powers until a real Russian presidency was created. He said he needed these powers "to lead the country out of crisis, to protect Russian sovereignty, to protect the transition to a market economy, to stop social conflicts and to suspend strikes."

His opponents howled in anger. "Boris Nikolayaevich, you have unmasked yourself!" deputy speaker Svetlana Goryacheva said.

"Your only goal is presidential power. To attain it you are ready
to trick, to lie – you're ready for any adventure. You don't even
hesitate at the possibility of pushing the country into crisis. You're
ready for anything!"[35]

It was, said another opposition deputy, the moment of truth for
the Congress. And in that moment of truth, the deputies capitulated
before the psychological force of Yeltsin. They voted 607 to 228
to grant him those powers and to organize the first presidential
election on 12 June.

Yeltsin would win that election with 58 per cent against six other
opponents, easily beating a field that included the former Soviet
prime minister Nikolai Ryzhkov and an unknown politician leading
an unknown party – Vladimir Zhirinovsky. And it was in his new
role as president of Russia that he would face his greatest challenge
yet: the putsch of August 1991.

But the Third Congress of Russian Deputies was a mirror of
crises to come. As it unfolded, it revealed almost all of the charac-
teristics which would lead to dispute, deadlock, and finally
breakdown two years later in the hybrid parliament in Russia. Each
side in the struggle had approached the Congress not as a legislative
session, but as a military campaign. Troops had been mobilized,
secret plans for the seizure of power drawn up and distributed. In
the parliamentary battle itself, rules and procedure were twisted
and broken so as better to achieve the upper hand. The rhetoric
was violent. Compromise was unthinkable.

In this military campaign, however, there were no armies, no
parliamentary parties ready to obey caucus discipline. Instead there
were factions. Their number varied from fourteen to twenty-four
in the short, violent life of this legislature. Some, such as Democratic Russia and Communists of Russia, bore a faint resemblace
to embryonic political caucuses. Many, such as the groups "Far
East," "Central Russia," and "Professionals from the Army and
KGB," appeared to represent regional or sectorial interests. A few,
such as the group "For the Return of Solzhenitzyn," were no more
than political declarations of faith. In the beginning, none was
exclusive. Deputies often belonged to several. And a large proportion of the deputies – 30 per cent – belonged to none.

The sessions of the Congress itself resembled an uproarious political bazaar. Almost every day, there were insults, shouting matches,
shoving matches, and great confusion. Votes swung wildly, swayed
by waves of anger and emotion. In this vast hall, where 40 per cent

of the one thousand deputies were committed neither to Democratic Russia nor to the Communists of Russia, decisions were often based on being on the winning side.

Alexander Lyubimov, a young deputy who had won office because of his popular anti-establishment investigative television show, watched succeeding congresses with mounting disgust. "It's a herd. It reacts emotionally. So one day the deputies can vote to do one thing, and the next day to do exactly the opposite."[36]

Anatoli Shabad participated actively in the battles of this Congress and all the others. He said the setting, in the Kremlin where deputies huddled in corridors and corners of the ornate St George's Hall during breaks, was redolent of the czarist court.

There was an atmosphere of conspiracy and intrigue. So if Khasbulatov was breaking the rules or being rude to some other faction, that was fine if it served our purposes. If it didn't, then we protested. There were very few deputies who opposed such rule-twisting on principle. The Congress was a reflection of our society at that time. The structures had broken down, the rules could be broken. It also reflected our passion for gambling. Deputies approached these sessions like a game of chance. That was one of the failures of our democracy. Too many people reached the top overloaded with dreams and delusions.[37]

August 1991 was the hour of Boris Yeltsin's greatest triumph. On 19 August he mounted a tank in front of the White House to proclaim his defiance of the putsch leaders who had toppled Mikhail Gorbachev. Within three days he had routed them and restored Gorbachev to his office in the Kremlin, only to orchestrate his public humiliation in the Russian parliament forty-eight hours later. With Gorbachev now in his political debt, he took just two more weeks to ram through a new charter for the Soviet Union which made him its undeclared master.

Then, just as suddenly, he lapsed into lassitude and inertia. In September he disappeared to his dacha at Sochi on the Black Sea. It was a pattern of behaviour which had marked his life. He used an analogy from his days as a volleyball player to explain it. "If it was an easy game, you wouldn't see me. But if the result hung in the balance, then I could achieve miracles."[38]

The miracle had been achieved. Now, drifting in the wake of his victory, Boris Yeltsin proceeded to make what he later described as the greatest political mistake of his life. He decided not to dissolve the Russian Congress and call new elections.[39]

The idea was actively discussed by Yeltsin's Presidential Council. A member of the council and a founder member of the Interregional Group, Sergei Stankevich, campaigned hard for dissolution. The Communists were in disarray, he said. New elections would decimate them and reinforce the new democratic alliance. "We could have completed the political revolution peacefully in such a way that the public would fully support it."[40] But other advisers, such as the thirty-five-year old economist Yegor Gaidar and Yeltsin's *eminence grise*, Gennadi Burbulis, carried more weight and had other ideas. Their view was that Yeltsin had to use his enormous prestige to launch fundamental economic reform and to complete the destruction of the totalitarian Soviet state. A new election campaign would slow down, and possibly even derail, such ambitious plans.

They found a temporary ally in Ruslan Khasbulatov, the acting chairman of the Russian Congress. He had declared himself against the breakup of the Soviet Union and would soon become a bitter opponent of Yeltsin's economic reforms. Because of his key role defending the Russian White House during the putsch he still had great influence with Yeltsin. He was under pressure from the deputies of Democratic Russia to call an early session of the Russian Congress. He had no doubt that their goal was to introduce a resolution calling for the dissolution of the Russian parliament and new elections. He was an ambitious man and now a very powerful one; a new legislature would conceivably destroy his fragile base of power. And so he sought out Yeltsin and argued that not only the Russian president but also the Russian parliament had emerged from the crisis with its prestige enormously enhanced. Yeltsin could harness this prestige to pass his program. To dissolve the Congress and the local soviets at a time when the Communist Party and most Soviet state structures were collapsing was to risk chaos. Yeltsin was tired. This was the easier solution. He was persuaded.[41]

The Russian Congress was postponed until 28 October. Yeltsin's speech on the opening day (written by Gaidar and Burbulis, the men who were to become his two key deputy prime ministers) shaped the session and the events of the years to come. Yeltsin described the course he was proposing as "the most important decision of my life." He announced that most prices, controlled by the state for seventy years under the Soviet system, would be freed on 2 January 1992. In three days, on 1 November 1991, his government would stop paying for the upkeep of seventy Soviet ministries of what he described as "the former Union." This was the death knell for the Soviet system and its government.

Yeltsin then told the Congress that early elections would be "too large a luxury. Organizing a general election campaign and introducing fundamental economic reforms at the same time isn't possible! To try to do both would lead to the ruin of everything!" Instead he proposed an entirely different path: virtual one-man rule for one year. The president would assume the functions of prime minister with the power to rule by decree. He would not even be bound by existing legislation. His decrees could overturn any law.

Yeltsin invoked the emergency situation to justify emergency measures.

I am convinced that this is in the interests of the people, who are completely indifferent to our procedural quarrels. The people need decisive, energetic and fast action!

The time has come to say, loudly and clearly, that in Russia there is just one centre of power – the Russian Congress, the Supreme Soviet, the Russian government and the Russian President![42]

As Gorbachev before him, Yeltsin, at the pinnacle of his power, reverted to the politics of Leninism. The concept of the separation of powers between the executive and legislative branches was dismissed as a procedural quarrel. There was only one centre of power: it flowed downward from the president through the government which he now personally controlled to a subordinate and submissive legislature.

In the fall of 1991 the Russian Congress bowed before this logic. Only seventy of the 1,068 deputies opposed the proposal to give Yeltsin the sweeping powers he sought.

CHAPTER ELEVEN

Raskol

In the wreckage of the Soviet Union the line-ups grew longer. For many, money had almost ceased to have meaning, since there was nothing to buy. In the wet wind and snow of late December 1991, Russians waited to enter stores where shelves were completely barren. They hoped that, sometime during the day, a truck from a food depot would deliver something they could take home.

On 25 December the Soviet Union officially died; in less than a week, on 2 January 1992, the Soviet economic system which had bequeathed the bitter legacy of line-ups and empty stores would be swept away. This was to be the "big bang" of price liberalization announced by Boris Yeltsin on 28 October. His young Western-trained economists hoped that goods would return to the shelves when the market, not the government, set the prices. Yeltsin had not masked the pain to come: inflation, dropping production and rising unemployment would be the lot of Russians until the fall. Then, he had promised, things would begin to improve.

One leading Russian politician did not believe him. In interviews and press conferences, he thundered that in Russia there existed "neither government nor democracy, but only chaos and anarchy." Yeltsin himself was being manipulated by his first deputy premier, Gennadi Burbulis, the Robespierre of the revolutionary process that had destroyed the Soviet Union and its army and would soon destroy its economy.[1]

The critic was General Alexander Rutskoi, the vice-president of Russia, chosen by Yeltsin as his running-mate just six months earlier. Retribution was swift. On 19 December a presidential decree stripped Rutskoi of all executive responsibility, including the chairmanship of the committee on military reconversion.

The economic reforms of 2 January 1992 caused shocks as great as had been predicted. Prices leapt and leapt again. Line-ups, once ubiquitous, rapidly melted into memory. Once-empty shelves suddenly held food and other goods, and stores were filled with Russians looking at these wonders, although few could now afford them.

Yet within two months another Yeltsin lieutenant was criticizing his leadership. Parliamentary chairman Ruslan Khasbulatov judged the price reforms to have been disastrously implemented. Inflation wasn't running at 200 per cent, as the government claimed, but at over 1,000 per cent. The young team of economics ministers put together by Yegor Gaidar should be dismissed. Price and wage controls had to be put in place.

Both Khasbulatov and Rutskoi had a genuine political quarrel with Yeltsin. Both were believers in the Soviet idea. Immediately after the failed August putsch, Khabulatov told the Soviet parliament it was imperative to sign a new Union treaty to keep the Soviet Union together. He recorded later that he was severely taken to task by the radical democrats in Yeltsin's circle for that view.[2] In his Kremlin office, long after the demise of the Soviet Union, Rutskoi defiantly hung a wall map of the USSR behind his desk. And both men believed that radical economic reform was the wrong course. It did not deal with the restructuring of industry and agriculture; it would leave tens of millions impoverished.

But this conflict was more than a philosophical quarrel; it was a conflict of personal ambitions unchecked by institutions and enflamed by Soviet traditions. While the Soviet Union had died, these men were still prisoners of the Soviet political system: here compromise was failure, criticism was a capital sin, and victory could only be achieved by routing and humiliating the adversary.

The young Russian deputy Oleg Rumyantsev glimpsed these forces at work in the first winter of economic reform. Rumyantsev believed that radical reform was necessary but also that some of Rutskoi's criticisms of the program were valid. He urged Yeltsin not to isolate his vice-president, but to listen to him. "When I suggested this, his immediate reaction was: 'You're talking about compromise!' I realized that in his mouth this was an accusation and a serious one."[3]

Instead, as another session of the Russian Congress approached in April 1992, Yeltsin publicly demanded that his emergency powers be reinforced and extended for two or three more years.

Russia needed what he called a presidential republic. "In a republic of the parliamentary type," he told his supporters, "the president is no more than a figurehead. Endless talk and political games with pseudo-democratic rituals will start again. In conditions of crisis, such a policy is suicide. I, as president, will never agree to it!"[4]

Rumyantsev discovered that the price for talking of compromise was exclusion. In the weeks leading up to the Sixth Russian Congress in April, all his attempts to meet or to phone Yeltsin were blocked by the president's advisers. And so he sent one last message – by letter. "I wrote to him to say he had surrounded himself with bootlickers, that he could no longer accept criticism and that he had become a hostage of the 'apparatchik mentality'."

Some Yeltsin allies in parliament tried a different approach. On the eve of the Sixth Congress, leaders of the "association of democratic deputies" – the core of two hundred members which had provided him with essential support since his election as Congress chairman in 1990 – met with the Russian president. They warned him of growing hostility to his program and of attempts to force the resignation of Gaidar and other reform ministers. Together they and Yeltsin agreed on a pact to work together, consulting mutually on each political step to be taken during the session. "Instead of that," wrote one of the deputies, "information leaked out that the president's men were cold-bloodedly drawing up various scenarios for the early dissolution of parliament."[5]

This was the work of Gennadi Burbulis. In 1989, at the age of forty-three, Burbulis had arrived as a deputy in the capital from the provinces, a pure non-entity, on the eve of revolutionary ferment. By chance, Burbulis had been elected from the city of Sverdlovsk, Yeltsin's political base. The two men, however, scarcely knew each other. Burbulis was an intellectual, who at one time had taught Marxism-Leninism at a government institute in Sverdlovsk. Now he vehemently rejected that philosophy and its political results. Instead, he became one of small circle of advisers around the unofficial leader of the opposition before the Russian elections of 1990. It was Burbulis who organized Yeltsin's election campaign in Sverdlovsk which won him a seat in the Russian parliament. Short, gaunt, with a large head and a high-pitched, precise voice, he brought a single-minded conviction to his cause. And his cause was destruction.

In the fall of 1991, shortly after being named first deputy premier of Yeltsin's government, he described the team as "a government of military field-engineers preparing a blast which will be like a minefield exploding." He would continue to use the metaphor for the next two years, describing the mines as the vestiges of the Soviet system which had to be blown up to render them harmless.[6] "My radicalism is humanitarian," he proclaimed, when asked to describe his political philosophy, "I am against any compromise with the Soviet totalitarian past!"[7]

As the self-appointed intellectual strategist of this work of destruction, he developed a three-step scenario. The failed August putsch had led to the destruction of the first pillar of the Soviet system, the Communist Party itself, first suspended in August and then banned outright by presidential decree on 7 November 1991, the seventy-fourth anniversary of the Bolshevik revolution. Both in August and in November, Burbulis stood closest to Yeltsin, demanding the radical decrees.

The second step was the dismantling of the Soviet Union itself. As state secretary of the Presidential Council, he took the lead in urging Yeltsin to push for the creation of a Commonwealth of Independent States. In November Mikhail Gorbachev revealed that he had in his hands a secret memorandum, written by Burbulis, saying a surgical strike was necessary because Gorbachev was trying to recreate the old Union under the guise of a confederation. "Russia has already lost half of what it gained after the August putsch. Cunning Gorbachev is weaving a net to restore peace. The process must be stopped."[8] In December, at a weekend meeting of the presidents of Russia, Ukraine, and Belarus in a hunting lodge in the Byelovezhsky forest near Minsk, Burbulis and another Yeltsin adviser, Sergei Shakhrai, worked all night to draw up documents declaring the Soviet Union dead. On 8 December Boris Yeltsin and the leaders of Ukraine and Belarus signed them. Later, at a press conference in Moscow, Burbulis blandly insisted the new Commonwealth of Independent States, formed by the three leaders, hadn't killed the Soviet Union; it had already died. "Our declaration was a medical diagnosis," Burbulis said.

The final step was economic reform and the destruction of the political system of Soviet power still standing in Russia: the Congress, the Supreme Soviet, and the network of regional and local soviets, all dominated by Communist Party functionaries. In the winter of 1992 Burbulis argued vehemently that it was now time for more surgery, time to sweep away the existing parliament with new elections. Otherwise, the president and the people would remain hostages of these representatives of the old regime. But Yeltsin wasn't yet ready. One participant remembers a particularly heated cabinet meeting in March 1992 at which Burbulis started to unleash a diatribe against the Russian parliament. "Yeltsin immediately put a stop to it, saying: 'We have to find a way to work with the Supreme Soviet. Above all, we don't need another enemy!'"[9]

Burbulis's unrelenting pursuit of his goal had become a liability for Yeltsin's government. To placate the Congress, Yeltsin dropped Burbulis from his government post in April 1992, although keeping him on as a key adviser. But the damage had been done; by identifying the parliament as the enemy, Burbulis helped make it so. The Sixth Russian Congress in April 1992 was again the theatre of confrontation and dramatic gesture. The deputies voted a motion of no-confidence in the government's reform program. When the government threatened to resign the motion was rescinded. And for the crucial four days of this confrontation Yeltsin remained in mysterious seclusion, only emerging on the last day to unveil a government bill demanding for himself, once again, more powers. He told the Congress he had been ready to call a referendum on the dissolution of the parliament if it had not backed his reforms. (Under the existing Russian constitution, the president had no power to dissolve the legislature before the end of its term.)

"Russia has awakened," he declared. "The course of history cannot be stopped." And the course of history, he made clear, was directly linked to his authority. "The time of puppet governments is gone. Without strong executive authority there will be neither reforms, nor order, nor statehood, nor a dignified Russia."[10]

But this tactical victory for Yeltsin merely postponed a more savage battle to come. Burbulis, in his quest to build a society based on humanitarian radicalism without compromise, had ruthlessly excluded those who did not share his vision. In the wake of the failed August coup he reached the pinnacle of his influence, becoming, by Yeltsin's own admission, the de facto head of the Russian government.[11] In that capacity he blocked bids by both Alexander Rutskoi and Ruslan Khasbulatov to be named prime minister. Khasbulatov, in particular, was deeply offended. He was a Chechen, born in Grozny and deported by Stalin at the age of eighteen months in 1944, along with his family and most of his people, to Kazakhstan. He had come to Moscow to complete his university studies and became a leader of the Young Communist League. He remained in the capital to teach his specialty, economics. So he was further mortified by Yeltsin's choice, at Burbulis's insistence, of Yegor Gaidar, a round and balding economist who had once been *Pravda*'s economics editor, as deputy premier and leader of the team of economic reformers.

"He became very jealous, he felt diminished by the presence of Gaidar in the government," one deputy said. "He suffered when Gaidar spoke at the Congress. It was worse than jealousy between a man and a woman."[12] In the spring of 1992, with Gaidar's star on the rise (he would be named acting prime minister in June) and with Burbulis counselling an end to the Congress, Khasbulatov went into open opposition to Yeltsin's government.

The president was now opposed by the second and third figures in the political hierarchy of the Russian state, both men he had picked. In the second volume of his memoirs, Yeltsin revealed that he chose both men at the last minute, barely knowing either of them, and only for tactical reasons.[13] In choosing Khasbulatov as his deputy chairman in 1990, Yeltsin remained faithful to the Communist principle of personnel selection: the second secretary should represent the minorities. The selection of Rutskoi was a variation on the same theme: in choosing a military man, Yeltsin hoped to capture the military vote and the military's allegiance once in power.

Having chosen them, Yeltsin remained faithful to his communist past in another way. He simply assumed unswerving loyalty from grateful subordinates elevated, by his will, to high positions. That presupposed, however, a vast and rigid hierarchy in a frozen system of power. And it was Yeltsin himself who had destroyed the hierarchy and the system. In its place had been created something which resembled a court, swirling with intrigue and jealousies, where power depended on proximity to the remote and impulsive leader.

"I think Khasbulatov could have gone in any direction and I believe that Yeltsin himself was, in large measure, responsible for the fact that he ended up opposing him." The judgment is that of a senior deputy from the democratic wing, Viktor Sheinis, a man who remained loyal to Yeltsin. "Yeltsin behaved harshly toward the people he worked with. He was very quick to abandon people to whom he owed a debt and Khasbulatov was one of those people."

It was Khasbulatov who now began to realize that, with the old structure of power in ruins, he could create his own court in the

Russian parliament. Ironically, Yeltsin himself had left him the tools: a constitution making the Congress virtually irremoveable and the chairman a potentate with a vast budget and personal control of cars, dachas, Moscow apartments, committee appointments and foreign travel for the deputies. Yeltsin had originally justified this by arguing he needed more power in his battle with Mikhail Gorbachev and the Soviet power machine.

The final element in this mix was the personality of Khasbulatov himself: volatile, scornful, and above all, confrontational. In a book of interviews and essays, entitled *The Struggle for Russia*, written in this period, he offered this extraordinary definition of his job: "A Speaker extinguishes, prevents, and triggers conflict."[14]

Conflict in parliament there would be, as Khasbulatov would refuse to recognize deputies he disagreed with, refuse to allow votes on motions he disliked, countenance deputies and secretaries using borrowed electronic voting cards from absent members – in full view of spectators – to pass legislation he wanted, and order new votes on bills and motions until he got the result he desired. In one case, he called eleven votes on the same resolution; in another, he simply shelved a bill on privatization in the capital for almost a year, until deputies agreed to his version, giving control of the process to the mayor's office and not to Yeltsin's Ministry of Privatization.[15] And all this was accompanied by snide remarks and insults directed at deputies he didn't like.

His personal arrogance and aptitude for confrontation, combined with the refusal of Communist deputies to accept all forms of reform, led to legislative deadlock. Despite the government's commitment to sweeping economic change, the parliament threw up roadblock after roadblock to privatization and never amended the Soviet-era constitution to allow the free purchase and sale of land.

Having first installed himself in Leonid Brezhnev's colossal private apartment, Khasbulatov set about acquiring the other attributes of power. Obediently, the Supreme Soviet of the Russian Federation voted to create a five-thousand-member armed parliamentary guard, under the direct orders of the chairman. He copied Yeltsin's tactics in his struggle as Russian chairman against Mikhail Gorbachev. He created his own newspaper, *Rossiskaya Gazeta* (Russian Gazette) and demanded, and received, a nightly hour on prime time television. But that wasn't enough. He was infuriated by persistent criticism from Moscow's most prestigious newspaper, *Izvestiia*.

"One night in 1992, around 11:30, Khasbulatov phoned me from his limousine," recalled Mikhail Poltoranin, the government press and information minister. "'All right, let's close *Izvestiia*,' he said. 'They criticize everything!' I told him it wasn't possible. 'Then we'll take other measures!'"[16] The other measures became a bill to put the newspaper under the control of the parliamentary chairman. It was finally passed in July 1993 but never implemented.

An investigative parliamentary commission set up to uncover the roots of the August 1991 putsch was headed by two of the leaders of Democratic Russia, Lev Ponamarov and Father Gleb Yakunin. "We didn't report to him, we did our own research, we held press conferences to announce what we had discovered," Ponamarov said. "He couldn't stand the idea of some deputies being autonomous." The commission's preliminary report was published in February 1992. It revealed the extent of the penetration of the Russian Orthodox Church by the KGB. The commission leaders intended next to investigate KGB links to the Soviet and Russian parliaments where, they suspected, the security organs "controlled" at least 30 per cent of the deputies. But by the spring, Khasbulatov had sealed access to KGB archives and closed the commission. For good measure, he accused its leaders, in a newspaper interview, of Stalinist methods. "Look at Ponomarov and Yakunin. They say, give us a stadium and we'll shoot all the communists."[17]

Deputies of all persuasions, when asked to evaluate Khasbulatov, used terms like sick, paranoid, and mentally unbalanced. Even his close aide, Constantin Zlobin, who remained with him to the end, talked of "his lack of elementary political culture."

"As events unfolded, deputies from the 'democratic' wing who didn't want to submit to his orders began to rebel. And as he accumulated power, his 'oriental' side became more and more evident: his amour-propre, his intolerance of criticism, and his egomania."[18]

The opposition of the democratic deputies was gravely weakened, however, by internal splits, lack of discipline, and Boris Yeltsin's evident distaste for party politics and all things parliamentary. The cohesion of their principal political vehicle, Democratic Russia, had already shattered. In January 1992 two of its five co-chairmen had angrily quit. One of them was Yuri Afanasiev, the former co-chairman of the Interregional Group in the Soviet parliament. As he left, he published an incendiary open letter accusing the majority of creating an organization completely subservient to the Russian president who, in turn, was betraying the cause of democratization by preserving the political and economic power of the old nomenklatura. "This is the question: either Democratic Russia becomes a completely democratic force, both independent and constructive, or it becomes an empty shell."[19]

The majority wing was not helped by Yeltsin's periodic flirtation with the idea of creating and leading a new political party which would channel and discipline the chaotic energies of Demcratic Russia. It was an idea urged on him by Gennadi Burbulis, but each time he backed away. His reluctance might have sprung, in part, from the movement's glaring inability to organize itself properly. "We now have between 100,000 and 200,000 active members," announced Lev Ponamarov, the movement's co-chairman, after its third convention. "I can't give you an exact figure since we don't keep any record."[20]

The lack of discipline was equally apparent in parliament. The democratic deputies had split into four factions, Democratic Russia, Radical Democrats, Consensus for the Sake of Russia, and Rodina (Motherland) each with about fifty members. Often, by their own admission, the deputies arrived ill-prepared for debate. Binding decisions of the caucus constituted an alien concept. Each deputy voted as he saw fit. "We weren't ready for discipline," Anatoli Shabad said. "We equated it with the discipline imposed by the Communist Party. We were still in rebellion against it. And so things just happened by accident."[21]

By the end of 1992 there were ten other factions divided into two other major blocks: Russian Unity, an umbrella group of about three hundred deputies strongly opposed to Yeltsin and his policies, composed of the Communists of Russia, Agrarians, and Russian nationalists; and a block of centrists composed of groups such as Smena (Change), Workers Union (Reform without Shocks), Free Russia (the group originally formed by Alexander Rutskoi), and Left-Centre. Many of the centrists were for reform, with reservations, and for a republic with a strong executive. Their support for the president could have been secured but Yeltsin no longer made any effort to try to build a working parliamentary coalition. "It seems the American president spends an enormous amount of his time at breakfasts, lunches, and dinners with congressmen and senators. Good relations with them is one of his major priorities," another democratic deputy said. "Boris Yeltsin didn't consider it important at all."[22]

Yeltsin considered the normal work of negotiation and political horse-trading with the Russian Congress as if it was an unnatural act. "The coming battle would be hard. Not only would I have to sit through the sessions, I would also have to meet with caucus spokesmen and faction leaders. The Congress was an enormous drain on my energies. And all this to achieve one goal: to persuade them. Asking, begging, winning promises – simply so the government could work normally!"[23]

He preferred the path of patronage, which would prove calamitous. He co-opted deputies loyal to his program into the executive branch. Working in his personal office, or as ministers or deputy ministers, they were rewarded and they obeyed his orders. By June 1993 more than two hundred of the 1,066 deputies of the Congress had taken such jobs, although almost all continued to hold on to their status as deputies, just in case.[24] These men and women were the best of the democratic forces. The result was that those left defending the president's interests in parliament were reduced to a rump caucus. Two political groupings now faced each other in an atmosphere of open hostility: the party of the Kremlin and the party of the White House.

"People recognize me. They often don't know my name but they remember the incident." The incident took place in the Seventh Russian Congress and conferred a peculiar glory on Anatoli Shabad. At political meetings men and women pointed to him. That's the boxer, they said. Others, far less sympathetic to his views, muttered, there's the Jew, send him back to Israel. They whistled and stomped their feet when he rose to speak. But Shabad, as combative as in the maelstrom of the Congress Hall, shouted them down.

The battle had begun even before the Congress opened. Gennadi Burbulis and other Yeltsin advisers darkly announced to foreign journalists that the parliamentary leadership was planning a legal putsch. Yeltsin himself talked of the growing menace of fascism in Russia. Not surprisingly, opposition hardened. Tactical compromises offered by Yeltsin were rejected.

On the third day the deputies prepared to vote on whether to strip Yeltsin of his special powers. The democrats gathered the requisite 20 per cent of the deputies to demand a vote by electronic ballot. Khasbulatov refused their request and pushed through a vote by written ballot. "Such a vote would take two hours and give him more time to round up the deputies for the necessary two-thirds majority," Shabad said. "So we rushed the podium, because this was illegal. He yelled into the microphones: 'Protect me from these deputies!' And so the Leninists charged forward. They pulled and shoved and hit us. We fought. That incident symbolized that parliament."[25] All the more so because the fight in the aisles was broadcast over and over to the country.

The forces opposing Yeltsin fell just a few votes short of the two-thirds majority needed to strip him of his special powers. But Yeltsin and his advisers saw in the incident the confirmation of their worst fears. They drew up an "appeal to the people." It spoke of the menace of civil war. Reading it out at the Congress on 10 December, Yeltsin demanded a referendum in January to allow the people to answer the question: "To whom do you confer the responsibility to lead the country out of the economic and political crisis: the present Congress or the President?"[26] He then called on the deputies to follow him out of the hall. But, stunned and unprepared, only 150 straggled out behind him.

Almost immediately Vice-President Alexander Rutskoi stepped to the podium. "For me the highest order is the constitution, the Congress, and the people," he shouted to a storm of applause. Yeltsin's defence minister, Pavel Grachev, followed. He said the army would uphold the constitution and wouldn't mix in politics.

The actions of the rest of the Congress constituted a steady and ignominious retreat for the president. Angry deputies adopted a resolution condemning his program of reform. They amended the constitution to prevent a referendum on the future of the Congress. Yeltsin was forced to abandon Yegor Gaidar as prime minister. Only the intervention of the chief judge of the Constitutional Court, Valery Zorkin, allowed Yeltsin to emerge from the Congress with his special powers extended until the spring.

In the new Russia of the winter of 1993 inflation ran at 2,000 per cent a year, university professors earned less than $50 a month, while students abandoned their studies to become rouble millionaires, selling cigarettes, imported vodka, mace pistols, condoms – almost anything – from ranks of wooden cabins which seemed to have sprung like mushrooms on the sidewalks of Moscow. This was kiosk capitalism. Mercedes clogged the streets of major cities, most stolen in Western Europe and imported illegally to Moscow, almost all purchased there for cash. This was cash accumulated in mountains from the sale abroad of Russia's abundant riches, such as oil, timber, gold, metals. The licences to sell these resources abroad were purchased in bribes from compliant government officials. The state treasury received almost nothing from these sales. Customs officials had been bribed as well; the only taxes collected efficiently were for protection, by various mafia gangs.

The recently dismissed prime minister, Yegor Gaidar, voiced his suspicion and despair. His own police and security ministries were actively collaborating in the corruption. "We were walking a minefield. Agencies which should have been protecting the government's honour were actually involved in hushing up such activities."[27] A few months later Boris Yeltsin fired the Russian minister of security. He had been "bought" by a former Soviet citizen, Boris Birstein, now the holder of Israeli and Swiss passports and the founder of a murky trading company, Seabeco. The purchase of the minister had taken the form of a $US350,000 shopping spree in Switzerland organized for his wife and the wife of the deputy minister of the interior.[28]

Privatization was proceeding explosively but unevenly. According to the statistics of the committee on state property, by the end of 1992 a total of 2,250 large state firms had already been transformed into joint-stock companies. But only 7.7 per cent of the country's retail shops and 2.7 per cent of cafés and restaurants had been privatized.[29] The new breed of commercial bankers arrived at work in bullet-proof vests, accompanied by ranks of bodyguards (recycled KGB agents) carrying sub-machineguns. Half-a-dozen bankers had been murdered in the previous six months. The number of murders in Moscow had doubled in two years. Most violent deaths were now mafia-related.

The political elite of Russia was, however, locked in another world, deaf to the signals of disarray, fear, and frustration among voters. The political world had become a battlefield. Neutrality was no longer possible.

Boris Yeltsin was now determined to rid himself of the Russian parliament. Only the weapon remained to be chosen. On 20 March 1993, he delivered a speech on national television announcing that he was instituting presidential rule, depriving the Russian parliament of power until a referendum on new elections could be organized. A presidential decree would soon be issued to that effect.

Within minutes Ruslan Khasbulatov and Alexander Rutskoi were holding a press conference in the Russian parliament, the White

House, denouncing Yeltsin's initiative as illegal and declaring that they would remain in the building, as in August 1991, until the illegal putsch had been defeated. At their side now was Valery Zorkin, the chief judge of the Constitutional Court. He, too, proclaimed Yeltsin's initiative unconstitutional. This was judicial innovation. The legal decree had not yet been issued or even signed but judgment was already rendered.

It was, as it turned out, just a dress rehearsal. The decree, when it was finally issued four days later, contained no provisions bypassing parliament. Another raucous Congress, convened at the end of March, lurched wildly toward impeachment of Yeltsin but fell seventy votes short. In the end, one last compromise was reached. There would be a referendum in April containing four questions. The first two were questions of confidence: Did the voters support Yeltsin and his economic reform program? The last two asked whether voters wanted early elections for the presidency and the parliament. To be safe, the Congress stipulated that only a majority of all *registered* voters would make the results binding.

Yeltsin campaigned vigorously for what he called a "yes, yes, no, yes" result – that is, support for him and his reforms, rejection of early presidential elections and support for the dissolution of parliament. The result was as he had asked. Even his embattled reform program won a slim majority of support, 53 per cent. On closer examination, however, his victory concealed dangerous divisions. Ten out of Russia's twenty autonomous republics had voted against giving him confidence. And only in large cities was his economic program endorsed. In small towns and the Russian countryside it was rejected strongly.[30]

The victory also concealed rising voter apathy and disgust. The turnout was just two-thirds of the electorate, a drop of more than 10 per cent from the last vote for the Russian presidency in 1991. This reflected the findings of Russian political scientists and opinion pollsters. Sentiment had swung from sympathy for the Russian political elite and parliament in 1900 to indifference in 1992 to active dislike in the spring of 1993. In 1990 more than one-third of those polled declared themselves active supporters of political groupings such as Democratic Russia or the Communists. By 1993 the numbers were 7 per cent and 5 per cent respectively. Ninety per cent said they had little or no trust in political parties.[31] Nevertheless, the referendum was a political victory for Yeltsin. But, just as in the wake of the August putsch of 1991, he seemed exhausted by his efforts and unsure of what to do with his triumph.

As for the leadership of the Russian parliament, it simply denied reality. Victory for Yeltsin was in fact defeat, Ruslan Khasbulatov declared. More than half the registered voters had voted against him or hadn't voted at all. Fifty per cent of Russia's registered voters hadn't voted for the dissolution of parliament; it would carry on as before.

In fact, not quite as before. In the spring and summer of 1993 all semblance of normal politics evaporated. Both sides now practised the tactics of humiliation, retribution, and reward.

Boris Yeltsin had suffered humiliation at the hands of Mikhail Gorbachev. Now he would refine the art against his enemies. His first target was his own vice-president, Alexander Rutskoi. Yeltsin ordered his Mercedes limousine taken away from him. His phalanx of aides and bodyguards was reduced to six. His official phones at his office, home, and dacha were cut off. Russian prosecutors leaked documents purporting to show that he had a Swiss bank account worth $US 3 million (the documents were later judged to be forgeries). Finally, Yeltsin issued a decree suspending Rutskoi from his duties and locking him out of his Kremlin office, although there was no provision in the Russian constitution permitting him to do this.

The chief judge of the Constitutional Court was next. He had judged Yeltsin's 20 March speech to be unconstitutional; he would be punished. He, too, lost his limousine and bodyguards. He was not permitted to attend the annual Second World War victory ceremony along with the president and other senior state officials. At his dacha near Moscow, which bordered the president's, his pet cat was shot and killed by Yeltsin's bodyguards. Finally the dacha itself was taken away from him.

The counter-offensive was in the same vein. Alexander Rutskoi announced that he had eleven suitcases detailing corruption up to the highest levels of the government. Waving papers, but offering no proof, he told deputies of the Moscow City Council that fifty thousand gold coins and ninety tons of gold had disappeared from state coffers and suggested darkly that this was the work of Gennadi Burbulis.[32] A month later the Russian parliament voted to demand criminal proceedings for corruption against two senior Yeltsin ministers, Mikhail Poltoranin and Viktor Shumeiko.

Lacking the panoply of weapons available to the president to humiliate their adversaries, the parliamentary party compensated with language of violent excess. Immediately after the April referendum Sergei Baburin, a young parliamentary leader who sported a goatee and conjured up the vision of a young Lenin with hair, compared Yeltsin to a foreign usurper. "Like Napoleon after the Battle of Borodino, he sits in the Kremlin. But Moscow burned and Napoleon was driven out. Yeltsin, too, is a foreign presence, backed by foreign powers, and the people will soon rise up and rid themselves of him."[33]

Baburin was, at this time, co-chairman of the National Salvation Front, an alliance of neo-Communists and Russian nationalists which claimed the uneasy allegiance of a majority of Russian deputies. The Front's new strategy, published in July 1993, called for a "total offensive" against the Yeltsin government. "Either we assault them and replace the criminal regime, or we are crushed and lose the Motherland."[34]

Alexander Rutskoi used language just as harsh. The Yeltsin government was "an administrative-mafia dictatorship. Why do these people need a dictatorship? To justify their illegal actions, to launder the money they have stolen, to shut up the opposition and, later, the whole nation!"[35] So virulent was his language, and that of Ruslan Khasbulatov (he publicly described the Yeltsin ministers as "worms" and Margaret Thatcher, who had praised Yeltsin, as a *babyoshka* – something between a "broad" and an "old bag"[36]) that aides to both men tried repeatedly to rein them in. "It is impermissible to use terms like 'fuckers,' 'bandits,' 'fascists,' 'snivellers,' 'punks,' and 'library workers' (?). It would be better to tone down the critical thrust of speeches and turn to more constructive themes." This from a memo written to Rutskoi by a senior aide. It was ignored.[37]

Against this, Yeltsin employed the classic weapon of power: patronage. He dangled lucrative jobs in the executive before deputies, along with limousines, dachas, and apartments, in the hope of attracting so many that the Congress would, by the fall, no longer have the necessary two-thirds quorum to function. In this manner, the man who had come to power campaigning against privilege and the bloated apparatus of the Soviet state built a presidential administration 80 per cent larger than that of Mikhail Gorbachev.[38]

Not to be outdone, Khasbulatov countered with lavish promises to deputies at a June session of the Supreme Soviet. "Don't worry, you won't be forgotten. Your apartments, all that. It's in our hands. I know some of you want to be ambassadors. Just tell us about it and we'll give you the credentials. I'll write the decree myself."[39]

When Yeltsin finally decided on how to use the political capital from his referendum victory in April, it was to convene a constitutional assembly. The choice was significant; Yeltsin's obsession with sweeping away the detested Congress was now coupled with a search for a political structure that would confirm the legitimacy of his regime and reinforce the powers of his office. Ironically, it was a task he could have achieved three years earlier.

Yeltsin was later to write that the political deadlock in Russia had come about in part because there had been no time to adopt a new constitution in the agitated months before the end of the Soviet Union.[40] But Viktor Sheinis, a senior democratic member of parliament and deputy secretary of the Constitutional Commission which Yeltsin chaired in 1990–1, disputed that view. The Constitutional Commission had worked quickly, preparing a first constitutional draft within three months of its creation in the summer of 1990. The draft was ready for debate and preliminary passage at the Second Russian Congress in November 1990, but at the last minute, according to Sheinis, it was taken off the agenda, on the orders of Yeltsin. A new Russian constitution was, at the time, of secondary importance for him.[41]

The story was similar a year later. For Yeltsin, the priority in the wake of the collapse of the August putsch was to obtain emergency powers with which to implement economic reform. Only as an afterthought, on the last day of the Fifth Congress, was there a discussion of the constitutional draft. Yeltsin himself praised it in a speech to the Congress. "The constitutional draft starts from the position that Russia is a presidential republic ... The most important characteristic of this draft is the presence of the concept of a 'civil society.' A full-fledged civil society is the strongest guarantee against a return of totalitarianism. This is a strictly anti-doctrinaire, non-ideological document."[42] But after a short debate and a pro-forma vote to adopt the draft as a basis for discussion, the Congress closed. The Yeltsin team had other things on its mind.

As the struggle for power intensified in the next two years, constitution-writing suddenly became an obsession. By the time

Yeltsin addressed the opening session of his Constitutional Assembly in June 1993, there were no fewer than six drafts in circulation, four of them drawn up by allies of the president. In his opening address on 5 June Yeltsin presented the so-called Presidential Version and defended it as the last rampart against chaos now threatening Russia and its institutions. "It is not two branches of government which are now locked in bitter confrontation but two independent political systems," he proclaimed. On the one hand were the democratic institutions of presidential power, featuring constitutional control and the norms governing the separation of powers. On the other hand stood the Russian Congress and Supreme Soviet, successor institutions to the illegal Bolshevik Assembly which had dispersed at gunpoint the democratically elected Constituent Assembly of 1918 and seized power. The Congress was a monster, a forum without recognized rules and procedures, a place not of legislation but of sophisticated political manipulation. It and the Supreme Soviet were illegitimate in a democratic system, Yeltsin said. The presidential draft would rid Russia of this monster, and it would do more: it would lay the foundations of a society where "the state would serve as the guarantor of the freedoms and rights of the citizen and not of the right of the bureaucrat to rule arbitrarily."[43]

This was powerful rhetoric, but it was fundamentally misleading. The real choice was not between the presidential draft and chaos caused by Soviet-era parliamentary institutions, but between Yeltsin's version and the final constitutional draft prepared by Oleg Rumyantsev and Viktor Sheinis and approved by the Russian parliament. This draft, too, would sweep away the discredited Congress. It would establish in Russia a political structure with power divided between an executive president, a bi-cameral legislature, and the judiciary. The president would propose the members of the government to the legislature, which would ratify his choices. He would not have the right to dissolve the parliament before the end of its term or the right to assume special powers in an emergency. This was a recognizable imitation of the American presidential system.

But it was not what Yeltsin wanted. What he wanted was to be Russia's Charles de Gaulle, with a constitution tailor-made for a dominant president who would bestride the other branches of power like a colossus. And so, obediently, constitutional advisers like Sergei Shakhrai and Sergei Alexeyev had written that constitution.[44] It gave to the president the power Yeltsin craved: to call referendums on national questions, and to dissolve parliament and call early elections in the event of a political crisis. The president would name the prime minister; if the parliament rejected his choice three times, he could dissolve it. In time of crisis the president could declare emergency rule and ignore parliament altogether. And for good measure, the Yeltsin draft included Article 80, a provision that not even De Gaulle had written into the constitution of the Fifth French Republic. This provision would give the president the power to suspend legislation of the national or local legislatures he judged to have contravened the constitution. In the new Russia, the president would be both supreme leader and judge.

The need to enshrine human rights in a new fundamental law – the second major reason invoked by Yeltsin in his call for support of the Presidential Version – was, if anything, even more disingenuous. The Bill of Rights in the Rumyantsev draft was a carefully considered, meticulously crafted chapter guaranteeing the right to life, liberty, freedom of speech, conscience, and association, and detailing protections against arbitrary arrest, search, and seizure. It was so meticulous that Yeltsin's men simply borrowed large chunks of it, along with the preamble, and incorporated them into their draft.[45] Later Yeltsin even admitted that parts of the parliamentary Bill of Rights were more successful than his own team's efforts. Indeed, the only major addition to the Rumyantsev draft in the Presidential Version was a detailed clause guaranteeing to individuals and associations the right "to own, buy, sell, bequeath, give as a gift and otherwise dispose of private property."[46]

Ruslan Khasbulatov had come to the opening session of the Constitutional Assembly on 5 June at the head of a parliamentary delegation. At the end of Yeltsin's address, he demanded to speak in his turn. He planned to tell the Assembly, and the nation watching on television, that the Yeltsin draft was a worse version than the parliamentary draft, which Yeltsin had originally approved. He would propose a special coordinating commission to reconcile the two versions so that a final draft could be adopted by the Congress in the fall.

But Yeltsin would not let Khasbulatov speak. The chairman of the parliament stormed out. Other deputies followed him, shouting and denouncing what they considered Yeltsin's new abuse of power. There was pandemonium. Kremlin guards carried out one protesting deputy over their heads, only stopping to retrieve his shoe which had fallen off in the scuffle. All this was shown live on Russian television. According to Constantin Zlobin, Khasbulatov was "mortally offended." The rupture between the two men and the institutions they headed was complete.[47]

What followed that summer can only be described as preparations for constitutional war. In the parliament, committee chairmen and a deputy speaker suspected of sympathy for the president were stripped of their jobs. Plans were drawn up to strip deputies holding executive appointments of their right to vote. This would give the hard-core anti-Yeltsin wing in the Congress a two-thirds majority with which to pass constitutional amendments. The amendments being drawn up would transform Russia into a parliamentary republic with a figurehead president. It then adopted a state budget in which expenses would be more than double projected state revenues. The leadership group around Khasbulatov planned to invoke Yeltsin's expected veto of the budget as grounds for impeaching him.

The president made preparations of his own. In August he secretly drew up a draft decree to dissolve the Congress and hold early parliamentary elections. He then locked the draft in his personal safe.[48] He consulted not his advisers, but German Chancellor Helmut Kohl about potential Western reaction to his secret plan to end the life of the Congress.[49] On 19 August, at a Kremlin press conference to mark the second anniversary of the 1991 coup, he announced he had a two-month strategy to force early elections. "The new Russia must not have such a parliament, it must not," he said. September would be the crucial month. He refused to give details about the flurry of measures he promised. With a smile, he described them as "an artillery barrage."[50]

He spoke more prophetically than he knew.

For Russians the word *raskol* (schism) has profound historical resonance. "Russians are schismatics," the philosopher Nikolai Berdyaev proclaimed.

According to Soviet dissident writer Andrei Sinyavsky, the key lay with Lenin and his creation, Soviet civilization. "In a system of absolute violence there was a need of someone to crush. Without an enemy it could not function."[51] Yuri Afanasiev saw schism as a permanent theme of Russian and social life from the first split in the seventeenth century which divided the Russian Orthodox Church into modernizers and Old Believers. "It reappears in a new guise at each moment of fracture in our history."[52]

Others believed that the answer was to be found even further back in history, in the world view developed by the medieval Russian Orthodox Church. In contrast to the western Catholic Church, which saw life after death divided into heaven, hell, and a neutral zone of purgatory, Russian theology was markedly dualistic, dividing life beyond the grave into just two categories: heaven and hell.[53]

The political struggle now about to explode in violence contained elements of all of these ideas: the schismatic fury, the search for enemies, and the belief that, ultimately, this was a battle between good and evil.

CHAPTER TWELVE

A Higher Value

The end began as a surreal repetition of a previous putsch.

Inside the parliament building, Ruslan Khasbulatov, wearing a black suit, a black shirt and a polka-dot tie, looked like a bit player in a bad gangster movie. He was smiling. "I've organized one defence of the White House," he said to reporters, standing at a podium with a crest still proclaiming 'Workers of the world, Unite!' I'll just do what I did the last time."[1]

Less than two hours earlier on the evening of 21 September 1993, Boris Yeltsin addressed the country on television to announce that he had dissolved the Russian parliament. He admitted this decision was illegal. "The existing Constitution does not make this possible." But the constitution was only a document: "the security of Russia and her peoples is a higher value than formal compliance with regulations produced by the legislature, which has discredited itself." He said his authority to protect this higher value was conferred by the ballot box.

Then, after a dramatic pause to drink a cup of tea, he announced the dissolution of the Congress and new elections for a new Federal Assembly in December, an Assembly which would be "more competent, more cultured, and more democratic." He also promised an early presidential election after the new legislature met.

By 11 p.m. a crowd of two thousand people had gathered behind the White House. Most were middle-aged or older. Communist believers waved red Soviet flags. A knot of monarchists held up icons of Jesus Christ and the last czar, Nicholas II. Nationalists hoisted a banner which read "Army, Protect Your People from the President and his Zionists." Many began erecting makeshift barricades around the Russian parliament. Inside the building almost

150 deputies had defied Yeltsin's decree and were gathering for an emergency session of the Supreme Soviet. They discovered that the Kremlin had already cut off their official phones.

At midnight the session began. Khasbulatov led Alexander Rutskoi to the desk on the rostrum previously reserved for Yeltsin. The deputies burst into loud applause. By a majority of 142 to six they voted to strip Yeltsin of his post. "I am the acting president of Russia," Rutskoi proclaimed, after reading the presidential oath of office at the podium. Khasbulatov called for a nation-wide general strike and for massive civil disobedience, starting with soldiers of the defence and interior ministries. They should declare allegiance to the White House, where the legislature's leadership and the "acting president" would barricade themselves in until the crisis was resolved. But many defiant deputies decided to go home for the night. "We'll see what tomorrow brings," one said.

What the following days would bring was a confrontation of comic-opera unreality.

By the next morning unshaven men in military fatigues patrolled the corridors and demanded identification at the doors. They carried Kalashnikov sub-machineguns and scowled. On the thirteenth floor an aging gentleman emerged from a conference room clutching a document. He was dressed in a freshly-pressed camouflage uniform and black leather boots. This was General Vladislav Achalov. The document was Decree No. 3 from Rutskoi naming him defence minister of the Russian Federation. His first duty was to organize the defence of the White House. The irony was that in 1991 he had supported the coup against Gorbachev and had urged a bloody attack on the same building.

Rutskoi had also named his own interior and security ministers. His first "decree" had declared war on Yeltsin and his government, specifying the death penalty for officials who "violently disrupted" the constitution. Now, armed and isolated in their parliamentary fortress, Rutskoi, his ministers and Khasbulatov waited for the country to rally to them.

But the country was indifferent. Two streets away, a team of municipal workers desultorily paved a patch of road; two men worked while eight watched. Only three had even bothered to listen to Yeltsin's speech to the end. They were not concerned by the dissolution of parliament – they held it in bemused contempt. What was needed was order. Initial soundings showed the same reaction around the country. There was cautious support for Yeltsin, born of fatigue with incomprehensible political battles. But in the streets, and in the polls, many added a caveat: as long as there was no violence.

There would be no use of force and no violence, Yeltsin promised when he came out of the Kremlin that day to press the flesh on Pushkin Square. Beside him stood General Pavel Grachev, the defence minister, and Viktor Yerin, the interior minister. The message was clear: the armed forces and the police were behind Yeltsin.

But the White House was another world. "In those last two weeks, starting on September 21, Khasbulatov, Rutskoi and the others were completely out of touch with reality. They were in the grip of 'wishful thinking'," Constantin Zlobin said. He was Khasbulatov's press secretary.

It wasn't even clear they were in charge in the White House. On one of the first days of the siege, someone from Hungarian TV came in to see me. They wouldn't let his crew through the barricades. I went down and discovered it wasn't Yeltsin's police, it was our side. These were bizarre characters, unshaved and unwashed. We've got orders, they said, from the commander. I found the commander: he was a Cossack with a huge sabre.

I didn't even bother talking to him. I went upstairs to see Achalov. I found him in his huge office in his camouflage uniform with a bank of telephones on his desk. They were all dead. He was just playing soldier. He was the minister of defence but he wasn't even in control of the men outside.[2]

Yeltsin was better organized; he had the power structures on his side. But it quickly became apparent that, having cut the Gordian knot, he had given little thought as to what to do next. On 22 September Yegor Gaidar, newly reappointed as deputy prime minister, admitted there was no election law or election map ready for the December vote. It wasn't even clear what Russians would be voting for. Gaidar suggested the elections would only be for the lower house of the new parliament. The upper house, composed of two representatives from each republic and region would, he said, be appointed for its first term.[3]

By 23 September 638 deputies, now deprived of free air tickets and priority seating, had made their way to Moscow. That was not enough to form an official quorum to hold a Congress. The magic number was two-thirds of the deputies – 689. So the parliamentary leadership decided to expel all deputies who had shown support for Yeltsin. Now there was a quorum and the Tenth Congress could begin. It convened at 10 p.m. and by midnight had voted, by 636 to two, to impeach Yeltsin. "We've stripped the criminal of his powers," a deputy named Iona Andronov exulted.

Yeltsin quickly showed he still had power. Riot police were despatched to surround the parliament. Light, heat, and electricity in the building were cut off.

For another week the stand-off would continue. In the evenings, outside the perimeter of the barricades, crowds of parliamentary supporters scuffled with police. Inside the barricades, defenders lined up Molotov cocktails on the pavement. Their anger and resentment at what they had lost – an empire, economic stability, simple belief in the future – boiled over into expressions of xenophobia and racism. "The West wants us poor and broken. We were a great country; people were afraid of us. Now we're just another third-world nation," this from an impoverished lecturer in physics. "Jews are flourishing everywhere in Russia while we are dying," said a pensioner trying to live on the equivalent of $20 a month.

Hard men, former soldiers and policemen, arrived from Moldova, Georgia, Latvia, Siberia to join the fight. Alexander Rutskoi roamed the corridors inside in a sweatsuit, a Kalashnikov slung over his shoulder. Desks lay overturned in hallways as obstacles against invading forces. The stench of sweat and blocked toilets filled the air. Deputies dozed on chairs and tables.

Periodically Rutskoi emerged to review his troops, a rag-tag collection of men from sixteen to sixty dressed in everything from military fatigues to factory clothes. Then, clutching a bull-horn, he strolled about his "state," stopping to address the phalanxes of Yeltsin's riot police stationed just outside the barricades. "I'm talking to you as your president. Don't obey the orders of those sons-of-bitches, those swine!" The police stared back impassively.

Despite that bravado, Rutskoi had already offered the Kremlin a compromise: simultaneous legislative and presidential elections in February. He even guaranteed he wouldn't run. The idea was backed by the deputies and by the chief judge of the Constitutional Court, which had already condemned Yeltsin's action as unconstitutional. But Yeltsin brusquely rejected the plan. Once again there would be no compromise.

Russians watching the news on television saw almost none of this. Television was an obedient servant in Yeltsin's defence of a higher value. A typical newscast began with news of the president's latest decree, followed by reports about his prime minister, his defence minister, his spokesman, a Yeltsin adviser, and Yeltsin supporters. Towards the end, Khasbulatov was seen, but not heard, for five seconds. "They're urging people to take up arms," said the deputy director of Russian televison, Albert Pridhodko, of the leaders of the White House. "How can we give the floor to such people? Who's going to take responsibility for that? We're trying to provide a calming influence on society."[4]

Desperately seeking allies whose voice would be heard and reported, the White House leadership despatched the young deputy Oleg Rumyantsev to see Mikhail Gorbachev at his dacha outside Moscow. Tell him, Rutskoi wrote on a piece of paper (he was convinced the security services were electronically scanning all his conversations), that this is his chance to rehabilitate himself. Khasbulatov wanted Gorbachev to harness world public opinion in favour of the White House defenders.

On the evening of 27 September Rumyantsev spent three hours discussing the situation and drinking Greek brandy with the former president, while Raisa Gorbachev listened. "Three years earlier I had opposed him," Rumyantsev said. "Now I found I agreed with him on almost everything. I found he strongly resembled my father. He called the siege an authoritarian coup d'état and said he was ready to return to politics, in any capacity."[5] Gorbachev authorized Rumyantsev to report his views. But almost no one in Moscow was interested. And the next day, returning to the parliament, Rumyantsev found himself locked out.

Early on 28 September Yeltsin had ordered the White House sealed off. People inside would be allowed out; no one would be allowed in. The police set up loudspeaker trucks and began blasting rock music at the besieged defenders. The deputies replied with broadcasts of their speeches from a generator-powered radio station built from cannibalized television sets.

The mounting pressure only reinforced the resolve of the last angry knot of deputies, numbering perhaps one hundred. Their leaders proclaimed their moral invulnerability. Ruslan Khasbulatov said, "I am the bearer and the expression of the force of good." Their words were their remaining weapons. They denounced the "criminal regime" and the "monstrous lies" of Yeltsin. Khasbulatov crowned his talent for insult with one condensed description of the man in the Kremlin. "He is sick, drunk, and the leader of a banana republic."

A new barbarism of language was not the preserve of the leaders of the White House. The Russian foreign minister, Andrei Kozyrev, declared to the world, via CNN, that the parliamentary defenders "have been drunk for days. Some are mentally unstable. Rutskoi is very unstable, and very primitive."[6]

But for Yeltsin, the siege, now in its second week, was becoming counter-productive. The men and women in the White House were being transformed into martyrs in the eyes of Russians. Human rights associations began protesting at their treatment. Journalists raised their voices against the blanket censorship of Russian television. As the stand-off continued, regional councils such as the one in Novosibirsk, Siberia, threatened to cut off payment of taxes to Moscow.

The Kremlin agreed to talks with a White House delegation, mediated by the patriarch of the Orthodox Church. It agreed to turn the heat and electricity back on in return for the stockpiling in neutral hands of parliamentary weapons – up to two thousand rifles, machineguns, and grenade launchers, according to Kremlin officials. The lights were turned on in the White House but the defenders refused to hand over their guns.

On the weekend of 3 October the siege exploded. Far from the White House, on October Square, at the foot of the last and largest statue of Lenin erected by the dead Soviet regime, a crowd of ten thousand gathered in the bright sun of a Sunday afternoon. Many were young, many were angry, and many carried sticks, clubs, or iron bars. They were a volatile mixture of Communists and ultra-nationalists and their goal was to march to the parliament in defiance of Yeltsin's police.

They met the police on a bridge over the Moskova River near Gorky Park. At a signal from one of their leaders, the crowd charged the police line and simply overran the five-hundred-man contingent. The policemen fled; those who were caught by the pursuing crowd were beaten savagely. Reinforcements abandoned the buses they were sitting in. Some vehicles were smashed into instant wrecks by the mob, others were commandeered to pursue the fleeing forces of order. Twice policemen stopped to fire tear-gas at their pursuers. But the canisters were ancient and the gas had no effect. A water cannon was turned on the crowd; it only dribbled water. It, too, was abandoned on the Garden Ring Road.

At 3:35 p.m., using a commandeered truck as a battering ram, the mob burst upon the cordon of Interior Ministry troops round the White House. The troops cut and ran, abandoning weapons and armoured personnel carriers.

The siege was broken. Triumphantly, the crowds surged around the parliament building, shouting "Rutskoi, President!" The police and Interior Ministry troops had been routed. Their senior officers, lulled into a sense of security by the dwindling group of ineffectual protesters around the White House, had simply not believed the parliamentarians could rally such a crowd.

There was another reason for this defeat. Moscow's riot police were among the least capable in the world. They were poorly led, ill-trained, and badly equipped. But, above all, they and their officers had almost no practical experience of crowd control. Riots were simply unimaginable under Brezhnev. The huge crowds which had marched through Moscow in the late Gorbachev era had been peaceful. The nature of the problem had become glaringly evident just four months before the October events. On 1 May 1993, a much smaller crowd of Communists and nationalists had inflicted heavy casualties on riot police in a two-hour clash. One policeman died, and two dozen other people were hurt. Boris Yeltsin was outraged at the incompetence of his police. An inquiry was ordered, but nothing was learned, nothing changed.

Seen from inside the White House, the breaking of the siege was deliverance – and more. "Rutskoi and Khasbulatov had been living in a cocoon," Constantin Zlobin said. "When the crowd broke through the blockade, they thought the whole nation had risen up to defend them."[7]

Rutskoi now stepped onto the balcony of the White House and called for the violent overthrow of the Yeltsin regime. "Boys, it's time to take the mayor's building, Ostankino [the television centre] and the Kremlin!" The crowd roared its approval. It was not, indeed it could not have been, planned. It resembled rather the exultant call for revenge of the prisoner uncaged.

Within twenty minutes a firefight erupted around the mayoralty building, across the street from the White House. The battle was brief. When it was over, one policeman lay dead, at least three others were wounded, and the plate-glass front windows of the building lay in shards. The rebels had taken their first objective. A column of police, now prisoners, was led away under guard. On the balcony, the rebels raised the red hammer-and-sickle flag. In the street a convoy of buses and trucks and armoured personnel carriers, festooned with Soviet flags and filled with men armed with pistols, sub-machineguns, and grenade launchers set out for the Russian television complex ten kilometres away.

It was 5 p.m. and in the Kremlin the offices of president of Russia and his staff were virtually deserted. Anatoli Shabad was attending a meeting of liberal democrats to plan the coming election campaign when he heard the siege had been broken. He rushed to the Kremlin. "No one was prepared. No one was there. I went to the studio of the radio station Echo of Moscow to record an appeal to the people. It's right next to Red Square. The guards had run away. They thought they were going to be overrun any minute by the people from the White House. I went in and recorded my appeal and then ran back to the Kremlin. We barricaded ourselves in."[8]

Sergei Parkhomenko, a Moscow journalist, slipped into the Kremlin at the same time, with the help of a Yeltsin aide. He described a scene of confusion and recriminations as the president's advisers arrived. "The first hour after they all assembled was wasted on heated arguments over who had been the most naïve: those who believed in the possibility of compromise with the bandits or those who allowed the rebels to prepare their breakthrough.

"'So, what are you going to do now, you peacenik?' 'Me peacenik? Peacenik yourself!' were the type of epithets shouted into telephone receivers."[9]

The situation was equally chaotic at the Defence Ministry in central Moscow. As the White House mob roamed the streets, deputy ministers and three-star generals stood guard at the entrances, protecting the nuclear codes within. They had almost no troops to help them.[10]

At 7:15 p.m. a helicopter bringing Boris Yeltsin back from his presidential dacha outside Moscow landed inside the Kremlin. According to Sergei Parkhomenko, Yeltsin plodded into his office, closed the door, and disappeared for several hours.

Sergei Stankevich, a Yeltsin adviser, described the scene in the Kremlin at this time as one of "disarray and disorganization." He decided to drive in his car from the Kremlin to the television centre to assess the situation. "There were no police in the streets when I made my way across the city, just these groups of people, armed people. It was fearful. When I got to Ostankino, there was heavy shooting already. I met a group of military vehicles and I understood I couldn't get in." He turned and drove back to the Kremlin.[11]

The battle at the television centre would be the bloodiest of the day. Just minutes before the armed mob arrived from the White House, a small contingent of one hundred special forces troops loyal to Yeltsin reached Ostankino. They posted themselves at key points in the main building and in the building facing it.

In the expectation of another easy victory, many of the rebels were laughing as their leaders used a truck as a battering ram to break down the barricaded main doors. Then, after giving a warning of three minutes, they launched a grenade into the lobby. Immediately, the special forces replied with a murderous cross-fire. Two dozen people, several of them journalists, were cut down on the spot. By the end of the night, at least sixty people would be dead, according to ITAR-TASS.[12] Despite the resistance, the rebels broke into the main building and fought their way to the second floor. Shortly after 8 p.m. three of Russia's four main networks went off the air.

In the White House, Khasbulatov announced to cheering deputies that Ostankino had been taken and that the fortress of the Russian government would fall the next day. (In fact, the rebels never got higher than the second floor of Ostankino although the fighting continued into the middle of the night.)

At this point, Gennadi Burbulis and Mikhail Poltoranin, no longer in the government but still powerful advisers to Yeltsin, walked into the Kremlin. They found the presidential office in a panic. "The apparatchiks were racing around like cockroaches," Poltoranin said later.[13] Poltoranin and Burbulis took charge. They despatched armed Afghan veterans to the state news agency ITAR-TASS, where rebels were already at the door, and to the second Russian television network, which was still broadcasting. Then they set about rallying the population. From a secret studio, Sergei Stankevich, Yegor Gaidar, and finally the Russian prime minister, Viktor Chernomyrdin, broadcast televised messages that evening urging the people to demonstrate their support for the Yeltsin regime. Gaidar called on them to mass in front of the City Council building and start building barricades.

But Yeltsin was invisible. He explained in his memoirs that he had more important things to do than make speeches. "I was trying to rouse my valiant generals from their state of stress and paralysis."[14] The country, he wrote, was hanging by a thread. Amazingly, he and his senior ministers in charge of the armed forces and the police, in a secret meeting on 13 September to discuss his decree to dissolve parliament, never considered a contingency plan to deal with the eruption of violence such as had just occurred. Indeed, Yeltsin himself erupted in anger because his chief of Kremlin security suggested, in a private discussion on 19 September, the need for such a plan. "I was furious with Mikail Barsukhov," Yeltsin wrote later. "I saw his 'rebellion' as a sign of weakness. Now I know that he intuitively understood the danger."[15]

It is an extraordinarily revealing comment. One of the most dangerous decisions of Yeltsin's presidency was, quite simply, a terrifying leap into the dark. To point this out and to suggest that something might go wrong was to invite the wrath of the president, and accusations of rebellion and cowardice.

Later in the week, in an interview with the newspaper *Moskovsky Komsomolets*, the defence minister, Pavel Grachev, would offer an astounding reason for the army's absence from Moscow in the crucial hours of the evening of 3 October. It was harvest time and soldiers from key units stationed around Moscow were helping pick potatoes. They couldn't be rounded up quickly. And then, at the end of the afternoon, the general staff decided to delay sending the tanks and armed personnel carriers into the city to avoid traffic jams as Moscovites returned from their weekend at the dacha.[16]

But Yeltsin had an entirely different version of events: his defence minister lied to him in that chaotic evening, assuring him that tanks and troops were moving through the centre of city to protect key installations and government offices when, in fact, all army units had been halted in the suburbs. "My defence minister couldn't make up his mind," Yeltsin told an interviewer a month later. "Apparently he had been given too much responsiblity and he doubted whether the soldiers would follow his orders."[17] (Despite all this, Yeltsin never dismissed Grachev. Their relationship, during and after the crisis, is a psychological mystery.)

The problem ran far deeper than one man's inability to make up his mind. The army had been scarred and diminished by its participation in the August coup of 1991. Since that disaster, its leaders had repeated, like a prayer, that the army would uphold the constitution and not participate in political wars. Now the president was demanding that it intervene to save his regime. The military leaders knew the cost in blood and death would be high. They were being told to resolve a political confrontation that they believed should never have reached this stage. Still, the price of non-intervention could conceivably be even higher: the triumph of Rutskoi, who had not hesitated to begin the armed violence and would now be bent on revenge against the senior generals who had refused to help him during the two-week siege. And so, late into the night, the general staff dithered.

Yeltsin first sent his prime minister, Viktor Chernomyrdin, to the Defence Ministry to convince the generals to intervene. He was unable to persuade them. At 2:30 a.m Yeltsin himself drove from the Kremlin and walked into their meeting. Rather than take over, he sat off to one side, a silent, brooding presence demanding a decision. It wasn't until after 3:00 a.m. that the key question of how to deal with the White House was finally broached. The prime minister asked for suggestions. There was silence. Then, amazingly, Yeltsin's personal bodyguard took charge. Alexander Korshakov had been with Yeltsin since 1985, when he was assigned to guard him as a member of the Politburo. Over the years he had become the president's closest confidant. Now he stood up and told the general staff that, as one of the key defenders of the White House in 1991, he and a small group had considered all possible plans of attack and how to parry them. He then introduced another member of that group, a naval captain, who outlined the best plan. Within a few minutes the general staff had endorsed it.

But Grachev still hesitated. "Boris Nikolayevich, are you authorizing me to use tanks in Moscow?" Yeltsin stared at him in silence. Finally he stood up and said Grachev would have the written authorization within a few minutes. With that, he left the room and returned to the Kremlin.[18]

By 7 a.m. tanks and troops were in place around the White House. Within minutes the firing began. In the middle of the morning a tank fired two rounds into the upper stories of the White House, sparking a fire that would burn all day and leave the tower of the building a scorched black hulk. In the distance a huge plume of grey smoke could be seen rising into the sky. The fires from the attack on the Ostankino television centre were still smoldering.

At 9 a.m., with the battle raging, Yeltsin finally addressed the nation. The men and women in the White House were criminals. He described the actions of the previous twenty-four hours as a well-planned armed mutiny. "For them there is no forgiveness because they raised their hand against peaceful civilians, against Moscow, against Russia, against children, women and the elderly."

Inside the White House, as the battle dragged on, Khasbulatov seemed to withdraw into himself. Smoking a pipe, he muttered, "I've known Yeltsin for a long time. I never thought he could do this."

When the tanks opened up, Alexander Rutskoi, the man who had sworn to die defending the White House, began to panic. "I think he got a bit scared," said Constantin Zlobin, who watched that day. "He hadn't realized that playing with toy soldiers might lead to real tragedy."[19] Rutskoi used the one functioning cellphone to phone to generals in the Defence Ministry. They cursed him. He phoned the chief judge of the Constitutional Court, Valeri Zorkin, and pleaded with him to intervene. He had to support his aged mother, he had brothers and sons to take care of. "Valeri, they're firing at us with guns, with guns, do you understand? Call the foreign embassies, I implore you. Valeri, fuck your mother! Make the ambassadors come here immediately! Do something! You know I'm a hero! They won't have the courage to fire in front of international witnesses."[20]

Within the burning parliamentary fortress there were still more than a thousand people, about 250 of them armed fighters. By early afternoon elite units of the army and the Interior Ministry had penetrated to the first floor of the building. Zlobin was on the third floor with a walkie-talkie linking him to White House defenders. "I could hear them yelling: 'Long live Soviet power! We've run out of ammunition, scum, but we'll die for Soviet power.'"

Like Zlobin, deputies and others not fighting huddled in a windowless amphitheatre on the third floor. This was the Hall of Nationalities. Candle flames punctured small holes of light in the darkness. Among the deputies sat women – secretaries, cafeteria employees, and cleaning staff – and two dozen children, trapped with their mothers when the assault began. As the shooting intensified a group of members of the Ukraine Communist Youth League Choir were led in. According to one witness, "their faces wore the doomed but determined expressions of patriots ready to make the ultimate sacrifice for their motherland."[21]

Surrounded and under heavy fire, the participants began the final "session" of the Tenth Congress of People's Deputies. More than one hundred deputies, of the original total of 1,033, were there. Several, like Oleg Rumyantsev, returned the night before, after the siege had been broken.

Two years earlier Rumyantsev had also defended the Russian parliament against the plotters who had tried to topple Mikhail Gorbachev. He had negotiated the surrender of the tank and crew which had killed three defenders of the White House a kilometre from the parliament. Now, once again, he was suggesting a negotiated solution, the naming of a compromise president, the former Security Council secretary Yuri Skokov, "a figure who would suit everybody." But it was far too late for negotiation and compromise. A communist deputy dismissed the idea as "a road to nowhere." Debate drifted into silence.[22]

Some of the women sang peasant songs of lament and lost love; deputies sang songs of victory, like this one composed four days earlier:

Faith, Hope, Love,
Burns anew within us
Closer, ever closer, you approach,
The Victory of our dreams.[23]

It was not victory but Yeltsin's troops that were approaching. In the middle of the afternoon the leader of the Interior Ministry's elite commando group Alpha came into the Hall of Nationalities and stood at the candle-lit podium to propose surrender. It would take two more hours of shooting and negotiation before Rutskoi and Khasbulatov were led away to board a bus for Lefortovo prison. "Don't worry," said Sergei Baburin, the deputy from Omsk. "We'll all sleep at home tonight."

He was wrong. For most of the day Baburin, a veteran of Afghanistan, had been trapped in his office, on the floor, with eleven other people, including three women and a child. At the end of the afternoon he led his group out through the main entrance of the White House.

The special forces immediately separated me from the group. They pushed me up against the wall and began to argue about where they would shoot me, there inside the building or at another spot set aside for that. They began hitting me. After each blow, they asked me whether I was for capitalism or socialism. Then they hit me and asked me why I was smiling.

It was true, I realized I was smiling. It was as if I was watching this from the outside. I know Russian history, and I know the history of coups d'état. In a coup d'état you get rid of your political enemies. I was an adversary of Yeltsin, I understood they had to get rid of me.

But I was lucky. Several officers said I should be taken in alive. So they took me to a cell at Petrovka 38, the headquarters of the police. And twenty-four hours later I was released.[24]

Oleg Rumyantsev was taken by the special troops to a stadium near the White House and beaten, with blows to the ribs, the stomach, the testicles. A drunken policeman grabbed him and spat in his face.

"'It's over, you bastard, say goodbye to life,' he shouted at me. He told me to turn around and kneel down. Then he fired, over my head. I couldn't get up for several minutes, I was stunned."[25] In the confusion Rumyantsev managed to escape. He took refuge in a nearby apartment and didn't emerge for several days.

The bloody revolt was over.

With the White House still burning, decrees flowed from the Kremlin establishing emergency rule. Censorship was imposed, newspapers, like the nationalist *Den* and the Communist *Pravda*, were suspended. The chief judge of the Constitutional Court was hounded by Yeltsin's chief of staff until he resigned two days after the crushing of the revolt. Valery Zorkin was told that Yeltsin was furious at his "disloyalty"; only his resignation could save the court from extinction. His office was sealed up. The next day Yeltsin issued a decree which suspended the court's activities until the adoption of a new constitution.[26]

The outcry was immediate. Even Sergei Stankevich now said publicly that the times called for compromise. Russia couldn't be reformed "by a man standing on a tank." It became clear that there was profound disagreement within the government itself about how heavy a hand was acceptable. It erupted publicly when Yeltsin's press secretary criticized the prime minister for trying to create a propaganda ministry which would completely muzzle state television.

Censorship was lifted after Western governments, which had supported Yeltsin throughout the crisis, openly questioned the turn his government had taken. Yeltsin reaffirmed his commitment to legislative elections on 12 December. He publicly criticized aides and ministers who submitted decrees for his signature. "I am worried by the draft decrees people put on my table, many of which have nothing to do with the direction of reforms and push the authorities toward extremist measures."[27]

But Yeltsin was himself a mirror of the struggle within his government. He would play by the rules, as long as he could set them. Thus, his chief of staff announced in early November that Yeltsin no longer felt bound by his commitment to hold early presidential elections in June 1994. That, said Sergei Filatov, had been a compromise agreed to under pressure. It was another telling glimpse into Yeltsin's attitude towards compromise. It was also a shameless reinterpretation of recent history. Yeltsin had made the commitment to early presidential elections before the siege of the White House and had reaffirmed his promise in his speech dissolving the legislature. No pressure had been applied.

In this period of unlimited one-man rule, Yeltsin now promised self-limitation. He would only issue "operational" decrees that did not alter fundamental government policy. But at the end of October he signed a decree that constituted one of the most fundamental policy changes of all. After seven decades, he fully legalized private property and land and set the conditions for their purchase and sale. "This decision was overdue," he said. "The Congress had discussed it and put it off. The question was ripe. I know the people supported the idea. And I also wrote that it has to be confirmed by the new parliament, the Federal Assembly."[28]

In October Yeltsin also made up his mind to couple the elections with a referendum on a new constitution. He ordered his staff to put the final touches on a made-to-measure document he could submit to the people. That document, when it was unveiled in November, outlined an even more powerful presidential regime than the version he had introduced in June. The president would name the prime minister and his ministers "with the agreement" of the lower house, the Duma. If the Duma refused his choice of prime minister three times, he could dissolve the parliament. If the Duma voted no-confidence in his government twice within three months the president would have the option of dismissing the government or dissolving the legislature. Budget and tax measures could only be introduced by the cabinet, over which the president presided. In an emergency, he would have the power to rule alone. Impeachment of the president would be theoretically possible, but so complicated as to be almost unthinkable.[29]

This constitutional draft was also notable for what it omitted. Entirely eliminated was the Federation Treaty, signed just a year earlier by the central government and the eighty-eight Russian provinces and republics, which had granted to them a large measure of autonomy. In 1990 Boris Yeltsin had travelled around Russia, campaigning against Mikhail Gorbachev and the Kremlin and gathering support in the provinces and republics with the famous slogan "take as much sovereignty as you can." Now, abruptly, he was turning his back on the federalism he had fervently preached and restoring Russia to the status of a unitary state dominated by one man.

Like Mikhail Gorbachev before him, Yeltsin was looking for inspiration in a golden age of the past. It was "The Russia We Have Lost," as the title of a recently released documentary film put it. This was the Russia of Nicholas II, seen in nostalgic glow, a country whose economy had been growing rapidly under the benevolent, if autocratic leadership of the czar, who ruled with the advice and consent of a subservient Duma. In unveiling his draft, Yeltsin made no secret of his inspiration. "I don't deny the powers of the president in the draft are considerable," he said in an interview with *Izvestiia*. "But what did you expect in a country that is used to czars and strong leaders?"[30]

Twelve days after the storming of the White House, in the auditorium in Moscow's House of Cinema, ten minutes by foot from the blackened hulk of the parliament, a political convention was about to begin. Russia's Choice was holding its first convention.

With the aid of American image-makers and political consultants, the scene had been set. Above the stage hung an enormous party emblem, an equestrian Peter the Great, in looming silhouette, framed by the words "Liberty, Legality, Property." The stage itself was decorated with painted backdrops of Kremlin towers and Orthodox crosses and onion domes. A carillon of church bells, a Russian choir singing a patriotic lament and finally a wordless film, accompanied by swelling music, which showed the triumph of Russia and its flag over the Soviet Union and the hammer and sickle, constituted the solemn inauguration of the new party.

In the front rows sat the cream of the young elite that had presided over the rocky course of reforms: members of the president's staff, vice-premiers and ministers, former deputies from Democratic Russia, and the Interregional Group. These men and women believed that they were the present and future party of power. Like the czar on their emblem, they had opened a window on the West, but they wished the world to know their roots were firmly Russian. Their leader was Yegor Gaidar, the former prime minister and now deputy premier, and their organizer was Gennadi Burbulis.

Their speeches stressed that a new page in Russian history and politics was being written. Their party represented a decisive break with the Communist past, which had been finally defeated on 4 October. Now they underlined the need for discipline, unity, and honesty with the voters. Gaidar, in particular, insisted on the need for honesty: only by further slashing government subsidies to industry and agriculture – the Communist cushions which had smothered initiative – could Russia's economic transformation be completed.

But the reality of their party was, in many ways, a continuation of the recent past, not a break with it. The first indication of this was the absence of one man – Boris Yeltsin. Russia's Choice had been set up as a "presidential party" and Yeltsin had agreed to make the opening address to the convention. But, literally at the last minute, he had backed out, sending instead his chief of staff, Sergei Filatov, to speak on his behalf. Yeltsin could not abandon the role of the charismatic lone leader, above parties and political organizations.

Russia's Choice itself was already racked by divisions. The chief of these was between the presidential group and the populists. The presidential group was composed of ministers such as Gaidar and men in the president's office. Their distrust of the populists, most of them former deputies and leaders of Democratic Russia, was evident. They were undisciplined and stained by association with the disgraced parliament. The presidential group manoeuvred to reduce radically their representation at the convention and on the party's election list.[31] The populists were furious and threatened to walk out. Only a last-minute deal, brokered by Gaidar, kept Russia's Choice from splitting open even before it had held its first convention.

The leaders of Russia's Choice had called for unity and discipline. But the Yeltsin model charted another path. It would now wreak havoc in the "democratic" camp. In the election campaign, each powerful figure in that camp opted to form his own tiny political party. The roll-call of names was bewildering: Shakhrai, Sobchak, Yavlinsky, Travkin, Popov. Each had played his role in the ferment of the past five years. Now none would submit to the leadership of Gaidar or any other. Each saw himself as the Yeltsin of his political generation.

The result was that, of the thirteen parties finally allowed on the
12 December ballot, five were from the Yeltsin camp. All proceeded
to compound their error by running inept campaigns. In part this
was due to lack of money; in much larger measure it was due to
the belief – propagated in Moscow and abroad – that, with the old
parliament swept away, the democrats merely had to wait for the
voters to demonstrate their gratitude.[32]

And so these men sat in Moscow. Their campaigns consisted of
press conferences and television interviews. Candidates in the provinces reported they had no contact with the central headquarters
of Russia's Choice, nor was any money allocated to them. Candidates who adhered to the themes laid down by Gaidar discovered
their pitfalls. "People blame the government for all their hard-
ships," said Anatoli Shabad, running as a Russia's Choice candidate
in a riding outside Moscow. His message of more subsidy cuts to
come was unpalatable. "It's difficult to explain that it's bad with
Gaidar's reforms, but without them it would be much worse."[33]
After three years when, according to the government's own statistics, national output had dropped by 38 per cent and the number
of people living below the poverty line had risen to 30 per cent,
the voters were looking for a message to allay their fears and stoke
their hopes.[34]

Other parties were ready to provide it. Leaders of the Communist
Party and their close allies, the Agrarians, travelled the country,
evoking nostalgia for an empire lost and promising to restore the
security of the past.

And then there was Vladimir Zhirinovsky. He entered the campaign regarded condescendingly by the Kremlin as the mad clown
of Russian politics. He had been little heard of since the summer
of 1991, when he had finished a surprising third in the Russian
presidential elections and then had stood in the foyer of the Palace
of Congresses during the last Soviet parliamentary session, threatening the Baltic states with clouds of nuclear pollution, blown by
huge fans from Russia, if they tried to secede. He had taken no
part at all in the confontation between the Russian parliament and
president. Instead he had criss-crossed the country, speaking to
voters, building his Liberal Democratic Party.

Now all that would turn to his advantage. Zhirinovsky presented
himself as the new man, unstained by a Communist Party past or
by association with the bloody events of October. He was a brilliant
television campaigner, dominating the political debate with bizarre

wit and simple solutions. His history of the Communist state as sexual politics, delivered in one of his first free-time television broadcasts, was talked about for days. The Bolshevik takeover had been revolutionary orgasm, Leninism had been rape. Life under Brezhnev had been masturbation, and under Gorbachev – coitus interruptus.

He did not disguise his chauvinism or racism. He railed against foreign "pollution" on the airwaves and promised, if elected, to ban advertisements for Western candy bars and chewing gum. He also promised that only pure blond announcers, with kind blue eyes, would read the news on television. This was a barely veiled reference to what Zhirinovsky described as the "fact" that Jews exercised influence out of all proportion to their numbers in Russia. He promised a return of huge state subsidies to industry to put people to work. He promised cheap vodka. But above all, he preached the politics of resentment, of humiliation, and the dream of restored greatness.

Almost until the end of the campaign, the Yeltsin government encouraged him in this. Alone of the political leaders, he was offered paid television time on credit. The reason for such encouragement was that Zhirinovsky vociferously backed Yeltsin's constitutional draft. It was not until the final three days of the campaign, when government polls showed Zhirinovsky's party surging into the lead, that the Kremlin panicked and tried to reverse course. Government spokesmen warned, once again, of the danger of fascism. A documentary harshly critical of Zhirinvosky was hurriedly programmed on Ostankino Television. It only served to give him more exposure and consolidate his support.

On election night Zhirinovsky's Liberal Democratic Party list took almost 23 per cent of the vote. Russia's Choice limped home with just over 15 per cent. The Communists and the Agrarians together took 20 per cent. The other "democratic" parties lagged far behind.

It had been confidently planned as a Kremlin victory party for Yeltsinian democracy. Party leaders and the political elite were invited to a televised celebration on election night inside the fortress where they and the nation could watch the returns. But the first results from the Russian far east showed Zhirinovsky pulverizing Russia's Choice. Smiles on the faces of government leaders congealed. Abruptly, the flow of returns dried up, apparently on orders from presidential advisers. Then the Kremlin spokesman declared, on the basis of "unofficial" returns and long before many ballots had been counted, that Yeltsin's constitutional draft had been adopted. Having declared constitutional victory, he walked out.

The image that would remain with viewers was of Vladimir Zhirinovsky, gulping champagne, toasting his rivals and grinning wolfishly.

CHAPTER THIRTEEN

Russia Returns to Its Roots

Vladimir Zhirinovsky entered protesting. His theme was humiliation. The scene was Moscow's Metropol hotel, just outside the Kremlin walls. In 1918, when Lenin moved the revolutionary government from Petrograd to Moscow, it became home to Bolshevik Politburo members. Now, renovated by the Finns, it was the most luxurious business palace in the Russian capital.

"English, only English!" Zhirinovsky was shouting in the lobby as he took off his coat, surrounded by five aides and bodyguards. "All the signs here are in English! This is outrageous. This is Russia. There must be Russian! Change it!" All this at the top of his voice, addressed to no one in particular. Startled hotel guests looked up as he and his retinue swept by.

The leader of the party with the largest number of votes in Russia's 1993 legislative elections had taken to holding court in the dining room of the Metropol. This was the man who had threatened the Baltics with nuclear pollution, the United States with nuclear war. Now he issued more threats and judgments. When he, Vladimir Zhirinovsky, came to power, Yegor Gaidar, the man who had launched Russia's reforms, risked prison ("we'll begin criminal investigations!") He brushed aside accusations that he was an authoritarian fascist; he believed in pluralism. But in the next breath he said his plan, on coming to power, was to suspend all parties for one year "to clean up the mess."

Any question launched a monologue; it was a performance and the performer understood well its impact. "You have to make noise if you want to get a reaction from Russians! Look at the others, the so-called democrats. They played by the rules, they were polite. And where are they? I'm glad people in the West are worried.

Russians have been humiliated. It does them good to see the West reacting with fear, not condescension."

The head waiter arrived. He had been personally serving Zhirinovsky. Now he whispered that in this hotel, where the richest and most powerful from the West stayed, 90 per cent of the staff had voted for him. Could he, in turn, autograph copies of his autobiography, *The Last Push to the South*, for them? For Vladimir Zhirinovsky, it would be a pleasure.[1]

The book is a mirror of the man. Zhirinovsky enters his autobiography shouting and protesting. "I am Vladimir Zhirinovsky. My name is Russian – Vladimir!" There follow, in the first three pages, no fewer than fifteen more references to his "Russianness." But his is the Russianness of the colonizers, the Russians of Kazakhstan, who built the capital Alma-Ata, and now in the post-Soviet world, are dispossessed. "For some reason Russians are not allowed to keep their state where they were born and grew up, where their ancestors died, where they built their city." A tone and a theme have been established.[2]

The early pages of this life contain a distinct, if distorted, echo of the autobiography of Boris Yeltsin. Like Yeltsin, Zhirinovsky believed himself set apart by fate from birth. Like Yeltsin, he underlined that he was alone from the start. The boy would grow up to be a political rebel, and, as with Yeltsin, a catalyst would be unjust treatment by a teacher in school. In the ninth grade he was stripped of his post as Komsomol (Communist Youth) class representative by a teacher who turned on him because she realized he was too independent. (She was, Zhirinovsky writes, a Jew who russified her name.)

"It was perhaps from this moment that I went into 'opposition'. I didn't like her authoritarian style." But the tone of heroic adventure and struggle which permeates Yeltsin's book is wholly absent in Zhirinovsky's. This is rather a catalogue of persecution and injustice, of a life "filled with wounds from childhood and hostility on every side." At the end he spells out the message plainly. "Ours was the fate of the whole nation: a people uprooted by revolution and war, constantly being pushed, moved from Europe to Asia. A whole nation in a cart, squeaking down rutted roads, throughout the century. Every family was split and broken. How many people were lost, destroyed. And how well we had lived at the beginning of the century!"[3]

This was the message of shared suffering and resentment he was to hammer home in his election campaign: "I am one of you. I am the very same as you!"

The headquarters of the Liberal Democratic Party were situated in Fisherman's Lane in central Moscow. The building was decrepit, the elevator broken. It was necessary to climb the steps past the store selling rock music and leather jackets set up by the party to the fourth floor. There, in the wake of his electoral success, Vladimir Zhirinovsky ruled like an autocrat in his tiny political kingdom. He would slouch in at noon, yelling orders and insults. Aides trailed obsequiously. His word was unquestioned. His party newspaper was called *Zhirinovsky's Truth*.

His office was vast and lit like a stage set. Spotlights highlighted icons, flags (the czar's imperial banner, the flag of St George, the patron saint of Russia) and the desk of the party leader. Above it hung a stylized map of "Zhirinovsky's Russia." It included a chunk of Poland, Finland ... and Alaska.

In the outer office reporters and television crews waited like supplicants to receive the summons. Inside, Zhirinovsky unveiled his vision. It was the vision already outlined in *The Last Push to the South*. "I see Russian soldiers gathering for this last march south," he wrote. "I see submarines surfacing in the Indian ocean and fleets of ships offshore. Soldiers of the Russian army and masses of tanks will converge on this final shore."[4] The final shore, for Zhirinovsky, was India.

This push, Zhirinovsky writes, is necessary "for the salvation of the Russian nation. Other parties which talk of cutting the links with Kazakhstan, Khirghizia, and Central Asia don't understand that we would be locking Russia into the tundra which only has mineral resources. Nothing can live and develop there."

The result of this enormous expansion of the empire would be to usher in a golden age of peace. Russia would have room and good relations with its new neighbours. "Hostility would cease forever."[5] Humiliation, the terror of his childhood in an outpost of the Russian empire, would be exorcized for the entire Russian nation.

It was a vision which appealed to thirteen million voters in the elections. At least one-third of the soldiers and officers in the Russian army, according to statistics supplied to Boris Yeltsin himself, voted for Zhirinovsky.[6] Opinion surveys showed that one-third of his supporters were men between twenty-five and forty, men who were educated and resentful. Oleg Karpenko was typical. He was thirty, a former army officer who set up a small but prosperous trading business in Volgograd. In December 1993 he voted for Zhirinovsky. In January 1994 he and a friend set up the Volgograd branch of the Liberal Democratic Party.

"I simply found it shameful what was happening to my country," he said. "Russia must rise again. Never in its history did Russia lose a war and now, without any war, it's been chopped into little pieces. Now all those little politicians want to be czars in their little republics. There should be one Great Russia, like before."[7]

Sergei Abaltsev had once served in the Soviet special forces. He looked the part. At thirty-four he was built like a bouncer tailored in an expensive suit. He had a head like a football, with hair shaved to a stubble. His hobby was collecting priceless historical icons. He was the vice-chairman of a giant commercial, and formerly collective, farm just outside Moscow. He was also a deputy elected on Zhirinovsky's list, the man the leader had named his shadow security minister. In his office, under the benign gaze of a Byzantine Virgin Mary, he outlined the Zhirinovsky vision of order.

"We'll rewrite the laws and ban political parties. Then we'll strike such a blow that we'll break the backbone of organized crime in Russia. And we'll erect a monument on Dzerzhinsky Square in front of the KGB building – a monument commemorating the last criminal in Russia. And everyone will say an enormous thank-you to us for freeing Russia from the filth that the false democrats brought with them."[8]

The restoration of the empire and the brutal eradication of crime: these were issues that touched the nerve of uncertainty and fear among Russians. The historian of Stalinism, Roy Medvedev, said Zhirinovsky's achievement was to integrate the message and the man. "Exploiting the cult of personality has always brought political advantages here. The focus has always been on the leader, not the party: Lenin, Stalin, Brezhnev, Gorbachev: there were cults for all of them, even for Yeltsin. Zhirinovsky simply seized on this tendency."[9]

In his book, Zhirinovsky describes himself as "an artist," designing his ideas, creating possibilities, seeking an audience.[10] The artist was also an outsider who never joined the Communist Party, despite the difficulties this caused him. He was, he writes, relegated to a lesser caste, that of the non-party member.[11]

There is much evidence that Zhirinovsky's autobiography is, in large part, a creation of his "artistic" mind. The man who so vehemently protested his Russianness and who so frequently criticized the vast and perfidious influence of Jews in Russia was, perhaps, the son of a Jew. A birth certificate unearthed by reporters in Alma-Ata indicated that his father was Wolf Eidelshtein, whom his mother had married five months earlier.[12] Zhirinovsky denied this, saying it was a fabrication of the Kazakh authorities to discredit him.

Zhirinovsky suggests in his book that he gained entry into the Institute of Oriental Languages in Moscow on intellectual merit alone. He offers no explanation for his assignment to Georgia during his period of compulsory military service, where he worked as a propaganda officer in the Transcaucacus Military Staff Political Directorate, nor for his eight-month posting to Turkey in 1969.

Oleg Kalugin was a senior officer in the KGB in this period. He eventually rose to the rank of general before leaving the service in 1990 and publicly denouncing its abuses. Kalugin said KGB sources told him that, far from being an outsider and a man alone, Zhirinovsky was recruited while a student to do low-level work for military counter-intelligence, the Third Directorate of the KGB.[13]

Zhirinovsky writes that it was his decision not to join the Communist Party. Yet his superior at the state legal agency where he worked in the 1970s and 1980s remembered that Zhirinovsky applied to join the party and was turned down. He was considered dangerously undisciplined.[14]

Zhirinovsky's political chance came at a time of gathering political collapse. In April 1991, with Boris Yeltsin having pushed through the Russian Congress the principle of presidential elections, Mikhail Gorbachev and the Soviet leadership drew up a strategy to stop him. They would encourage and help as many candidates as possible to try to force Yeltsin into a second, runoff round by depriving him of 50 per cent of the vote. Zhirinovsky was one of the first to benefit from that decision. On 12 April his Liberal Democratic Party was officially registered, despite the fact that it had had only 146 official members.[15] According to Roy Medvedev, then a member of the Central Committee of the Communist Party, Zhirinovsky was invited to meet one of Gorbachev's most senior advisers, the speaker of the Soviet parliament, Anatoli Lukyanov, and his aides. He also met the head of the KGB, Viktor Kryuchkov.

His posters, leaflets, and program were all printed by the Communist Party publisher on the presses of *Pravda*.[16]

In the end, however, help from hidden friends could only advance Zhirinovsky so far. He had not succeeded in gathering the ten thousand signatures he needed to be placed on the presidential ballot. The only other route was to obtain the support of 20 per cent of the deputies of the Russian Congress. He petitioned parliament to plead his case. Three weeks before the 12 June vote he was allowed to speak to the Congress. According to Roy Medvedev, who was there, he gave a good speech, restrained, moderately populist in tone and devoid of anti-communist slogans. In reply to a question about his KGB links, he gave an evasive answer. His candidacy was supported by 477 deputies.[17]

In the election three weeks later, his promise of simple solutions and his mastery of television won him 6.2 million votes – 8 per cent of the participating electorate.

Ironically, in the 1994 election campaign Boris Yeltsin would, in his turn, offer hidden help to Zhirinovsky. His party this time would win 23 per cent of the vote, humiliating Yeltsin's declared allies.

The word *samozvanets* in Russian means both pretender and impostor. It describes a phenomenon with a long and colourful tradition in Russian history, the periodic appearance of so-called false Dmitris – rebels claiming to be the incarnation of lost or murdered czars. The power of these rebels sometimes threatened to topple the leadership of the state.

In 1994 Vladimir Zhirinovsky had become a modern-day *samozvanets*. As the "artist" of his own life, he had ignored the facts while recreating himself in the leadership mould of Boris Yeltsin, that of the charismatic Russian man alone, harping on the theme of the abasement of a whole people and proposing drastic yet simple solutions to complex problems.

The first days of the Russian State Duma suggested that Russian legislators, like Bourbon kings, had learned nothing and forgotten nothing. Vladimir Zhirinovsky swept into the building on opening day like a conquering hero, leading a legion of journalists and admirers and taking his seat at the head of his parliamentary delegation of sixty-four deputies.

Almost immediately the wrangling and recriminations began. Because of the vagaries of the new electoral system – with each voter casting two ballots, one for a party list and one for his choice of local deputy – Zhirinovsky's party had won far more votes than any other, but fewer seats than Russia's Choice. The bulk of Russia's Choice deputies had been elected as local members, propelled into office by their reputation or local position as a Yeltsin-appointed administrator. The result was that the caucus of Russia's Choice counted seventy-six members, twelve more than Zhirinovsky's group.

The other main groups were the Communists with forty-five seats and the Agrarians with fifty-five. These last two were, in fact, two wings of the same political party. There were also sixty-five deputies elected independently who banded together to form a deputies' group called New Regional Policy. They were, for the most part, local barons, most of them former members of the Communist Party of the Soviet Union. There followed four other parties, each with between fifteen and thirty members in the Duma. Three of these offered conditional support to the course of economic reform while proclaiming that it had been implemented too brutally. Thus the new Duma was composed of nine political groupings, plus forty-seven independent members for a total of 444. Only seventy-three of the deputies had been members of the Russian or Soviet Congresses but their influence was out of proportion to their numbers; they formed the leadership group of almost every faction except Zhirinovsky's.[18]

It quickly became apparent there was no working majority, even to deal with procedural issues. The opening day of the Duma was marked by long arguments about how to elect the new speaker while the assembly's oldest member and by this fact the man presiding, a Zhirinovsky deputy named Georgi Lukava, tried ineffectually to direct the debate. By the end of the day more and more deputies were demanding publicly that he be replaced. Suddenly Zhirinovsky stood up and demanded the floor for the first time. "Turn off all the microphones in the hall! Let no one approach the podium! No one leaves this hall, no one is going anywhere until these questions are decided!"[19]

This speech created an instant uproar which increased dramatically when Zhirinovsky's deputy dutifully tried to implement his leader's orders. The effect was only to add to the atmosphere of confusion and carnival which Zhirinovsky seemed to revel in.

Two days later, at the Duma's second session, his caucus nominated Zhirinovsky for the post of speaker. His speech was a triumph of provocation. "In every other country of the world the leader of the party with the most votes becomes the speaker of parliament or the head of government. But we're still taking our first (parliamentary) steps. In 1917 we went to grade one, now we're in grade two. But the rest of the world is in university! On one side of this chamber there are a lot of candidates for psychiatric examination," he said, pointing at deputies from Russia's Choice. "You are waging war on Russia!"

With that he withdrew his candidacy for the job of speaker. "I will wait for the election for the Russian presidency. Then I'll have a little talk with you again."[20]

It captured the headlines, but the speech of another candidate for speaker illustrated more graphically the road travelled since the days of excitement and optimism in the first Soviet Congress of May 1989. The candidate was Yuri Vlasov, a former Olympic weight-lifting gold medallist. At the first Soviet Congress it was he who, in a speech everyone remembered, had named the crimes of the KGB and called for its destruction. Now, less than five years later, he denounced the democrats who had dismantled the Communist machine and its secret police apparatus. They had led the country to brink of civil war. "I spoke out against the hold of the Communist nomenklatura on the country," he said, "but when the democrats disposed of the nomenklatura, they immediately set about to break up Russia. I never agreed to smash Russia and I will speak out against you and I will fight you with all my power to prevent this."[21]

The divisions in the new Duma promised to be as sharp as in the old Congress. The election of the speaker seemed to provide further proof. Vlasov narrowly lost to Ivan Rybkin, who had been a leader of the Communist group in the Russian Congress and had remained in the White House until the last day of the siege. His principal proposal in his nomination speech was for an immediate amnesty of Khasbulatov, Rutskoi, and the other parliamentary leaders in jail. The deputies of Russia's Choice tried to block his election by abstaining to prevent him obtaining half the votes of all sitting members, as required by the rules. His victory was assured when Zhirinovsky ordered his deputies to vote for Rybkin, and Russian commentators concluded that an unofficial coalition of Zhirinovsky's group, the Communists, and the Agrarians would dominate the lower house.[22] To complete the tableau of tumult,

Zhirinovsky got into a fist fight in the parliamentary cafeteria with a deputy from Gaidar's faction, Russia's Choice.

The same week the upper house, the Federation Council, elected a close political ally of Yeltsin and a former deputy premier, Vladimir Shumeiko, to the post of speaker. Shumeiko immediately declared that his election meant that Yeltsin could ignore the Duma if it disintegrated into a political battleground. The upper house, he said, would take care of passing legislation needed to underpin Yeltsin's reforms.[23] That completely ignored the constitution which had come into effect just one month before. By its terms, the upper house could initiate almost no legislation. Its function was to review bills initially passed by the Duma.

The consequences were clear, at least to some. The prime minister, Viktor Chernomyrdin, had studied the election results and was working to reshape his policies and his team to accommodate the nationalists and the Communists. Both groups were demanding less reform and more protection for the state sectors of the economy. For Chernomyrdin, a former Soviet bureaucrat and minister of the state natural gas complex, this was a course he found easy to endorse. He announced that the era of market romanticism was over. Within days Yegor Gaidar and other reformers had resigned from the government. Gaidar wrote in his letter of resignation, "I cannot be in the government and in opposition to it."[24] Other reformers, like Finance Minister Boris Fyodorov, left predicting economic catastrophe by the fall.

Boris Yeltsin seemed curiously unconcerned. As he and his aides saw it, he now had a tailor-made constitution which allowed him to rule while virtually ignoring parliament. In the three months since smashing the former parliament, he had issued 934 decrees. Despite his promise, several of these decrees – including those on land, privatization, the budget, and the overhaul of the tax system – had altered or set fundamental policy without reference to parliament. One of Yeltsin's legislative aides, Igor Bezrukov, stated the Kremlin's position with no attempt at diplomacy. "It's practically impossible to overcome the president. Under the new constitution the parliament should know its place."[25]

In his speech marking the opening of the new parliament on 11 January, Yeltsin had proclaimed, "Russia returns to its roots, and restores its lost traditions." The roots and traditions he was referring to appeared to be those of the period of Nicolas II, when the czar treated the Duma he had been forced to create with disdain. Yeltsin signalled his attitude towards the new Duma by refusing to address it. At the last minute his office announced he would speak only to the upper house, the Federation Council, half of whose members were appointed, many by him personally. His prime minister was sent to address the Duma.

There were other obvious signs of the president's lack of respect. The new Duma was housed in the former mayoralty building which bore the scars of the October attack. On some floors wrecked furniture still lay in corridors. The winter wind blew in through windows where plate glass had been shattered by gunfire and not replaced. Deputies dodged debris as they looked for empty offices in which to meet. The Communist Party leader complained that his caucus of forty-five members had neither an office nor a phone. Meanwhile squads of Turkish workers had worked around the clock for three months with specially-imported materials to restore the Russian White House, at a cost of $100 million. On 4 January 1994 it officially became the new home of the Russian prime minister and his cabinet.[26]

The deputies responded to this scarcely concealed contempt with a grand gesture of defiance. On 23 February a large majority voted to grant a complete amnesty to the leaders of the Congress, including Alexander Rutskoi and Ruslan Khasbulatov, who had been awaiting trial in Lefortovo prison since the storming of the White House on 4 October 1993. The resolution had been sponsored by the Communist caucus and by Vladimir Zhirinovsky, who arrived for the session in the dress uniform of an army captain. He was, he said, marking Russian Army day. The vote was 252 to 67 and was greeted by a standing ovation by the deputies. Late on the afternoon of 26 February Rutskoi and other imprisoned parliamentary leaders strode out of prison to be greeted by two hundred cheering supporters. A few minutes later Zhirinovsky arrived to share the spotlight and to announce the amnesty was the first step towards restoring social peace.

That was not how Yeltsin's men saw it. His press secretary declared the vote a challenge to Russian democracy. "The Communists and the Zhirinovskiites have discovered a total unity of purpose: to take power through destabilization." Their fury was all the greater because on the day after the amnesty vote Yeltsin was scheduled to deliver his first State of the Union address to a joint session of the new parliament. Its impact was all but submerged by the controversy over the amnesty. Statesmanlike, Yeltsin made no mention of the vote in his speech.

But behind the scenes his aides worked furiously to prevent the release of Yeltsin's enemies. Their pressure tactics blew up in their faces when, hours before Rutskoi and the others were set free, the Russian state prosecutor, Alexei Kazannik, angrily resigned. He said he'd come under great pressure from Yeltsin and his men to subvert the constitution and simply ignore the amnesty vote. He had refused.[27]

The day after his political enemies walked free Yeltsin dismissed the minister of security, Nikolai Golushko. According to the Russian news agency ITAR-TASS, he was fired for failing to foresee the amnesty and for failing to prevent the prisoners' release.

The failure was, however, almost entirely the fault of the president's office, according to a Yeltsin ally in the Duma. Viktor Sheinis had sided with the president in the October confrontation and had worked on a presidential legislative commission preparing the legal groundwork for the new parliament before the December elections. He pointed out that the Kremlin had had ample warning. A first amnesty vote on 12 February had failed to rally a majority of deputies. "If Yeltsin's advisers had collaborated properly with the parliament, if they had held discussions with deputies, if they had tried to persuade them, there never would have been a majority in favour of the amnesty. The saddest thing in this is the obvious indecision, weakness, and lack of organization displayed by the executive branch."[28]

But predictions of a new period of confrontation between the president and the parliament did not come to pass and this for several reasons. The physical destruction of the Russian Congress in October 1993 loomed large in the memory of all deputies, as did the provisions in the new constitution giving the president wide latitude to dissolve the Duma and hold early elections, notably if the deputies directly challenged the government by passing a vote of no-confidence.

The Duma was also severely fractured politically. By the spring of 1994 there were not nine, but ten factions sitting in the Duma. The former finance minister, Boris Fyodorov, had split with the former prime minister, Yegor Gaidar, and had left the Russia's Choice faction to form his own group in the lower house, the Liberal Democratic Union. But although split, the reformist democrats could block most measures they fundamentally disagreed with. They were helped by the rule in Russia's parliaments that, to pass, any measure had to have the majority of all elected members. That meant at least 223 members of the Duma. As a united block the Communists, the Agrarians, and their allies from the New Regional Policy could only pool about 155 votes. Even in concert with Zhirinovsky's party they didn't have a clear majority.

The grind of parliamentary politics and the political spotlight soon proved unhelpful to Zhirinovsky. His trips abroad were carnivals. He was thrown out of Croatia. In Finland he visited strip clubs, trailed by photographers. In France, in front of the European parliament, he threw mud at demonstrators. In Moscow in April his party held a convention. It opened with a parade onstage of "Zhirinovsky's Falcons," a squad of young men in blue uniforms and black boots, each with a pistol strapped to his military belt. Guests were introduced: a German neo-fascist, a delegation from Iraq's Saddam Hussein. Zhirinovsky spoke: "The leader and the party are one and the same! The regime is in its final agony and when a sick man is lying on the operating table, you need a single doctor, not a team of consultants." The delegates voted, without a dissenting voice, to make him leader and virtual dictator of the party, with total control over finances and appointments, for the next ten years. The evidence suggested this disturbed and frightened Russians. A survey of fifteen hundred people by the Russian Centre for Public Opinion and Market Research in March 1995 showed that 63 per cent said they didn't trust Zhirinovsky.[29] By June six members of his parliamentary caucus had announced they were quitting. Half a dozen others talked of doing the same thing in disgust at his autocratic, unpredictable ways.

Despite Zhirinovsky, the new Duma was less anarchic than its predecessor. Most of the deputies had been elected as members of political parties now sitting in the legislature and party discipline was apparent. Issues were discussed in caucus and most votes went along party lines. This assembly was no longer a "mob" which could be stampeded in one direction or another by impassioned speeches from the podium.

Nor was there to be a repeat of the systematic flouting of rules of procedure to slip through controversial resolutions which had characterized the Russian Congress. The Council of the Duma, representing all factions and chaired by the new speaker, decided procedural questions and drew up the agenda for the assembly. Detailed discussion of bills took place in committees. The full Duma met only twice a week for more wide-ranging debates on legislation. The result, according to deputies from almost every faction, was a far more competent and professional parliament.[30] Working this way, the Duma drew up and passed a new criminal code for Russia within a year. The problem was that the state bureaucracy, taking its cue from the president, simply ignored many legislative measures.

The new legislative competence was due, in large measure, to the speaker, Ivan Rybkin. Despite his experience as a Communist faction leader in the Russian Congress, or rather because of it, he declared after his election that the Duma must not repeat the errors of the previous parliament. His task was "to restore the continuity of Russian parliamentary democracy." He had studied Russian history and knew how difficult that would be.

I read the memoirs of the speaker of the last Duma under the czar, Mikhail Rodzianko. On the second page there is a photograph of him speaking at the podium surrounded by several deputies, all standing and shaking their fists at him. It's the Russian mentality. Of the five chairmen of the Dumas under the czar, two ended up in prison. There are a lot of similarities with today. The key is avoid the same outcome as in 1917.[31]

In conscious contrast to his predecessor, Ruslan Khasbulatov, Rybkin was studiously polite to all political factions. He proclaimed his intention and ability to work with Boris Yeltsin, whom he described as necessary for the consolidation of Russia's institutions. It was Rybkin who first advanced the idea of an Agreement on Civil Accord, a sort of political peace treaty for Russia. It was an idea seized upon by Yeltsin and his advisers and it led to a grandiose ceremony on 29 April in St George's Hall in the Kremlin. More than two hundred leaders of political parties, regions, and social organizations sat at long wooden tables waiting patiently to sign the document while Russian television broadcast the ceremony. Vladimir Zhirinovsky arrived for the ceremony with a bottle of "Zhirinovsky Vodka" under each arm. They were, he announced, gifts for the president. There were other bizarre touches. In its determination to demonstrate that all Russia was in favour of the document, the Kremlin invited almost anyone, from the Association of Private Detectives and the Seventh Day Adventists to the Union of Women of the Russian Navy, to sign. The agreement itself was little more than a collection of pious wishes accompanied by one commitment – not to press for early elections. Despite Rybkin's championing of the pact, the Communists and the Agrarians, the parties that had nominated him to the post of speaker, refused to sign. Nevertheless, Boris Yeltsin presented the document as a landmark in modern Russian history. "In signing this pact, we confirm that only peaceful, constitutional methods are permitted in Russian politics. It will not be easy to achieve. Confrontation still lives in our souls."[32]

The angry rejection of the agreement by the Communists, the Agrarians, and allies of the recently released Alexander Rutskoi seemed to confirm the truth of that last sentence. The rhetoric of refusal was extreme. "The thing called the Russian Federation is not a state, it is a backyard full of criminals and drug addicts," said Gennady Zyuganov, the Communist leader in the Duma. He described the leadership of Russia as "as half-mad people who describe themselves as democrats and drunkards who cannot control their own behaviour."[33]

Yet the gap between rhetoric and action was significant. In the twelve months after the elections for the Russian parliament the Duma had two occasions to take on the government directly. It ducked them both. In June, despite angry speeches of denunciation, a majority of the Duma approved the 1994 budget of relative austerity submitted by the government. In October, even after Black Tuesday when the rouble plunged 25 per cent against the American dollar in one day, the Duma debated but did not pass a motion of no-confidence in the government.

The man in the Kremlin was increasingly isolated and unpredictable, but his power continued to inspire fear among the legislators.

In the first week of May 1994 Boris Yeltsin published the second volume of his memoirs. The self-portrait contained in *The Memoirs of a President* bore little resemblance to that of the heroic rebel in his first book. One analyst wrote that it seemed to be an attempt to create a new genre of political memoir – "the president as victim."[34] It was, rather, the president as Prometheus. The mythical Greek hero had defied the gods by offering freedom in the form of fire to his people. As punishment he was chained to a rock by Zeus where his flesh was eaten by carrion birds. Yeltsin, too, now presented himself as the hero who had offered freedom to his people only to be pursued by the carrion birds of Russian politics.

The solitude of life at the summit was conveyed in tones of intense self-pity.

The debilitating bouts of depression, the grave second thoughts, the insomnia and headaches in the middle of the night, the tears and despair, the terrible sadness at the appearance of Moscow and other Russian cities, the flood of criticism from the newspapers and television every day, the harassment campaign at the Congress sessions, the entire burden of decisions taken, the hurt from people close to me who did not support me at the critical moment, who didn't stay the course, who deceived me – I have had to bear all of this.[35]

So many had betrayed him, so many had disappointed him. His vice-president, Alexander Rutskoi, had turned on him, his *eminence grise*, Gennadi Burbulis, had become so infatuated with power and its accoutrements that the sight of him had become unbearable.[36] His ministers, the deputies – almost all had failed him as he struggled to transform Russia, so long in the hands of usurpers, into a normal country. Nevertheless, his belief that he was destined, even divinely destined, to rule was, if anything, stronger. "To be Number One must be in my nature ... Everything unfolded as if some one or some force always came to my aid. I was obliged to believe that I had special protection."[37]

The populist who had once denounced the hidden privileges of the Communist elite now invited Russian television to follow him through his grandiose presidential villa. In this luxurious setting, when the interviewer bluntly asked if power had corroded or coarsened him, he answered: "If you're talking about the moral question concerning privileges, let's say that I'm much calmer about this than before. These things happen."[38]

Yeltsin was not in good shape. After two serious car accidents and a plane crash in the previous five years, he had serious back problems. He drank and disappeared from view for days, sometimes weeks at a time. Rumours of his drinking and depressions swirled through Moscow. The man deceived by so many former allies now relied on a tight little circle of advisers. Chief among them, by Yeltsin's own admission, was his bodyguard, General Alexander Korshakov. The president's praise for Korshakov was unstinting. "More than once I have called on him for advice. Thanks to his intelligence and his acute sense of observation I have come see many situations and problems in a new light."[39] Korshakov became a power in his own right, at the head of the presidential guard, a force of almost four thousand men by the end of 1994. In total disregard of the law, Korshakov ordered these soldiers to intervene against Yeltsin's adversaries, notably Most Bank, the majority owner of NTV, the first independent Russian television station whose news programs had displeased the president. On 2 December 1994 they raided Most Bank, carted off many files, and beat up its security guards. It was Korshakov, according to former chief prosecutor Alexei Kazannik, to whom aides now turned if they wanted a decision from the president.[40]

The absences, the rumours, the increasing dependence on Korshakov and the small core of loyal advisers, decrees issued and then cancelled – all this gave rise to speculation about a seriously weakened leader being manipulated by his entourage. "Everyone in the administration knows and says that if Korshakov wants, he can propose a draft decree," Kazannik said. "And Yeltsin, not reading it, will sign it."[41]

For most Russians, that called up memories of another aging and enfeebled leader, Leonid Brezhnev.

He was incapable of drafting the document himself. He said to me, "Just dictate what I should write." So of course I dictated it to him: "Instruction of the Politburo to prepare a draft decree..." He wrote what I had said, signed it, and gave me the piece of paper. In the last phase of his life Brezhnev had no idea what he was doing, signing or saying. All the power was in the hands of his entourage.

That description of Brezhnev in his political dotage was written by Yeltsin himself.[42]

The reality, in Boris Yeltsin's case, was much more complex. He was certainly diminished and distracted. As he himself admitted, in times other than those of crisis, he was detached to the point of negligence about the day-to-day administration of affairs.[43] But he was also a politician who had shifted ground dramatically before. Now, with the radical democrats out of favour and largely out of government and with Zhirinovsky's brand of neurotic nationalism on the rise, Yeltsin was shifting ground again.

His state of the nation speech to the parliament on 24 February 1994 showed the new direction he was taking.

Strengthening the state is a clear goal that can and must unite all Russian people at this dramatic moment...

A strong state is essential to fighting crime...

Russia is too dear to us in order to admit even the possibility of its disintegration.[44]

Yeltsin was transforming himself into an uncompromising neo-nationalist. There would be no quarter offered to criminals or separatists in the pursuit of a strong Russian state. In Yeltsin's new strategy, strengthening the state meant measures which flouted the Duma and his own constitution. Deputies discovered this when he issued a flurry of decrees in late May reducing tax exemptions for firms, reforming state enterprises, and cutting export quotas for raw materials. These were all decisions which should have been initiated or ratified by the Duma. The president's office defended the decrees by saying that the Duma wasn't working fast enough in the rapidly changing economic sector. Despite the clearly unconstitutional nature of the decrees, only 189 deputies – not even a majority – voted in favour of a resolution of protest.[45]

Two weeks later Yeltsin went much further. He published a draconian anti-crime decree. It contained provisions granting the police broad powers of search and seizure and stipulating that they could hold suspects up to thirty days without charge. This was in direct violation of Yeltsin's own constitution, which stated that no citizen could be held longer than forty-eight hours without being charged. Yeltsin was deaf to the protests of the deputies. The times demanded a general offensive against crime. Hadn't two deputies of the Duma already been murdered by hitmen for the many mafias in Moscow?

In the wake of the destruction of the Russian White House, opposition politicians had warned darkly that Boris Yeltsin was intent on creating what, in Russian, they called a *karmanniy* parliament – a parliament he could put in his pocket. Now the liberal democrats who had ardently supported a new constitution wondered aloud whether the fears they had dismissed just nine months earlier might not be justified.

On 27 May 1994, exactly five years after the first parliament in modern Russia opened, Alexander Solzhenitzyn returned to his homeland after twenty years in exile. He had stood alone against the Soviet regime which had punished him. He had confidently predicted that it would die before he did. Now the latter-day prophet bowed his head and touched the soil of Russia. But Solzhenitzyn's tone was not one of thanks or triumph. He had returned to denounce the rot in the state of Russia.

"We have chosen the most absurd, the most clumsy and the most destructive path for our people and our way of life. We must begin with repentance!"[46]

CHAPTER FOURTEEN

Confrontation Still Lives in Our Souls

On 11 December 1994 Boris Yeltsin issued an order to the Russian armed forces to enter the breakaway republic of Chechnya and pacify it. He then disappeared into hospital for ten days for what aides described as a nose operation. Seven months earlier he had said, "Confrontation still lives in our souls." He had meant it as a warning. His actions now transformed those words into a prophecy fulfilled.

Since its unilateral declaration of independence in 1991 the Chechen regime, under former Soviet airforce general Djhokar Dudayev, had refused all negotiations with Moscow. The Russian government accused Chechnya of being a renegade state, of protecting and encouraging criminal gangs across the country. In Russia the word "Chechen" became synonymous with "mafia." Moscow's aid to opposition groups in Chechnya could not topple Dudayev. A covert coup attempt, using undercover units of the Russian security services, failed miserably in November 1994 and two dozen Russian soldiers and officers were captured and displayed to the media. It was then that the decision to mount an invasion was announced.

As a military operation, the advance into Chechnya was a disaster. There had been no planning, no preparation – only the idle boast of the defence minister, Pavel Grachev, that two crack regiments could take the capital, Grozny, in three hours. Instead three weeks went by and the Russian army did not even enter Grozny. The army was torn by dissension. Senior generals, even the vice-minister of defence and the former commander of Soviet troops in Afghanistan, Boris Gromov, publicly criticized the offensive. On 31 December, according to Russia's most authoritative newspaper, the order was given to invade Grozny. The setting was a drunken birthday-New Year's party for Defence Minister Grachev. In the midst of revelry Grachev declared that the commander who seized the Chechen presidential palace would be decorated on the spot with three stars as a Hero of the Russian Army.[1]

The attack misfired catastrophically. Untrained recruits, many of whom had fired fewer than five rounds with a rifle in their lives, were sent on a mission of suicide. They were not even provided with maps of Grozny. They were slaughtered by Chechen fighters who mounted a well-armed, well-planned guerilla counter-attack. Dozens of Russian soldiers were cut down or burned alive in their tanks and armoured personnel carriers. In the panic to escape, their comrades left their bodies in the streets. Many soldiers died hours or days later in the winter snow and mud, their wounds untended and their cries unheard. Russians read about this and saw brutal images of carnage on Russia's first independent channel, NTV, and later on the second state channel. For the first time the Kremlin had launched a war with an unfettered press watching.

The Chechen presidential palace remained in the hands of Chechen fighters. In the basement bunker they continued to hold prisoner two dozen Russian officers and soldiers. In response to the international outcry over the indiscriminate aerial bombing of civilian targets in and around Grozny, Boris Yeltsin announced an end to the bombing on 4 January. His military commanders took no notice.

On 7 January, Russian Orthodox Christmas Day, the second offensive in Grozny began. One Russian military analyst said that the Russian army now relied on Stalingrad tactics, blasting all before it with heavy artillery before advancing slowly, street by street, house by house, through the devastated city.[2] By early February the dead numbered twenty-five thousand, almost all civilian casualties, according to Russian deputies who had travelled to Grozny to verify for themselves the sanitized version of events offered by the Kremlin.[3]

If the carnage in Chechnya showed the woeful inability of the Russian army, it also exposed the faultlines of Russia's fragile democratic institutions. The Duma held an emergency debate when Yeltsin ordered his troops to enter Chechnya in December. On 13 December, by a vote of 289 to four, the deputies passed a resolution criticizing the use of the army to handle the Chechnya problem. It urged the government to use "all available political and legal means" to resolve the conflict. The resolution was ignored. And with that, the lower house simply adjourned until the new year. Even radical democrats, now the fiercest critics of Yeltsin's military adventure, seemed resigned to parliament's passive role. "The Kremlin didn't listen to us. Once the war started there was nothing the Duma could do. So there was no point in sitting," Anatoli Shabad said.[4]

Yegor Gaidar, the man who once had been Yeltsin's prime minister and leading lieutenant, said the president refused even to listen to his criticisms. "I used to call the president's office and tell the secretary I wanted a word with him. He always returned the call within one, two or three hours. I called him when troops were sent to Chechnya and I'm still waiting for his call."[5]

As Yeltsin became increasingly remote, speculation and ever more bizarre stories about his behaviour filled the Russian press. "Believe me, Boris Nikolayevich, your fondness for liquor is a secret only to yourself," wrote Yegor Yakovlev, editor of the *Obshchaya Gazeta* and the man Yeltsin once named to run Russian state television.[6] He was referring to the president's escapades on the international stage. In Berlin, at ceremonies to mark the final withdrawal of Russian troops in September 1994, he stumbled down steps, loudly sang along with a children's choir, and grabbed the baton from the director's hand to conduct with gusto a military orchestra. In Shannon, Ireland, later the same month, his plane touched down on his return from Washington but Yeltsin did not emerge for an official lunch with the Irish prime minister. Yeltsin later blamed his aides for failing to wake him from a nap.

A leading Moscow daily, *Komsomolskaya Pravda*, revealed that one of Yeltsin's closest personal aides, Lev Sukhanov, had taken to organizing regular sessions with astrologists for the president. Sukhanov, reported the newspaper, "is serious about the importance of the other world and does not tolerate jokes on this matter."[7]

And, as the Chechnya crisis dragged on, *Izvestiia* blazoned the question of the influence of Yeltsin's bodyguard in its front page headline on 21 December 1994: "Who is running the country, Yeltsin, [Prime Minister] Chernomyrdin or General Korshakov?" It reported that Korshakov had taken to writing letters to Chernomyrdin demanding that the government protect Russian oil and gas resources from foreign invasion.[8]

"When bodyguards begin to set the government agenda, then the state is in trouble," said Vladimir Kvasov, a deputy in the Duma and a man who could confirm the enormous influence of Korsha-kov. For almost two years, in 1993 and 1994, he had been the prime minister's chief of staff in charge of 4,500 senior function-aries, and thus one of the most powerful civil servants in the country. His very power, Kvasov said, had incurred the wrath of Korshakov, as had his refusal to bow to suggestions from Kremlin advisers about policy.[9] In November 1994, at Korshakov's urging, Yeltsin signed a decree firing Kvasov as the prime minister's chief of staff.

Even Yeltsin's own chief of staff, Sergei Filatov, warned publicly of Korshakov's shadowy and growing power. Filatov said the head of the presidential guard had become a law unto himself. In the Kremlin the atmosphere was one of deepening paranoia, with political advisers convinced the president's security service was spying on them. "It is true that in my office some people are using pen and paper to communicate, for fear of talking out loud," Filatov said.[10]

As the Kremlin took on the trappings of a semi-monarchy, with access controlled and decisions determined by courtiers closest to the president, many radical democrat deputies reverted to the role first played by their predecessors in Mikhail Gorbachev's Soviet Congress – that of elected dissidents. Led by Sergei Kovalyov, a former prisoner in the gulag, a friend and acolyte of Andrei Sakharov, and the man appointed by Boris Yeltsin as Russia's human rights commissioner, a group of deputies travelled to Grozny in December 1994 to witness and to denounce the wanton excesses of the Russian military, and in particular the aerial bombardment of Grozny suburbs and Chechen villages.

In Moscow Yegor Gaidar, the leader of Russia's Choice, called for street demonstrations and demanded an emergency session of the Duma to take measures to stop the conflict. But the demon-strations were small, despite the fact that opinion polls showed a large majority of Russians opposed to the army's offensive. Political involvement no longer fired the enthusiasm of Russians; politics was something dirty and cynical, something to avoid.

Sergei Kovalyov returned from Chechnya to criticize in withering terms the invasion and the official version of events as recounted by the Kremlin, the defence minister, and the main channel of Russian state television. It was "lies, all lies."[11]

The next day Yeltsin heard a personal report from his human rights commissioner. He ignored it. Pavel Grachev later referred to

Kovalyov and other radical democrat deputies who had criticized the invasion as "the scum of the earth" and "slimy toads."[12]

For Galina Starovoitova, a democratic deputy in the first Soviet Congress and an adviser to Yeltsin in 1990–1, modern Russian history was repeating itself. "Yeltsin has removed himself from the democrats, he's finally in the camp of the nationalists. In his Security Council he praised the action of the army in Chechnya as disciplined and orderly. He can talk such nonsense only if he is deliberately being misinformed. That's exactly how the army and the security services isolated Gorbachev and Brezhnev."[13]

Gaidar and other radical democrats obtained the support of ninety-two members (just over the one-fifth necessary) to convene a special session of the Duma. Their goal now was to limit what they believed was the unchecked power of the president. To that end they had prepared a bill which would prohibit the use of the army within Russia's borders to deal with civil conflicts and a second bill to increase sharply the control power of parliament over the president.

But Starovoitova's suspicion was correct; Yeltsin had concluded a working alliance with the nationalists. On 10 January 1995 his prime minister met not with Yegor Gaidar but with Vladimir Zhirinovsky. And when the special session of the Duma opened the next day it was Zhirinovsky who quickly stood up to proclaim: "This is not a debate on the Chechnya crisis but on reinforcing the Russian state. The territorial integrity of Russia must be preserved!"

A few minutes later a Zhirinovsky deputy named Vladislav Marychev donned a military cap, hung a placard around his neck and asked to speak. The placard said "Hands off the army!" He demanded that Sergei Kovalyov be tried for slandering the army. Led by the Zhirinovsky faction, a large majority voted for an agenda which did not even include discussion of the bills proposed by Gaidar's group. In fact, almost all deputies believed that Chechnya was an integral part of the Russian Federation and had no right to leave. They had voted overwhelmingly in favour of a resolution stating that in December. And while the Communists and Centrists had criticized the way the Chechnya offensive had unfolded, they were not willing to condemn it. Thus the democrats found themselves isolated in opposition to the policies of the man they had once defended as the rampart of democracy in Russia.

Significantly, however, they refused to introduce a motion of no-confidence in the government. That refusal was born of fear. "Our choice now isn't between very good and the best," said Yegor Gaidar. "It's between the very bad and the worst." A successful no-confidence motion and the subsequent resignation of the government, Gaidar explained, could further destabilize the political situation in Russia and lead to outright authoritarian rule.[14]

And so the killing in Chechnya continued while the parliament stood by. On 19 January the Russian flag was finally raised over the shell of the Chechen presidential palace. Boris Yeltsin issued a statement declaring that the military operation was all but over. Weeks later Russian forces were still shelling and bombing suburbs and and villages around Grozny.

"The situation," Boris Yeltsin said on 9 February 1995, "is unfolding normally."[15]

In the ten years from 1985 Russia was transformed. It was a transformation dominated by two men and poisoned by their rivalry. Both Mikhail Gorbachev and Boris Yeltsin compared themselves to Peter the Great, the czar who set out to change his country, to modernize his government, and to open a window on the West at the beginning of the eighteenth century. Both established new parliamentary institutions but each man was as much a prisoner of his past as a herald of the future. They brought to their legislatures the Soviet style of command; decisions were imposed from above and recalcitrant deputies were browbeaten, or tricked into submission. Gorbachev and Yeltsin saw their creations principally as instruments to achieve their goals, to advance their power, and to humiliate their enemies. The collapse of the Soviet state and its consequences meant that the work of these parliaments almost always took place in an atmosphere of crisis. The rivalry of the two leaders was such that they did not hesitate to heighten the crisis by using their legislatures as weapons in their personal war for power. The result was to erode the legitimacy of parliamentary institutions in Russia.

In this Boris Yeltsin must bear a much larger share of responsibility. He proclaimed himself a rebel and a true democrat. Having ousted his rival and defeated and disbanded the Communist Party, he stood in the rubble of the Soviet Union with a unique opportunity to build a new political structure which would reflect his announced democratic ideals. Instead he proposed to Russia a leadership model where one man alone would make all important decisions, where compromise would be disdained and confrontation actively pursued. It was a recipe for political instability and violence. If Gorbachev's dislike of Yeltsin was intense and his wish to humiliate him clear, he stopped short of banishing him from political life when he had the opportunity. Yeltsin would show no such mercy to Gorbachev or other opponents. Even in retirement, Gorbachev excited his jealousy and anger. Aides reported that Yeltsin grew furious simply at the mention of his name. He ordered Gorbachev's passport seized temporarily in 1992. He deprived him of the limousine provided by the state and evicted his think tank from most of the offices originally provided by the Russian government. No humiliation was too small: in February 1995 he ordered the modest Volga sedan used by Gorbachev's bodyguards returned to the government. The message was evident: politics in Russia under Yeltsin remained a battle where no quarter would be given.

Surveying the political experiment they had helped launch six years earlier, many democrats still active in politics in 1995 were gloomily apocalyptic. "It's a tragedy for Russia," Galina Starovoitova said. "We have lost the historic battle for democracy in this country."[16]

"Some form of authoritarian power will be built up," Sergei Kovalyov said. "There will be a catastrophic widening of the gulf between the government and the people."[17]

"The future of our institutions is at risk," Anatoli Shabad said. "Yeltsin cannot win another democratic election."[18] Shabad and other radical democrats wondered openly if Yeltsin would therefore agree to hold a presidential election as scheduled in June 1996. That uncertainty and gloom was fed by an active campaign of rumours orchestrated by Kremlin aides about the possible declaration of emergency rule and the postponement of the presidential election.[19]

In his Duma office Vladimir Kvasov said talk of losing the battle for democracy missed the point. "Look at the people around the president in the Kremlin. They're all former Communist Party members. Most of them worked for the Central Committee. They continue to act just the same way." He started drawing on a piece of paper: two boxes, one above the other. The upper box, he said, was the old Central Committee and the lower box was the former Council of Ministers, the Soviet cabinet. "In the old days all the orders and all the pressure came from the Central Committee and the Council of Ministers simply obeyed. Now the top box is the presidential administration. And they operate in exactly the same way."[20]

In contrast to the gloomy politicians, television and newspaper editors in Moscow talked calmly, even derisively, of the men in the Kremlin. For the editors the conflict in Chechnya had been a war of sorts as well, a war they believed they had won. For the first time, despite threats of censorship and punishment, an independent press and an independent television channel had reported on a war waged by Russian troops from their point of view and not that of the government. NTV, Russia's first private television channel, was also the first Russian channel, and for ten days the only one, to send reports from Chechnya. It weathered a barrage of Kremlin criticism. Oleg Dobrodeyev was its managing editor. "Our history is tragic," he said, "but our present political leaders are simply tragi-comic. It's hard to take them seriously."[21]

The editor-in-chief of *Izvestiia*, Oleg Golembiovsky, offered a more nuanced judgment. "Yeltsin understands what free speech is, and what a market economy is, but not democracy as a whole. He makes decisions using communist methods."[22]

"Yeltsin has no core ideas and is dominated only by the search for power," said Sergei Markov, a professor of Russian politics at Moscow State University. "He is an excellent example of the post-totalitarian politician. He spent almost thirty years as a loyal Communist apparatchik. He became a socialist-populist, and then a free market democrat. And finally he began to transform himself into a Russian authoritarian nationalist, believing that was the surest way to keep power."[23]

The goal was to supplant Zhirinovsky as the chief spokesman of sullen Russian nationalism. Thus the newly bellicose attitude towards the West ("the Cold War is being replaced by a Cold Peace") and thus the war in Chechnya. As he evolved, Yeltsin retreated to his first circle of advisers who shared his authoritarian instincts. The atmosphere around him increasingly resembled that of the court of a nineteenth-century czar. But outside the Kremlin walls another dynamic was at work. Vigorous political dissidence first unleashed by Mikhail Gorbachev continued to flourish even in a weak parliament, and above all in a press unchained. The portrait was of two political systems co-existing schizophrenically in one society.

Of the four Russians who had launched and led the Interregional Group, the first democratic opposition in the Soviet Congress, only Boris Yeltsin remained active in politics. Andrei Sakharov was dead.

And Gavriil Popov and Yuri Afanasiev had retreated to the university world.

Popov had served as a member of Yeltsin's first presidential council and as the first elected mayor of Moscow. But as early as August 1992, just a year after the defeat of the putsch which had sought to restore traditional Soviet rule, Popov was warning that a false and dangerous illusion had taken root in Russia and the West: the illusion that the democrats had come to power in the Kremlin. "In fact we never took power. We found ourselves in a coalition (with the reformist wing of the senior state bureaucracy, the so-called nomenklatura). And in that coalition we would never be the leaders."

Yet in the heady, tumultuous months after the failed putsch it was difficult in Russia not to believe the illusion. Did not their leaders – men like Yegor Gaidar, Boris Fyodorov, Gennadi Burbulis, and Anatoli Chubais – hold the key economic posts in the Russian government? But, Popov wrote, they held nothing else. Real power remained in the hands of the state nomenklatura, now freed from the control of the Communist Party. The myth of the democrats in power was such that as inflation exploded, as corruption and crime festered, as trade with other republics of the former Soviet Union collapsed, it was the democrats who took the blame. In words which read like a blueprint for the next three years, Popov wrote in 1992: "As it spread the smokescreen of the democrats in power, the nomenklatura prepared to take formal as well as real control of the post-Communist transformation of Russia."[24]

Afanasiev echoed that analysis. The 1917 Bolshevik revolution, he believed, had frozen Russia in the shape of a pre-democratic society. The creation under Mikhail Gorbachev of parliamentary institutions had released decades of pent-up energy and enthusiasm but these institutions rested upon no concrete social foundation. "The basis for democracy in most countries is the middle classes, but we've never had them in Russia and we don't have them now. So democracy here begins and ends in our own feelings and ideas, but it doesn't have roots in the social structure and economy."[25]

The historian James Billington once offered this analysis of Russians' attempts to transform their society through the centuries:

Repeatedly, Russians have sought to acquire the end products of civilizations without the intervening process of slow growth and inner understanding. Russia took the Byzantine heritage en bloc without absorbing its traditions of orderly philosophic discourse. The aristocracy adopted the language and style of French culture without its critical spirit ... The radical intelligentsia deified nineteenth-century Western science without recreating the atmosphere of free criticism that had made scientific advances possible.[26]

In the late twentieth century Russians once again rushed without preparation to import another Western institution. Parliamentary democracy would resolve decades of repression and bring about the country's evolution to a normal state. Instead, the existing state structure imploded and half a decade later the country found itself led by an erratic, authoritarian president while leaders of its parliament quarrelled loudly but ineffectually. Politically, Russia at the end of the century resembled nothing so much as Russia at the beginning of the century. It had become a democracy of despots.

Notes *

1 Mikhail Gorbachev, interview with BBC World Service radio, February 17, 1995

1 Interview with G. Shaknazarov, 26 December 1991.
2 *Moscow Times*, 5 October 1993.
3 U. Gosset, and V. Fedorovsky, *Histoire secrète d'un Coup d'État* (Paris: Lattès 1991), p. 95.
4 *Moskovsky Komsomolets*, 8 October 1993.
5 Interview with S. Stankevich, 19 October 1993.
6 This was not the largest parliamentary delegation in the Duma. The new Russian electoral law imitated the German system, giving voters two ballots, one for a party list and a second for a constituency candidate. The seats in the Duma were split evenly between party list votes (222 seats) and constituency votes (222 seats.) Based on the party list votes, Zhirinovsky's party won fifty-nine seats. In the constituency voting, however, Zhirinovsky's candidates were largely unknown and won only five seats. Thus, although Russia's Choice, the party formed to back Boris Yeltsin's policies, won only 15 per cent of the vote, it entered the Duma with seventy-six deputies, thanks to the strong showing of its candidates in the constituency voting.

---

* (Unless otherwise indicated, all interviews referred to in the notes are with the author.)

7 Debates, Russian State Duma, 13 January 1994, Bulletin No. 2, p. 25.
8 Isaiah Berlin, *Russian Thinkers* (London: Hogarth Press 1978), p. 97.
9 Interview with G. Shaknazarov, 6 August 1993.
10 News conference, V. Zhirinovsky, 14 December 1993.
11 Berlin, *Russian Thinkers*, p. 126.

CHAPTER TWO

1 Alexander Yakovlev, *Predisloviye, Obval, Poslesloviye* (Moscow: Novosti 1992), p. 268.
2 Interview with A. Yakovlev, 2 August 1993.
3 Interview with A. Lukyanov, 13 October 1993.
4 *Komsomolskaya Pravda*, 5 June 1990.
5 Jonathan Steele, *Eternal Russia* (London: Faber and Faber 1993), p. 175.
6 Dusko Doder and Louise Branson, *Gorbachev: Heretic in the Kremlin* (London: Futura 1990), p. 48.
7 Interview with A. Lukyanov, 13 October 1993.
8 Interview with G. Shaknazarov, 6 August 1993.
9 Interview with A. Chernayev, 3 December 1993.
10 Interview with R. Medvedev, 14 August 1993.
11 Doder and Branson, *Gorbachev*, p. 190.
12 *Pravda*, 28 January 1987.
13 Ibid., 29 January 1987.
14 Angus Roxburgh, *The Second Russian Revolution* (London: BBC Books 1991), p. 57.
15 Debates of the First Congress of People's Deputies of the USSR, in *Pervi Siezd Narodnich Deputatov USSR* (Moscow 1989), vol. 1, p. 152.
16 Interview with G. Shaknazarov, 2 August 1993.
17 Michel Tatu, *Gorbachev: L'URSS, Va-t-Elle Changer?* (Paris: Le Centurion 1987), p. 163.
18 Interview with Y. Ligachev, 22 October 1993.
19 Minutes of Politburo meeting, 25 March 1988, in Mikhail Gorbachev, *M.S. Godi Trudnix Reshenii* (Moscow: Alpha-Print 1993), p. 106.
20 Ibid., p. 110.
21 Interview with V. Medvedev, 5 August 1993.
22 Lukyanov would later deny they had been "close" friends. He had been two years ahead of Gorbachev at university. As for the story made famous by Roy Medvedev at the First Congress of People's

Deputies in 1989 that Lukyanov had been Gorbachev's superior in the faculty Komsomol organization, that, he said, was a myth. Medvedev had confused him with a second Lukyanov then studying at the university. Interview with A. Lukyanov, 4 February 1994.

23 Interview with A. Lukyanov, 13 October 1993.

24 Later, almost to a man, these advisers would change their minds, claiming the elections from "social organizations" had proven their worth by allowing intellectuals like Andrei Sakharov to find seats in the Congress. Without this so-called third chamber, they said, the Congress would have been dominated by Communist Party bureaucrats.

25 *Konstitutionii Vestnik* 16 (May 1993), p. 137. Stalin's constitution of 1936 erased the Congress.

26 Interview with A. Yakovlev, 2 August 1993.

27 Andrei Grachev, *La Chute du Kremlin* (Paris: Hachette 1994), p. 154.

28 Valeri Boldin, *Ten Years that Shook the World* (New York: Basic Books 1994), p. 96.

29 Anatoli Chernayev, *Shest Let s Gorbachevym* (Moscow: Progress 1993), p. 317.

30 Ibid., p. 131.

31 Interview with G. Shaknazarov, 6 August 1993.

32 *Moscow Times*, International Weekly Edition, 12–17 April 1994 p. 37.

33 Chernayev, *Shest Let s Gorbachevym*, p. 216.

34 See Steele, *Eternal Russia*, p. 89.

35 *Resolutions and Declarations of Congresses, Conferences and Plenums of the Central Committee of the* CPSU, 15, 1985–88, (Moscow: Politizdat 1989), p. 609.

36 Interview with Y. Ligachev, 22 October 1993.

37 Nikolai Ryzhkov, *Perestroika, Istoriya Predatelstv* (Moscow: Novosti 1992), p. 275.

38 Interviews with G. Shaknazarov, 6 August 1993, and A. Yakovlev, 2 August 1993.

39 Interview with I. Laptev, 2 November 1993.

40 Interviews with G. Shakhazarov, 6 August 1993, and A. Yakovlev, 2 August 1993.

41 Interview with A. Yakovlev, 2 August 1993.

42 *Materials, Nineteenth Conference of the* CPSU (Moscow: Politizdat 1988), p. 102.

43 *Obshchaya Gazeta*, 21 May 1993.

CHAPTER THREE

1 Ryzhkov, *Perestroika*, p. 282.
2 Interview with A. Chernayev, 3 December 1993.
3 *Pravda*, 19 March 1989.
4 Interviews with V. Medvedev, 5 August 1993, A. Chernayev, 3 December 1993, G. Shaknazarov, 6 August 1993.
5 Andrei Sakharov, *Moscow and Beyond* (New York: Vintage Books 1992), p. 98.
6 Boris Yeltsin, *Against the Grain* (New York: Summit Books 1990), p. 59.
7 Interview with Y. Ligachev, 22 October 1993.
8 Vladimir Kolossov et al., *Vesna 1989* (Moscow: Progress 1990), p. 32.
9 *New York Times*, 26 March 1986.
10 Interview with N. Kotsenko, 24 January 1994.
11 Kolossov, *Vesna 1989*, p. 81.
12 Interview with A. Chernayev, 3 December 1993.
13 Ryzhkov, *Perestroika*, p. 284.
14 Chernayev, *Shest Let s Gorbachevym*, p. 284.
15 *New York Times*, 28 April 1989.
16 Interview with G. Shaknazarov, 6 August 1993. The statistics underline his point. In 1985 the Politburo met officially thirty-eight times. In 1990 it met just nine times. The figures are found in V. Stepankov and Y. Lisov, *Kremlovsky Zagovor* (Moscow: Ogonyok 1992), p. 45.
17 Interview with G. Popov, 15 January 1994.
18 E.H. Carr, *The Bolshevik Revolution* (London: Penguin 1982), vol. 1: p. 97.
19 See ibid., p. 220; and M. Heller and A. Nekrich, *L'Utopie au Pouvoir* (Paris: Calmann-Lévy 1985), p. 37; Richard Pipes, *The Russian Revolution 1899–1919* (London: Fontana Press 1992), p. 553–55; Robert Payne, *The Life and Death of Lenin* (London: Grafton Books 1987), p. 432.
20 Interviews with G. Popov, 15 January 1994 and A. Murashev, 4 December 1993. See also Sakharov, *Moscow and Beyond*, p. 107.
21 Interview with A. Chernayev, 3 December 1993.
22 Interview with A. Lukyanov, 4 February 1994.
23 Anatoli Sobchak, *Chozhdenie vo Vlast* (Moscow: Novosti 1991), p. 35.
24 Interview with G. Popov, 15 January 1994.

25 Sakharov, *Moscow and Beyond*, p. 115; interview with Mikhail Poltoranin, 22 February 1994.
26 David Remnick, *Lenin's Tomb* (New York: Random House 1993), p. 146; Boldin, *Ten Years that Shook the World*, p. 95.
27 Payne, *Lenin*, p. 328
28 Chernayev, *Shest Let s Gorbachevym*, p. 294.

CHAPTER FOUR

1 *New York Times*, 26 May 1989.
2 Transcript of proceedings of the First Congress of People's Deputies of the USSR, in *Izvestiia*, 26 May 1989.
3 *Izvestiia*, 26 May 1989, p. 1.
4 Interview with G. Shakhazarov, 6 August 1993.
5 He explained that a working group of deputies had endorsed his decision to change the rules on the eve of the Congress. When that didn't satisfy his questioners, he brusquely called for a vote which, as expected, overwhelmingly confirmed his position.
6 Transcript of proceedings, *Izvestiia*, 26 May 1989.
7 Ibid.
8 Sakharov, *Moscow and Beyond*, p. 121.
9 Transcript of proceedings, *Izvestiia*, 27 May 1989.
10 Ibid. According to an aide to Boris Yeltsin, Obolensky was supposed to have nominated Yeltsin as chairman. The plan was worked out between Yeltsin and Obolensky at a midnight meeting on the eve of the Congress. Instead, Obolensky nominated himself. Yeltsin was later nominated by another deputy, but immediately withdrew. "As a communist," he said he would support Gorbachev. See Lev Sukhanov, *Vmestye s Yeltsinym* (Nicosia: Kniga Pervaya 1994).
11 *Izvestiia*, 27 May 1989.
12 Sakharov, *Moscow and Beyond*, p. 122.
13 Transcript of proceedings, *Izvestiia*, 26 May 1989.
14 Ibid., 27 May 1989.
15 Ibid., 29 May 1989.
16 Ibid.
17 *New York Times*, 31 May 1989.
18 *Izvestiia*, 31 May 1989. Kazannik's noble gesture would be rewarded, not in another life, but in another country. In September 1993, having fired the Russian prosecutor general along with the recalcitrant Russian parliament, Yeltsin named Kazannik the new prosecutor general.

19 *New York Times*, 27 May 1989.

20 Transcript of proceedings, *Izvestiia*, 31 May 1989.

21 Interview with S. Stankevich, 19 October 1993.

22 Sakharov, *Moscow and Beyond*, p. 132.

23 Sobchak, *Chozhdenie vo Vlast*, p. 48.

24 Yeltsin, *Against the Grain*, p. 245.

25 James Billington, *The Icon and the Axe* (New York: Vintage Books 1970), p. 589.

26 Marquis de Custine, *Empire of the Czar* (New York: Anchor Books 1990), p. 346.

CHAPTER FIVE

1 *New York Times Magazine*, 15 November 1989.

2 TASS, 27 June 1989.

3 Sobchak, *Chozhdenie vo Vlast*, p. 98.

4 Ibid., p. 60.

5 Edouard Shevardnadze, *Moi Vybor* (Moscow: Novosti 1991), p. 324.

6 Yuri Afanasiev, *Ma Russie Fatale* (Paris: Calmann-Lévy 1992), p. 56.

7 Boris Yeltsin, *Sur le Fil du Rasoir* (Paris: Albin Michel 1994), p. 231. The existence of the documents was confirmed by Yuri Afanasiev, a member of the commission.

8 *New York Times*, 8 October 1989.

9 Ibid., 13 February 1989.

10 Interviews with R. Medvedev, 14 August 1993, 3 February 1994.

11 Interview with V. Korotich, 11 November 1989.

12 *Izvestiia*, 17 January 1991; *New York Times*, 17 January 1991.

13 Sakharov, *Moscow and Beyond*, p. 147.

14 Ibid., p. 149.

15 Interview with G. Popov, 15 January 1994.

16 John Morrison, *Boris Yeltsin* (New York: Dutton 1991), p. 112.

17 Interview with M. Poltoranin, 22 February 1994.

18 Sakharov, *Moscow and Beyond*, pp. 115–16.

19 Interview with Y. Afanasiev, 28 May 1994.

20 Interview with V. Alksnis, 18 October 1993.

21 *Izvestiia*, 28 August 1991.

22 Interview with V. Alksnis, 18 October 1993.

23 "Between Dictatorship and Anarchy," in the *New Yorker*, 25 June 1990.

24 Interview with A. Lukyanov, 4 February 1994.

25 Interview with A. Murashev, 5 December 1993.

CHAPTER SIX

1 Billington, *The Icon and the Axe*, p. 8.
2 Henri Troyat, *Pouchkine* (Paris: Perrin 1976), pp. 757–59.
3 A.N. Wilson, *Tolstoy* (London: Penguin 1988), p. 517.
4 Payne, *The Life and Death of Lenin*, p. 616.
5 Ibid., p. 618.
6 Quoted in Heller and Nekrich, *L'Utopie au Pouvoir*, p. 423.
7 Interview with A. Lukyanov, 13 October 1993.
8 Hedrick Smith, *The New Russians* (New York: Avon Books 1991), p. 477.
9 Afanasiev, *Ma Russie Fatale*, p. 138.
10 Morrison, *Boris Yeltsin*, p. 112.
11 A biography of Yeltsin says he was beaten up by Kremlin body-guards and tossed in the river after he crashed a birthday party for Nikolai Ryzhkov and got into an argument with Gorbachev. See Vladimir Solovyov and Elena Klepikov, *Boris Yeltsin* (Moscow: Bagrius 1992), p. 237.
12 Smith, *The New Russians*, p. 478.
13 *Izvestiia*, 14 November 1989.
14 Ibid., 17 November 1989.
15 Interview with G. Shaknazarov, 6 August 1993.
16 *Izvestiia TsK KPCC* No. 4, 1990, p. 46.
17 Ibid., p. 58.
18 Ibid., p. 69.
19 Comments to reporters by A. Sakharov, 12 December 1989.
20 Interview with A. Lukyanov, 13 October 1993.
21 CBC News, 21 November 1989.
22 *Le Monde*, 31 January 1990.
23 *Izvestiia*, Proceedings of the Third Soviet Congress of People's Deputies, 14 March 1990.
24 *Pravda*, 6 February 1990.
25 *Izvestiia*, 28 February 1990.
26 Stankevich was later able to persuade Gorbachev and his advisers to accept about half of the amendments he proposed, including one establishing an impeachment procedure and another allowing the legislature to override a presidential veto. See the *New Yorker*, 25 June 1990.
27 Sobchak, *Chozhdenie vo Vlast*, p. 170.
28 David Shipler, "Between Dictatorship and Anarchy," the *New Yorker*, 25 June 1990, p. 44.

29 *Izvestiia*, 14 March 1990.
30 Interview with Y. Afanasiev, 30 May 1994.
31 Ibid.
32 Shipler, "Between Dictatorship and Anarchy," p. 54. The deal fell apart the next day when Gorbachev announced there could be no talks with Lithuania, because states only negotiated with other states.
33 *Izvestiia*, 15 March 1990.
34 Sobchak, *Chozhdenie vo Vlast*, p. 179.
35 *Izvestiia*, 15 March 1990.

CHAPTER SEVEN

1 Ryzhkov, *Perestroika*, p. 365.
2 Yeltsin, *Against the Grain*, p. 203.
3 Chernayev, *Shest Let s Gorbachevym*, p. 337.
4 Shipler, "Between Dictatorship and Anarchy," p. 51.
5 Chernayev, *Shest Let s Gorbachevym*, p. 337.
6 The Soviet electoral law allowed politicians to hold two legislative mandates simultaneously. Thus, Yeltsin became a deputy of both the Soviet and the Russian legislatures.
7 Interview with A. Lukyanov, 13 October 1993.
8 Steve Crawshaw, *Goodbye to the USSR* (London: Bloomsbury 1993), p. 132.
9 Debates of First Russian Congress of People's Deputies, Bulletin No. 10, 22 May 1990, p. 35.
10 *Izvestiia*, 25 May 1990.
11 Interview with A. Lukyanov, 13 October 1993.
12 Interview with L. Ivanchenko, 23 September 1993.
13 *Izvestiia*, 4 September 1990.
14 Interview with A. Yakovlev, 2 August 1993.
15 *Izvestiia*, 18 September 1990.
16 Ibid., 22 September 1990.
17 Chernayev, *Shest Let s Gorbachevym*, p. 374.
18 Interview with A. Yakovlev, 2 August 1993.
19 *Izvestiia*, 16 November 1990.
20 Interview with I. Laptev, 2 November 1993.
21 Interview with A. Chernayev, 3 December 1993.
22 *Izvestiia*, 16 January 1991.
23 Ibid., 14 January 1991.
24 Chernayev, *Shest Let s Gorbachevym*, p. 415.

25 Proceedings of the USSR Supreme Soviet, 17 June 1991, Bulletin No. 82, p. 28.

26 Interview with V. Alksnis, 13 October 1993.

27 Stepankov and Lisov, *Kremlovsky Zagovor*, p. 59.

28 Interview with I. Laptev, 2 November 1993.

29 Interview with A. Yakovlev, 2 August 1993.

30 Chernayev, *Shest Let s Gorbachevym*, p. 453.

31 Interview with Ivan Laptev, 2 November 1993.

CHAPTER EIGHT

1 *Izvestiia*, 26 August 1991.

2 Yeltsin, *Sur le Fil du Rasoir*, p. 65.

3 Stepankov and Lisov, *Kremlovsky Zagovor*, p. 56.

4 Yeltsin, *Sur le Fil du Rasoir*, p. 61.

5 Interview with A. Lukyanov, 14 March 1993.

6 Stepankov and Lisov, *Kremlovsky Zagovor*, pp. 93–103. Unless otherwise indicated, information and quotations in the following paragraphs are from this book. It is based on interrogations and evidence gathered by the Russian Prosecutor's Office for the trial of the coup plotters. Stepankov himself was the chief prosecutor and Lisov was his deputy. Stepankov professed to see no ethical problem in publishing an account of the evidence gathered by the state a full year before the trial began. He told reporters that, on the contrary, the book had helped defence lawyers in preparing their cases.

7 James Billington, *Russia Transformed* (New York: Free Press 1992), p. 32.

8 Interview with M. Poltoranin, 22 February 1994.

9 Yeltsin, *Sur le Fil du Rasoir*, p. 35.

10 Billington, *Russia Transformed*, p. 39.

11 Martin Sixsmith, *Moscow Coup* (London: Simon and Schuster 1991), p. 36.

12 Yeltsin, *Sur le Fil du Rasoir*, p. 97.

13 Stepankov and Lisov, *Kremlovsky Zagovor*, p. 97.

14 Gosset and Fedorovsky, *Histoire Secrète d'un Coup d'État*, p. 135.

15 Ruslan Khasbulatov *The Struggle for Russia* (London: Routledge 1993), p. 182.

16 Gosset and Fedorovsky, *Histoire Secrète d'un Coup d'État*, p. 213.

17 Billington, *Russia Transformed*, p. 132.

18 *Izvestiia*, 28 August 1991.

19 Ibid.

CHAPTER NINE

1 Yeltsin, *Sur le Fil du Rasoir,* p. 153.
2 Interview with I. Laptev, 2 November 1993.
3 *Izvestiia,* 2 September 1991.
4 Proceedings of the Fifth Congress of People's Deputies of the USSR, in ibid., 3 September 1991.
5 Proceedings of the Fifth Congress, 4 September 1991, in ibid., September 5, 1991.
6 Proceedings of the Fifth Congress, in ibid., 6 September 1991.
7 Interview with I. Laptev, 2 November 1993.
8 Yeltsin, *Sur le Fil du Rasoir,* p. 58.
9 Andrei Grachev, *Histoire Vraie de la Fin de l'URSS* (Paris: Editions du Rocher 1992), p. 61.
10 Chernayev, *Shest Let s Gorbachevym,* p. 494.
11 Grachev, *Histoire Vraie,* p. 82.
12 Ibid., p. 99.
13 Ibid., p. 254.
14 Interview with A. Murashev, 4 December 1993.
15 Interview with G. Popov, 15 January 1994.
16 Chernayev, *Shest Let s Gorbachevym,* p. 490.

CHAPTER TEN

1 Vladimir Bukovsky, "Born and Born Again," in *The New Republic,* 10 September 1990.
2 Catherine Durand-Cheynet, *Moscou Contre la Russie* (Paris: Ramsay 1988), p. 228. She describes the *yurodivy* this way: "Often reviled, sometimes stoned, the objects of fury of the official clergy, they were frequently revered as saints and feared for their prophetic powers. Even the sovereign hesitated to punish them when he was attacked."
3 Afanasiev, *Ma Russie Fatale,* p. 292.
4 Nikolai Berdyaev, *The Russian Idea* (Hudson: Lindisfarne Press 1992), p. 24.
5 Yeltsin, *Against the Grain,* p. 154.
6 Interviews with Y. Ligachev, 23 October 1993, and Vadim Medvedev, 2 August 1993.
7 Yeltsin, *Against the Grain,* p. 129.
8 Ibid., p. 179.
9 Ibid., p. 191.
10 Boldin, *Ten Years that Shook the World,* p. 236.

11 Yeltsin, *Against the Grain*, pp. 185–201.

12 Interview with Mikhail Poltoranin, 22 February 1994.

13 Yeltsin, *Against the Grain*, p. 234.

14 Ibid., p. 192.

15 Boldin, *Ten Years that Shook the World*, p. 236.

16 Sukhanov, *Vmestye s Yeltsinym*, p. 36.

17 Proceedings of the First Russian Congress of People's Deputies May 22, Bulletin 10, p. 36.

18 Interview with Alexander Golz, 8 October 1993.

19 Interview with Anatoli Shabad, 16 November 1993.

20 Proceedings of the First Russian Congress of People's Deputies, May 22, Bulletin 10, p. 31.

21 Ibid., p. 36.

22 Interview in *Nezavisimaya Gazeta*, 10 June 1993.

23 Interview with O. Rumyantsev, 16 November 1993.

24 Proceedings of the First Russian Congress of People's Deputies, June 8, 1990, Bulletin 36, p. 16.

25 Interview with O. Rumyantsev, 16 November 1993.

26 Morrison, *Boris Yeltsin*, p. 218.

27 Interview with Andrei Golovin, 31 January 1994; interview with Vladimir Isakov, 16 February 1994.

28 Morrison, *Boris Yeltsin*, p. 232.

29 *Izvestiia*, 21 February 1991.

30 *Plan Deistvie 28* (Action Plan 28) published as an annex to the *Report of the Parliamentary Commission of the Russian Federation into the Causes of the Putsch August 1991*, February 1992

31 Proceedings of the Third Russian Congress of People's Deputies, March 29, Bulletin No. 2, p. 3.

32 Ibid., 29 March 1994, Bulletin 3, p. 14.

33 Ibid., 30 March, Bulletin 4, p. 13

34 Ibid., 30 March, Bulletin 5, p. 16

35 Ibid., 4 April 1991, Bulletin 14, pp. 4–6.

36 Interview with A. Lyubimov, 29 March 1993.

37 Interview with A. Shabad, 16 November 1993.

38 *Ostankino Television*, interview with Boris Yeltsin, 9 November 1993.

39 Boris Yeltsin, press conference, 19 August 1993.

40 Interview with S. Stankevich, 19 October 1993.

41 Ruslan Khabulatov, *Zapiski iz Belovo Doma (Notes from the White House)* in *Pravda*, 10 January 1994.

42 Proceedings of the Fifth Russian Congress of People's Deputies, 28 October 1991, Bulletin 13, p. 7.

CHAPTER ELEVEN

1 *Le Monde*, 30 December 1991.
2 Khasbulatov, "Zapiski iz Belovo Doma" in *Pravda*, 10 January 1994.
3 Interview with O. Rumyantsev, 16 November 1993.
4 Associated Press, 6 April 1992.
5 Viktor Sheinis, "Sudorogi Rossiskovo Parlamentarisma (Convulstions of Russian Parliamentarism)" in *Polis* (Journal of the Russian Academy of Sciences) 3 (1992), p. 54.
6 *Rossiskie Vesti* 172 (1993), p. 2, interview with Gennadi Burbulis.
7 Interview with G. Burbulis, 16 March 1994.
8 Steele, *Eternal Russia*, p. 230.
9 Interview with M. Poltoranin, 22 February 1994.
10 Reuters, Moscow, 22 April 1992.
11 Yeltsin, *Sur le Fil du Rasoir*, p. 256.
12 Interview with A. Shabad, 16 November 1993.
13 Yeltsin, *Sur le Fil du Rasoir*, p. 50 and 290.
14 Khasbulatov, The *Struggle for Russia*, p. 31.
15 Interviews with Russian deputies M. Astafiev, S. Baburin, A. Golovin, L. Ivanchenko, A. Shabad, V. Sheinis, and personal observation.
16 Interview with M. Poltoranin, 22 February 1994.
17 Interview with L. Ponamarov, 9 September 1993.
18 Interview with C. Zlobin, 18 October 1993.
19 Afanasiev, *Ma Russie Fatale*, p. 162.
20 *Rossiskaya Gazeta*, 17 August 1993.
21 Interview with A. Shabad, 16 November 1993.
22 Interview with V. Sheinis, 5 December 1993.
23 Yeltsin, *Sur le Fil du Rasoir*, p. 295.
24 *Moscow Times*, 10 June 1993.
25 Interview with A. Shabad, 16 November 1993.
26 *Izvestiia*, 10 December 1992.
27 Yegor Gaidar, interview in *Nedelya* 35 (September 1993), p. 13.
28 Yeltsin, *Sur le Fil du Rasoir*, p. 345.
29 Steele, *Eternal Russia*, p. 309.
30 *Guardian* (London), 30 April 1993.
31 Mark Urnov, et al. "The Present and Future Party System in Russia, 1993," paper prepared for the Presidential Council of Russia.
32 *Pravda*, 10 June 1993.
33 Interview with S. Baburin, 27 April 1992.
34 *Izvestiia*, 27 July 1993.
35 Alexander Rutskoi, in *Rossiskaya Gazeta*, 20 August 1993.

36 Interview with C. Zlobin, 18 October 1993.

37 *Moscow News*, 26 November 1993.

38 The figure comes from Mikhail Maley, a Yeltsin adviser and former deputy himself. Interview with M. Maley, 14 October 1993.

39 *Moscow Times*, 10 June 1993.

40 Yeltsin, *Sur le Fil du Rasoir*, p. 295.

41 Interview with V. Sheinis, 5 December 1993.

42 Proceedings of the Fifth Russian Congress of People's Deputies, November 2, 1991, Bulletin No. 23, p. 6.

43 Boris Yeltsin, Address to the Constitutional Assembly, June 5, 1993, in *Konstitutionnoyoe Soveshanie*, Information Bulletin No. 1, August 1993, pp. 12–13.

44 Interview with S. Alexeyev, 7 December 1993.

45 Interview with Mikhail Gorbunov, 7 December 1993. Gorbunov was a constitutional lawyer attached to the president's office who helped draft the Presidential Version. A reading of the different drafts confirms his statement.

46 Presidential draft, Clause 21, in *Konstitutionny Vestnik*, No. 16, May 1993, p. 70.

47 Interview with C. Zlobin 18 October 1993. The text of Khasbulatov's speech was published on 8 June 1993, in the newspaper *Sovietskaya Rossiia*.

48 *Ostankino Television*, interview with Boris Yeltsin, 9 November 1993.

49 Yeltsin, *Sur le Fil du Rasoir*, p. 190.

50 *Moscow Times*, 20 August 1993.

51 Andrei Sinyavsky, *La Civilisation Soviétique* (Paris: Albin Michel 1988), p. 106.

52 Afanasiev, *Ma Russie Fatale*, p. 208.

53 J.M. Lotman, and B.A. Uspenskij, *The Semiotics of Russian Culture*, edited by Ann Shukman (Michigan Slavic Contributions 1984), p. 3. "There is no provision for an intermediate zone. And correspondingly, behaviour in this life is either sinful or holy. This dualism extended also to concepts unconnected with the Church. The secular authorities might be regarded as divine or demonic, but never as neutral in relation to these concepts."

CHAPTER TWELVE

1 Ruslan Khabulatov, press conference, 21 September 1993; author's notes. Unless otherwise specified, other quotes and descriptions in this chapter are from my notes taken at the time.

2 Interview with C. Zlobin, 18 October 1993.

3 In the end, Yeltsin advisers would adopt an even more peculiar solution. Half of the upper house would be elected for its first, transitional two-year term. The other half would be composed of officials already appointed by Yeltsin to their positions.

4 *Washington Post*, 24 September 1993.

5 Interview with O. Rumyantsev, 16 November 1993.

6 CNN, 29 September 1993.

7 Interview with C. Zlobin, 18 October 1993.

8 Interview with A. Shabad, 16 October 1993.

9 Sergei Parkhomenko, article prepared for the 5 October 1993, edition of the newspaper *Segodnya*. Under emergency rule imposed by Yeltsin after the crisis, it was entirely censored. It eventually appeared in the 8 October 1993, edition.

10 *International Herald Tribune*, 10 October 1993.

11 Interview with S. Stankevich, 19 October 1993.

12 *New York Times*, 4 October 1993.

13 Interview with M. Poltoranin, 22 February 1994.

14 Yeltsin, *Sur le Fil du Rasoir*, p. 403.

15 Ibid., p. 376.

16 *Moskovsky Komsomolets*, 8 October 1993.

17 Yeltsin interview with ARD, German Television, as reported by Reuters, 12 November 1993.

18 The scene at the Defence ministry is described in detail by Yeltsin in *Sur le Fil du Rasoir*, pp. 404–7.

19 Interview with C. Zlobin, 18 October 1993.

20 *Moskovsky Komsomolets*, 8 October 1993.

21 *Moscow Times*, 8 October 1993.

22 Ibid.

23 "Faith, Hope, Love," composed by V. Mikhailov, Russian deputy, 30 September 1993, photocopy in author's possession.

24 Interview with S. Baburin, 17 February 1994.

25 Interview with O. Rumyantsev, 27 January 1994.

26 *Moscow News*, No. 42, 15 October 1993; *Nezavisimaya Gazeta*, 12 November 1993; interview with V. Zorkin.

27 *Moscow Times,* 3 November 1993.

28 *Ostankino Television*, interview with Yeltsin, 9 November 1993.

29 "Proekt Konstitutsia Rossiskoi Federatsii" (Draft of the Constitution of the Russian Federation) submitted for approval at the 12 December 1993 referendum.

30 *Izvestiia*, 15 November 1993.

31 Interview with A. Shabad, 16 October 1993. Russia's new election law called for a German-style vote. Voters would vote for a candidate in their district and for a party list. Half the seats in the new Duma would be allocated by party vote. The top candidates from the party lists would be allocated seats according to the percentage of votes the party received. Thus the importance of representation on the list of Russia's Choice.

32 The American historian of Russia and the Russian Revolution, Richard Pipes, wrote in the *New York Times* of October 5: "Judging by what we know of Russian opinion, the likelihood is that [Yeltsin and the democrats] will win a comfortable majority, perhaps as much as two-thirds of the deputies."

33 Interview with A. Shabad, 3 December 1993.

34 See 1993 economic development figures, Russian Statistics Committee, printed in *Segodyna*, 12 January 1994.

CHAPTER THIRTEEN

1 Interview with V. Zhirinovsky, 9 January 1994.

2 Vladimir Zhirinovsky, *Posledni Brosok Na Jug (Last Push to the South)* (Moscow: LDP 1993), pp. 5–7.

3 Ibid., p. 20.

4 Ibid., p. 143.

5 Ibid., p. 64.

6 Boris Yeltsin, press conference, 17 December 1993.

7 Interview with O. Karpenko, 21 January 1994.

8 Interview with S. Abaltsev, 19 January 1994.

9 Interview with R. Medvedev, 20 January 1994.

10 Zhirinovsky, *Posledni Brosok Na Jug*, p. 44.

11 Ibid., p. 49.

12 Associated Press, 4 April 1994. The same information was reported by CNN.

13 Interview with O. Kalugin, 1 February 1994.

14 Maureen Orth, "Nightmare on Red Square," in *Vanity Fair*, September 1994.

15 Zhores Medvedev, "The Nationalist Factor," in *Moscow Times*, 15 January 1994.

16 Interview with O. Kalugin, 1 February 1994. See also comments by Alexander Kichikhin, former KGB colonel, in *Vanity Fair*, September 1994.

17 Interview with R. Medvedev, 20 January 1994.

18 Proceedings of the State Duma, Bulletin No. 2, 13 January 1994, p. 3.

19 Ibid., Bulletin No. 1, 11 January 1994, p. 31.

20 Ibid., Bulletin No. 2, 13 January 1994, pp. 24–26.

21 Ibid., p. 43.

22 *Izvestiia*, 15 January 1994.

23 *Moscow Times*, 14 January 1994.

24 Ibid., 18 January 1994.

25 Ibid., 6 January 1994.

26 After a vote of protest by Duma members, the Kremlin found space in the former Gosplan building (the Soviet Ministry of Central Planning) and the lower house moved there in June 1994.

27 In interviews after his resignation, Kazannik revealed the extent of the hatred of Yeltsin's men for the parliamentary leaders. He told the newspaper *Komsomolskaya Pravda* on 12 April 1994 that after the storming of the White House in October 1993 a scenario was outlined to him whereby he would investigate the events for three or four days, charge all those held with conspiracy to murder and turn them over to the military tribunal of the Supreme Court. "The case was supposed to last for two or three days and everyone was supposed to be sentenced to death. The president's team put a lot of pressure on us."

28 Interview with V. Sheinis, 15 March 1994.

29 *New York Times*, 5 April 1994.

30 Interviews with A. Murashev, 10 March 1994; V. Sheinis, 15 March 1994; S. Stankevich 14 March 1994; A. Lukyanov, 12 February 1994.

31 Interview with I. Rybkin, 12 February 1994.

32 Reuters, Associated Press, 29 April 1994.

33 *The Economist*, 30 April 1994.

34 David Remnick, "Autumn of the Patriarch," in the *New Yorker*, 9 May 1994.

35 Yeltsin, *Sur le Fil du Rasoir*, p. 248.

36 Ibid., p. 260.

37 Ibid., p. 303.

38 *Ostankino Television*, interview with Boris Yeltsin, 7 November 1993.

39 Yeltsin, *Sur le Fil du Rasoir*, p. 11.

40 *Moscow Times*, 22 May 1994.

41 Ibid.

42 Yeltsin, *Against the Grain*, p. 69.

43 *Ostankino Television*, interview with Boris Yeltsin, 7 November 1993.
44 Boris Yeltsin, State of the Nation Speech to the Russian Federative
   Assembly, transcript on ITAR-TASS, 24 February 1994.
45 *Moscow Times*, 28 May 1994.
46 Ibid., 31 May 1994.

CHAPTER FOURTEEN

1 *Izvestiia*, 12 January 1995.
2 Interview with Pavel Felgengauer, military analyst for *Segodnya*,
   8 January 1995.
3 Reuters, 7 February 1995.
4 Interview with A. Shabad, 6 January 1995.
5 Quoted in *Newsweek*, 9 January 1995.
6 *Obshchaya Gazeta*, 27 October 1994.
7 *Komsomolskaya Pravda*, 7 February 1995.
8 *Izvestiia*, 21 December 1994.
9 Interview with V. Kvasov, 14 January 1995.
10 *Argumenty i Fakty*, 1 March 1995.
11 Sergei Kovalyov, press conference, 5 January 1995.
12 *Moscow Times*, 21 January 1995.
13 Galina Starovoitova, interview in *Der Spiegel*, 2 January 1995.
14 Yegor Gaidar, conversation with reporters, 11 January 1995.
15 *International Herald Tribune*, 10 February 1995.
16 *Newsweek*, 9 January 1995.
17 *Financial Times* (London), 10 February 1995.
18 Interview with A. Shabad, 6 January 1995.
19 In a front-page article on 14 January 1995, *Izvestiia* reported a
   detailed scenario, which it said was being whispered to deputies by
   Kremlin advisers. The Duma would be dissolved and early elections
   held in the summer of 1995. Then a majority of the new Duma
   would agree to a Kremlin proposal to hold simultaneous presidential and legislative elections – in 1999.
20 Interview with V. Kvasov, 14 January 1995.
21 Interview with O. Dobrodeyev, 19 January 1995.
22 *Newsweek*, 9 January 1995.
23 Interview with S. Markov, 13 January 1995.
24 Gavriil Popov, *Avgust Devyanosto Pervovo (August '91)*, in *Izvestiia*, 25 August 1992.
25 Interview with Y. Afanasiev, 28 May 1994.
26 Billington, *The Icon and the Axe*, p. 595.

Bibliography

Afanasiev, Yuri. *Ma Russie Fatale*. Paris: Albin Michel 1992.

Berdyaev, Nikolai. *The Russian Idea*. Hudson: Lindisfarne Press 1992.

Berlin, Isaiah. *Russian Thinkers*. London: Hogarth Press 1978.

Billington, James. *The Icon and the Axe*. New York: Vintage Books 1970.

– *Russia Transformed*. New York: Free Press 1992.

Boldin, Valeri. *Ten Years that Shook the World*. New York: Basic Books 1994.

Chernayev, Anatoli. *Shest Let s Gorbachevym (Six Years with Gorbachev)*. Moscow: Progress 1993.

Crawshaw, Steve. *Goodbye to the USSR*. London: Bloomsbury 1993.

Custine, Marquis de. *Empire of the Czar*. New York: Anchor Books 1990.

Doder, Dusko and Louise Branson. *Gorbachev: Heretic in the Kremlin*. London: Futura 1990.

Gorbachev, Mikhail. *Perestroika*. London: Collins 1987.

– *Augustovsky Pusch (August Putsch)*. Moscow: Novosti 1991.

– *Dekabr 91 (December 91)*, Moscow: Novosti 1992.

– *Godi Trudnix Reshenii (Years of Difficult Decisions)*. Moscow: Alpha-Print 1993.

Gosset, Ulysse, and Vladimir Fedorovsky. *Histoire Secrète d'un Coup d'État* Paris: Lattes 1991.

Grachev, Andrei. *Histoire Vraie de la Fin de l'URSS*. Paris: Editions du Rocher 1992.

– *La Chute du Kremlin*. Paris: Hachette 1994.

Heller, Mikhail, and Alexander Nekrich. *L'Utopie au Pouvoir*. Paris: Calmann-Lévy 1985.

Khasbulatov, Ruslan. *The Struggle for Russia*. London: Routledge 1993.

Kolossov, Vladimir. *Vesna 1989 (Spring 1989)*. Moscow: Progress 1990.

Ligachev, Yegor. *Zagadka Gorbacheva* (*The Gorbachev Riddle*). Novosibirsk: Intervuk 1992.

Lukyanov, Anatoli. "Perevorot Mnimyi i Nastoyoshii" (The Real and the Fake Coup). Moscow: Manuscript 1993.

Morrison, John. *Boris Yeltsin*. New York: Dutton 1991.

Payne, Robert. *The Life and Death of Lenin*. London: Grafton Books 1987.

Pipes, Richard. *The Russian Revolution, 1899–1919*. London: Fontana 1992.

Remnick, David. *Lenin's Tomb*. New York: Random House 1993.

Roxburgh, Angus. *The Second Russian Revolution*. London: BBC Books 1991.

Ryzhkov, Nikolai. *Perestroika, Istoriya Predatelsv (Perestroika, A Story of Betrayals)*. Moscow: Novosti 1992.

Sakharov, Andrei. *Moscow and Beyond*. New York: Vintage Books 1992.

Shevardnadze, Edouard. *Moi Vybor* (*My Choice*). Moscow: Novosti 1991.

Sinyavsky, Andrei. *La Civilisation Soviétique*. Paris: Albin Michel 1988.

Sixsmith, Martin. *Moscow Coup*. London: Simon and Schuster 1991.

Smith, Hedrick. *The New Russians*. New York: Avon Books 1991.

Sobchak, Anatoli. *Chozhdenie Vo Vlast* (*Coming to Power*). Moscow: Novosti 1991.

Steele, Jonathan. *Eternal Russia*. London: Faber and Faber 1994.

Stepankov, Vladimir and Yuri Lisov. *Kremlovsky Zagovor* (*Kremlin Plot*). Moscow: Ogonyok 1992.

Sukhanov, Lev. *Vmestye s Yeltsinym* (*Together with Yeltsin*). Nicosia: Kniga Pervaya 1994.

Yakovlev, Alexander. *Predisloviye, Obval, Poslesloviye* (*Foreword, Collapse, Afterword*). Moscow: Novosti 1992.

Yeltsin, Boris. *Against the Grain*. London: Cape 1990.

– *Sur le Fil du Rasoir*. Paris: Albin Michel 1994.

Index